BIG BROTHER

THE ORWELLIAN NIGHTMARE
COME TRUE

BIG BROTHER

THE ORWELLIAN NIGHTMARE COME TRUE

Mark Dice

The Resistance
San Diego, CA

Printed in the United States of America
First edition published in March 2011

Visit www.MarkDice.com

ISBN: 0-9673466-1-4

Table of Contents

About the Author

As a child Mark Dice spent many Wisconsin winters in his parents' basement disassembling toys and electronics, wondering how these seemingly magical devices worked. His father was an engineer and had a wide variety of tools, hardware, and mechanical devices that were at Mark's disposal to tinker with and build whatever he could imagine. He would turn his old radio controlled cars into radio controlled boats using scrap Styrofoam slabs from nearby construction sites and tested them on a local pond. When at the mall, instead of being interested in getting the latest tennis shoes or designer t-shirts, Mark would spend time at Radio Shack buying an odd array of switches, lights, and other electrical components to build whatever device he and his friends had dreamed up after watching films like *Short Circuit* (1986) or an episode of *MacGyver*.

Before the Internet and personal computers became as common as the telephone, Mark was fortunate enough to convince his parents to buy him a computer in 1991, which if you were born before 1980, perhaps you remember that PC computers consisted of a black screen displaying only a white C:/> which would respond with "bad command or file name" unless you entered in an exact command that few people knew how to do. This was called the C prompt. So while his parents couldn't get the computer to do anything but say "bad command or file name," Mark and his friends had discovered bulletin board systems (BBSes) and found themselves on the cutting edge of the coming computer revolution. Before most people had heard of the Internet or websites, Mark was downloading videogames and software from the different BBSes he found and developed a fascination with Bill Gates, the founder of Microsoft, and at the time, the richest man in the world.

With all the wonders and possibilities of advancing computer hardware and software, Mark also saw a dark side to the technology. He had a natural inclination that with the power Bill Gates had, he or another individual or group could cripple society, or one day create and implement the very kinds of Orwellian systems Mark had seen in science fiction movies growing up. Seeing the logical progression of technology in the hands of power-hungry megalomaniacs worried him. As the years went by, technology advanced at a more rapid rate each year, and as a young adult Mark began reading in mainstream publications that he was not alone in fearing what unregulated technology could do to our privacy, freedoms, and to mankind.

Mark Dice is the author of several books on the occult and secret societies, including *The Resistance Manifesto*, *The Illuminati: Facts & Fiction*, and *The New World Order: Facts & Fiction*. His criticism of pop culture, media, and politics has made news around the world. Mark has a bachelor's degree in communication and lives in San Diego, California.

Introduction

When George Orwell (pen name of Eric Blair) first published his famous novel, *Nineteen Eighty-Four*, it was the year 1949, and it told a dark story of what he envisioned life may be like in the future—in the year 1984. His book, as well as his name, have become synonymous with privacy concerns involving technology and also an all-powerful, oppressive ruling elite that strictly governs the activities of the population with an iron fist.

Orwell's book is where we get the term *Big Brother* from, such as when people say "Big Brother is watching you." When people say this, they're referring to the omniscient surveillance system described in the novel that continuously watched and listened to people—even in their own homes. When we call something *Orwellian* to describe the invasiveness of certain technology or government policies, we are also referring to George Orwell's nightmarish vision he described in his novel. There are several other terms that Orwell himself coined in *Nineteen Eighty-Four,* such as *doublethink, thoughtcrime,* and *memory hole*, which have also become part of our vernacular.

Even if you have not read the book or seen the film, you are still undoubtedly familiar with the issues that make up the storyline, such as the high-tech surveillance system watching and listening to everyone in order to keep them in line with the government (called the Party in the novel). You are probably also familiar with the concept of a small elite ruling class (what Orwell calls the Inner Party) living in luxury and wielding unimaginable power over lower level citizens. In the novel, people have lost their freedom, their critical thinking skills, and even the ability to love due to the cultural depths society has sunk to as a result of Big Brother's control. The reason *Nineteen Eighty-Four* remains so popular, and the reason society has adopted vocabulary from the book, is because it serves as more than merely a fictional novel for the reader's entertainment. The novel served (and continues to serve) as a stark warning of what the future may hold if we don't resist invasive technology and oppressive government policies, or if the population at large becomes so lost in a world of pop culture, sports entertainment, or our own selfish desires, that we simply don't care.

Big Brother: The Orwellian Nightmare Come True looks at technology that now exists or is under development and will exist in the near future, that threatens to make our world just as horrific or even worse than the world George Orwell described. This book will provide information from mainstream news sources, industry experts, and even patent numbers of the most invasive and sinister Orwellian devices anyone could dream of. We will also look at actual government programs and policies that seem as if they came right out of Orwell's dark imagination, such as the government secretly paying mainstream media reporters to act as gate-keepers and propagandists for the establishment, and the FBI illegally spying on and smearing peaceful political activists who were seen as problematic.

This book is certainly not anti-technology. Technology is a fantastic tool which can benefit those who use it, or harm them, depending on the intentions of the person designing it or using it. Technology has brought us amazing inventions that would seem supernatural to civilizations that lived just a few hundred years ago. Arthur C. Clark, the author of *2001 a Space Odyssey*, was correct when he said, "Any sufficiently advanced technology is indistinguishable from magic."

While this magical technology has brought us the convenience of calling our friends or family on our cell phones, allowing us to talk with them from virtually anywhere in the world, and given us the ability to watch events on the other side of the earth unfold live on television, and other wonders such as the Internet, DVR recorders, YouTube, Excel spread sheets, word processors, e-mail, Facebook, and more; it has also brought us identity theft, illegal wiretaps, Peeping Toms using hidden video cameras, cyber stalkers, and worse. If you have ever left your cell phone at home when you've left the house for the day, you've realized how much we depend on technology for what have become common and necessary activities. If you've ever been at home when the electricity unexpectedly goes out, you have also realized how much we take for granted in our modern world.

Unfortunately, with tremendous advances in technology often come unforeseen consequences. Nobody could have envisioned young teenage girls taking nude photos of themselves with their cell phone cameras and sending them to their boyfriends, and then having the boyfriends forward them to others, eventually ending up on the cell phone of someone over the age of eighteen, resulting in what is essentially child pornography in their possession. The music and film industries certainly didn't anticipate millions of Internet users downloading music and movies for free, sometimes before the products are even officially released. And when Albert Einstein was searching for the laws of physics to learn how our Universe functioned, he could have never imagined that his work would be used to design weapons capable of destroying the entire earth. It seems that the dark minds of men in power always strive to build sinister devices designed to enable them to hold onto their power, no matter how disastrous the consequences.

In the following pages we will look at some of the sinister inventions currently in operation, as well as the ones on the drawing boards, and the ones mad scientists are hoping to one day create. Facial recognition video cameras that can pick you out of a crowd of tens of thousands of people in a split second, machines that can read your mind, high-tech killer-robots, psychotronic weapons that can literally put voices in people's heads, and more. You will see beyond a doubt that George Orwell's description of Big Brother was chillingly accurate, and perhaps not as horrific as the reality we may one day face. Like a Pandora's Box, once much of this technology is created, there will be little hope of stopping it or even regulating it.

While some of the technology discussed in this book is known to exist in small and specialized industries (and to a growing extent the mainstream public), one must wonder about the technology that is classified as top secret and the experiments that go on in the hidden laboratories funded by the deep pockets of government. Knowing just a small fraction of the past abuses by the United States government (and others around the world) regarding human test subjects and goals, we should all be concerned about the continued illegal and immoral research and experiments that are undoubtedly continuing to occur in secret.

If one reads old *Popular Mechanics* magazines from the 1950's, one can realize how wrong, and even silly, the techno-utopian dreamers were in the past. Many were led to believe that by the twenty-first century we would all be living lives of luxury like the *Jetsons,* with large blocks of free time to enjoy ourselves as we had most manual labor and menial tasks taken care of by robots and computers.

Yet more than a decade into the twenty-first century, we still need to spend time cooking and cleaning, and commuting to work and raising the kids, and fixing up the house and countless other tasks and obligations that are required of us in our daily lives.

Our cars must still continuously be maintained, the oil needs to be changed, the engine serviced, the tires rotated and replaced, and the average vehicle now costs as much as a house did for people just two generations ago. The grass still needs to be cut, the bushes need to be trimmed, and things around the house continue to break and need to be fixed or replaced. People are working longer hours, having less time with their families, having to retire later in life, and are having less savings than past generations. Where is this techno-utopia that so many had promised would come in the near future?

Instead of living lives of luxury and leisure, now many people can't escape their job even after they leave the office. Where once we left work and were outside of the reach of our boss, now he or she can call us on our cell phone at anytime day or night and expects a promptly returned phone call or e-mail.

People are being turned into numbers and statistics, and mathematical formulas are used by employers to determine whether an employee is being efficient enough. It's difficult to get a person on the phone when calling a company's customer service department, and social networking sites such as Facebook and Myspace have turned everyone into their own favorite celebrity and supplement actual friendships and interactions. People don't need to get together for a dinner party to catch up on each other's lives anymore; we just monitor their newsfeed on Facebook from the comfort of our own home while sitting in our favorite chair getting fatter from lack of exercise and a poor diet.

Where we once discussed politics and religion with our friends and neighbors, such topics have become taboo and are replaced with the enticing entertainment of celebrity news as most people feel that it is more important to know about who our favorite celebrities are dating than it is to know what bills are being introduced and voted on in the halls of Congress or our own city council. It's interesting that while people seem to be getting dumber, computers are getting smarter.

We are becoming a nation of morons who can't think for themselves, and are being dehumanized into nothing more than a mentally enslaved workforce who are constantly being monitored, databased, and kept in line by the fear of the omniscient Big Brother technology that has gotten so advanced and so cheap, that the watchful eyes of surveillance cameras are mass produced, almost as if they were disposable.

At a presentation at the 2010 DICE Summit (Design, Innovate, Communicate, Entertain), an annual meeting of videogame executives, Jesse Schell, the former Creative Director of the Disney Imagineering Virtual Reality Studio, gave a speech on the future of gaming and talked about how in the future, "Before too long we're going to get to the point where every soda can, [and] every cereal box is going to be able to have a CPU, a screen, and a camera on board it, and a Wi-Fi connecter so that it can be connected to the Internet."

He concluded his speech by saying that our children and grandchildren will be able to know exactly what books we've read, what foods we ate, and practically everything we've done in our entire lives. He gave this speech not to warn people about these Orwellian technologies, but he was extremely excited about them, and looked forward to them.

"You have no idea what books your grandparents

read, or where they went on a daily basis, but these sensors that we're going to have on us and all around us everywhere are going to be tracking and watching what we're doing forever," Schell said. He concludes by saying that because we will all be constantly watched and our actions and interests databased forever, that we'll possibly be better people and be nicer and make better decisions because of the fear of judgment from others. Is this the kind of world you want to live in? Well, it's the kind of world that's rapidly approaching.

This book is meant to serve as a warning for what is already here, and what is soon to come. It is to encourage people to think about how to possibly prevent or minimize dramatic hazards to our lives by the very technology we have created. It is my goal to give you an accurate forecast of the coming storm so that you as an individual, and we as a society and species, may be better equipped to handle it when it hits. It is my hope that we do not lose our privacy, freedom, or our humanity in this 1984-style New World Order.

Surveillance Cameras

Surveillance cameras have been common in banks, department stores, gas stations, and government buildings for decades in order to prevent shoplifting and robberies, or to identify those who commit crimes after the fact. Society has largely ignored these cameras and barely notices they are watching us and we have come to accept them as commonplace. Even the most adamant privacy advocate would have to admit that such systems help to prevent shoplifting and catch bank robbers, but as technology advanced, these basic video cameras have been evolving into a high-tech surveillance grid almost identical to the Big Brother system described in *Nineteen Eighty-Four*.

Early in the twenty-first century, Britain became the most surveilled country on the planet with an estimated 4.2 million CCTV (Closed Circuit Television) cameras watching in government buildings, private businesses, and on street corners. What concerns privacy advocates, and frequently average citizens, is not necessarily the existence of ordinary security cameras, but the new and invasive ways that they are being used. As you will read in this chapter, security cameras have been installed in school bathrooms, private homes, and the built-in cameras on laptop computers have even been used by school officials to watch students when they were home without them even knowing it.

Facial recognition cameras are now becoming popular, and will soon be a standard feature in surveillance systems. You will also see surveillance systems on public streets that listen to you and detect "hostile" speech and will automatically dispatch the

9

police to investigate. Big Brother *is* watching you, and you might be startled to find out exactly what he sees and hears.

"The telescreen received and transmitted simultaneously. Any sound that Winston made, above the level of a very low whisper, would be picked up by it, moreover, so long as he remained within the field of vision which the metal plaque commanded, he could be seen as well as heard…You had to live—did live, from habit that became instinct—in the assumption that every sound you made was overheard, and, except in darkness, every movement scrutinized."[1] —*Nineteen Eighty-Four*

While Britain has been known for its millions of surveillance cameras that watch over nearly every street and alley in major cities, the United States of America had lagged behind in terms of the size and scope of a Big Brother system. Such cameras were, for a long time, relegated to parking lots and inside businesses such as banks and department stores, but Chicago had pioneered a Big Brother system in America which became a model for other cities.

After 9/11, the city began installing a massive surveillance system on city streets, in schools, around skyscrapers, and even on busses and in train tunnels. The system is so advanced that police officers can tap into practically any security camera from their squad car and watch the feed from a monitor on their dashboard.

"I don't think there is another city in the U.S. that has as an extensive and integrated camera network as Chicago has," said Michael Chertoff, the former head of the Department of Homeland Security.[2]

---

[1] Orwell, George—*Nineteen Eighty-Four* page 2

[2] *Associated Press* "Cameras Make Chicago Most Closely Watched US City" By Don Babwin April 6, 2010

The Chicago Big Brother system even links private security cameras into their grid, something unique compared to London and other cities. If someone calls 911 to report a crime, accident, or fire, police and 911 dispatchers can instantly tap into the nearest video cameras and monitor the scene in real time to assess the situation. In 2010, the city had an estimated 10,000 cameras feeding into their central system, most of which are clearly visible security cameras, but the city also hopes to install numerous hidden cameras as well, according to Police Superintendent Jody Weis. Mayor Richard Daley said he could put 10,000 more cameras up and "nobody would say anything."[3]

Not everyone thinks the cameras are a good idea. Edwin Yohnka, a spokesman for the ACLU wondered, "What protections are in place to stop a rogue officer from taking a highly powerful camera and aim it in a way to find or track someone who is perhaps a former love interest or something like that?"[4]

On May 1, 2010 an SUV filled with explosives was discovered in Times Square in New York City and lucky failed to detonate, causing officials to immediately call for a massive high-tech surveillance system to be put in place all over the city. Mayor Michael Bloomberg said the system "will greatly enhance our ability and the ability of the police to detect suspicious activity in real time, and disrupt possible attacks."[5]

At the time of the incident on May 1, 2010, dubbed the "attempted Times Square bombing," there were

---

[3] *CBS News* "Chicago Most Closely Watched U.S. City" (April 6, 2010)
[4] Ibid
[5] *AFP* "Police Cameras to Flood Manhattan to Prevent Attacks" By Sebastian Smith (May 3, 2010)

already 82 different devices installed around Times Square that watch and catalog footage and can identify license plate numbers from any targeted vehicles. A program called Operation Sentinel scans and logs every license plate from every vehicle entering Manhattan Island in order to spot targeted vehicles. The program also has hidden radiation detectors designed to identify if any nuclear weapons are smuggled into the city.

New York Police Chief Raymond Kelly wanted more federal funding for such operations and said they were looking to implement "analytic software" that would analyze information in real time in order to identify possible threats. For example, cameras that can detect if there is an unattended bag left on the ground, or if a car circles the block too many times. The new system was estimated to have cost more than $100 million dollars.

At some point in the future, ordinary security cameras will be completely outdated and seem like primitive ancient devices compared to pre-crime cameras, facial recognition systems, and other behavior analyzers that are being implemented.

UK Government Installs Surveillance Cameras in Private Homes

The UK government actually spent $700 million dollars to install surveillance cameras inside the homes of citizens to monitor whether their children attend school, eat proper meals, and go to bed on time.[6] It's part of a government program called "Family Intervention Projects," which also includes social workers making regular visits to see if parents are raising their children

---

[6] *Wired.com* "Britain To Put CCTV Cameras Inside Private Homes" (August 3, 2009) by Charlie Sorrel

properly.

Approximately 2,000 families were initially targeted by the program when it launched in 2009 and British authorities planned to expand the number to 20,000 within the following two years, with all expenses being paid by taxpayers. Parents and children subjected to this Orwellian program are also forced to sign a "behavior contract" called the Home School Agreement, which outlines what the government expects of them.

Britain was invaded by millions of CCTV cameras decades ago on the streets of London and elsewhere which have become hardly noticed and a part of everyone's daily life, but this move to put them inside the private homes of citizens shocked and disturbed people and is not something that is only happening in England.

Back in February 2006, the Chief of Police in Houston, Texas wanted to install video cameras inside apartments and homes in order to "fight crime" because he said there was a shortage of police officers. Chief Harold Hurtt told reporters, "I know a lot of people are concerned about Big Brother, but my response to that is, if you are not doing anything wrong, why should you worry about it?"[7]

A spokesperson at the Houston Apartment Association supported the idea, saying many people would, "appreciate the thought of extra eyes looking out for them."

School Spied on Students with Video Cameras in Laptops

In February 2010, a news story spread around the

---

[7] *Associated Press* "Houston Eyes Cameras at Apartment Complexes" (February 16, 2006)

country about a school in Philadelphia that was spying on students by secretly activating the video cameras in their laptops. These laptops were given to the students by the district and were taken home as if they were their own computers. Almost every laptop computer, as you probably know, has a tiny video camera located on the top, as well as a microphone, which are used for video chats or to record video blogs. Few people know that they can also be remotely activated and used to watch and listen to anyone in their range.

The parents of one student filed a class-action lawsuit against the school on behalf of 1,800 students who were issued the laptops and were not told that school administrators had the ability to secretly activate the laptop webcams remotely, no matter where the laptop was located as long as the computer was online. The lawsuit seeks damages for invasion of privacy, theft of private information, and unlawful interception and access of electronic information.

The parents of Blake Robbins, who are responsible for the lawsuit, found out that school officials were using the computers to spy on students when an assistant principle confronted their son about "improper behavior in his home" and showed him a picture taken from his school-issued laptop's webcam.

Most people only close their laptop when packing it up and transporting it, and a lot of people have their laptops sitting on desks in their bedroom, with their bed or bathroom often in clear view of the video camera, never suspecting that anyone could be watching from the webcam. School officials could have been watching the students undress in their own bedrooms, or even watched them as they sat in front of their laptops masturbating to porn on the Internet. If school officials had seen a student doing such a thing, which is a common occurrence for many teenagers and adults, it would constitute watching child pornography.

School officials tried to say that they would only use the remote activation feature if a laptop was lost or stolen, but shortly after the lawsuit was filed and news about this story made it around the world, the lawyer for the Robbins family alleged that school officials had taken thousands of pictures of students while in their homes using the remote activation feature of the built-in camera, and also had lists of the websites they visited and transcripts of their online chats.

The case, Blake J. Robbins vs. Lower Merion School District, was filed in the United States District Court for the Eastern District of Pennsylvania on Tuesday, February 16, 2010. The lawsuit also says that the camera on Blake Robbins' laptop took photos of the boy partially undressed and as he slept in his bed and says the camera was set up to take a new picture every 15 minutes, along with a screen shot.

One school employee allegedly sent an e-mail to Carol Cafiero, the administrator in charge of the spy program, saying the software was like, "a little LMSD [Lower Merion School District] soap opera," to which Cafiero is quoted as replying, "I know, I love it."[8]

It is alleged that Cafiero copied some images from the spy system onto her home computer, a claim she denies. Eight months later the lawsuit was settled and the school district agreed to pay $610,000 in damages, including $185,000 to two students it was proven were secretly spied on by the school using the webcams.

Blake Robbins, whose family brought the first lawsuit, was reported to have had $175,000 of the teen's

---

[8] *Philadelphia Inquirer* "Lawyer: Laptops Took Thousands of Images" By John P. Martin (April 15, 2010)

settlement put in trust for him, presumably for college.[9] The school district also had to pay $425,000 in legal fees to the plaintiff's attorney.

The school board decided to settle the case after their insurance company agreed to pay the $1.2 million dollars in fees, a settlement they had initially refused to pay. As a result of the case, the school disabled the spying software, apologized to students and parents, and suspended two employees. The school district even tried to demonize the Robbins family, who first filed the lawsuit against the school, attacking them by saying that if they were so worried about their son's privacy then they shouldn't have released photos of him to the media.

While this case was a major victory against Big Brother and helped raise awareness for what technology was now capable of, this is just the tip of the Orwellian iceberg.

Schools Installing Video Cameras in Bathrooms

While it is common for surveillance cameras to watch over businesses and even city streets and sidewalks, most people would never imagine that video cameras would be installed in bathrooms, especially at a school, but that is exactly what has happened in numerous schools around America. Channel 13, WMAZ in Central Georgia, reported that an 8th grader found a video camera installed in the school bathroom at a Jasper County school in 2005. The boy and his friends took the camera down and brought it home to show his parents. He was later suspended for stealing school property.

---

[9] *Philadelphia Inquirer* "Lower Merion district's laptop saga ends with $610,000 settlement" by John P. Martin (October 12, 2010)

"It felt like the right thing to do...because it felt like we were being violated in every way in the bathroom," said the 13 year old Mac Bedor, one of the boys who helped remove the camera.[10]

When the boy's mother contacted the school, she was told that the principle, Howard Fore, had authorized cameras to be installed in the bathrooms, allegedly to stop vandalism. What's especially creepy about this, is that only Howard Fore (the principle) knew about the camera being installed, and none of the other administrators were informed. It makes you wonder whether he installed the camera for his own personal perverse enjoyment, or to sell the footage to online pedophiles or to websites that market what they call voyeuristic video feeds which are taken from secretly placed cameras where people would never expect them to be, such as bathrooms, locker rooms, showers, or dorms.

The mother of one of the boys who helped remove the camera was interviewed by the local news station and said, "I had told the high school principal, Mr. Fore, that he needed to come up with another solution. That this wasn't appropriate. His response to me was he was going to continue to film."[11]

She was proud of what her son did because it was the right thing to do, and described the camera as a cheap one, not a professional one, and said it looked like a spy camera that people can buy on the Internet. The Bibb County District Attorney, Howard Simms, said that cameras in public school bathrooms are perfectly legal.

At another school, Reynoldsburg High School in Ohio, police installed a video camera in a bathroom saying it was to catch a person who wrote graffiti on a

---

[10] Channel 13, WMAZ Macon, GA
[11] Channel 13, WMAZ Macon, GA

wall. The school's superintendent Richard Ross said the graffiti was "cryptic" and believed it was referring to a bomb threat.[12] The school's janitor removed the camera as soon as he discovered it. The Reynoldsburg Police Chief, Jeanne Miller, defended the camera, saying it was positioned to only videotape people from the chest up.

"I don't agree with the method because I believe it was an invasion of privacy," said Linda Rico, whose daughter attends the school. "My daughter was extremely upset about it, and I took her side. I'm glad to hear the camera is gone."[13]

A school superintendent in Texas named Dan Doyen was sentenced to five years felony probation and had to register as a sex offender after he installed a hidden camera in a women's bathroom at his school's administration office. The camera was disguised to look like an air freshener and was purchased with a school district credit card.

A school in Pine Bush, New York installed a fake video camera in a bathroom once in an attempt to fool boys into believing they were being videotaped, in order to discourage them from messing up the bathroom.[14]

These cases are not only isolated to schools in America. The Grace Academy in Britain, along with other schools, installed cameras in bathrooms as well. One mother told the *Sunday Mercury* newspaper, "She [her daughter] came home from school and told me security cameras had been installed in the girl's toilets but we didn't know anything about it. You would expect the school to have consulted parents first, yet we received no

---

[12] *The Columbus Dispatch* "Secret Camera Removed From High School Bathroom" by Julie R. Bailey (October 14, 1999)
[13] Ibid
[14] *Times Herald Record* "Some Things Make No Sense" (April 17, 2003)

information and no letters have been sent home explaining this decision."[15]

The school's principal, Terry Wales, told *Sky News*, "It's to safeguard our youngsters, many schools are using cameras now. We had a parents' forum last night, we explained the arrangements and the parents were satisfied. We've found that when it comes to health and safety, children want to feel secure."[16] The school already had 26 CCTV cameras watching other parts of the building.

Police were called to a school in Salford, England after parents learned that cameras had been installed in a locker room. Police seized the system.[17] The practice of installing video cameras in children's bathrooms would seem like the last thing that someone who is normal would do, yet we have seen this done on multiple occasions in the name of security, and people think it's OK. It is possible that at some point in the future, this Orwellian invasion of privacy may be considered perfectly normal, and many people may actually encourage it.

Talking Cameras

Some surveillance cameras in the United Kingdom are equipped with loudspeakers that can be used to shout at people on the streets by the officials who are monitoring the camera feeds if they see someone litter or if people are deemed to be loitering. Some of these loudspeakers are designed to sound like a child's voice in an attempt to make it more difficult for people to resist the commands by making them feel bad if they shout back

---

[15] *Sky News Online* "Parents Angry Over CCTV In School Toilets" by Roddy Mansfield (March 09, 2010)
[16] Ibid
[17] Ibid

at the loud speakers because they will feel like they are yelling at a child.[18]

The system enables workers at a control center to monitor different cameras that can all communicate with people on the street through the speakers. Secretary of State for the Home Department, John Reid, actually said that people liked the Orwellian system. "This is a hugely popular scheme in Middlesbrough and the vast majority of the people here are right behind it," he said.[19]

It was even reported that children from local schools were taken to the facilities and shown around as part of a field trip after the system was installed, thus indoctrinating them that such a Big Brother system is normal, and part of everyday life.

The telescreens in *Nineteen Eighty-Four* both watched and listened to everyone on the streets, and even in their own homes, and barked orders at people when they were slacking in their obedience to Big Brother.

Cameras with Microphones

Since surveillance cameras can watch you, and the human monitors can talk to you or shout at you through speakers built into the cameras, it shouldn't come as a surprise that these cameras are increasingly being equipped with microphones so they can listen to people too.

In 2006, it was reported that over 300 CCTV surveillance cameras in Holland were being equipped with high powered microphones that can detect and

---

[18] *The London Telegraph* "Oi! Talking CCTV cameras will shame offenders" by Philip Johnston (April 5, 2007)
[19] Ibid

record conversations from 100 yards away.[20] The creepiest part of this system is that it can automatically record conversations that it deems potentially aggressive based on 12 factors, including the volume level and the pitch and speed of people talking. The software does this all automatically and if the system detects what it considers to be hostility, then the police are dispatched to investigate.

Derek van der Vorst, who is the director of Sound Intelligence, the company that created the system, said "The cameras work on the principle that in an aggressive situation the pitch goes up and the words are spoken faster. The voice is not the normal flat tone, but vibrates. It is these subtle changes that our audio cameras can pick up on."[21]

The privacy laws in Holland allow this system to operate, although in other countries recording conversations without people's knowledge or consent would be the topic of much debate.

"It is technically capable of being live 24 hours a day and recording 24 hours a day," Van der Vorste said. "It really depends on the privacy laws in a particular country."

During a testing period the cameras were said to have detected 70 genuine alarms and led to four arrests. Harry Hoetjer, the head of surveillance at the Groningen police department said, for example, the system identified a gang of four men who were about to attack someone, and insisted the system stopped it.

In the buildup to the 2012 Olympics, a company called VCS Observation that markets the technology,

---

[20] *The London Times* "Word on the Street ... They're Listening" (November 26, 2006)

[21] Ibid

gave a presentation to London police officials hoping to convince the city to install the system there. Martin Nanninga of VSC Observation said, "There was a lot of interest in our system, especially with security concerns about the Olympic Games in 2012. We told them about both our intelligent control room and the aggression detection system."

British officials claimed that audio recordings from such a system would be treated the same as CCTV video footage under British law, saying that audio can be recorded for the purpose of the detection and prevention of crime and the apprehension and prosecution of criminals.

In Sylvester Stalone's 1993 film *Demolition Man*, the futuristic society is constantly monitored by audio surveillance equipment with voice and keyword recognition that automatically fines people if they swear or use inappropriate language. The film has several references to Aldous Huxley's novel *Brave New World*, including the naming of Sandra Bullock's character, "Lenina Huxley," which is a reference to Lenina Crown, a character in the *Brave New World* novel. At one point in the film, Wesley Snipes' character says, "It's a brave new world," as he picks up a futuristic ray gun.

I was surprised to find that in 2009 a local Subway sandwich shop had a microphone standing by the cash register, and when I asked the employees about it they informed me that the owner had installed it and can listen in on them from his laptop or cell phone at anytime, and says he does so to make sure that the employees are behaving themselves and treating customers the way he wants them to be treated.

Similar audio monitoring devices that include radio controlled cameras, and even speakers, are now frequently installed in businesses by the owners to intimidate employees into working harder and deter them from stealing or fooling around on the job.

The European Union has looked into Big Brother systems that involve installing cameras and microphones on the backs of seats on airplanes that would monitor the facial expressions of each passenger and even listen to their conversations to identify any suspicious behaviors or conversations taking place, in an attempt to thwart terrorism.

The EU has funded the technology and is working with several companies and universities to develop it. A European Commission spokesman confirmed that the European parliament had begun talks to actually form legislation "in order for these [security] measures to be applied across [all] airlines."[22]

The program is called Security of Aircraft in the Future European Environment (SAFEE) and would trigger an alert to airline personnel if the system detected specified combinations of facial expressions and other behavior that can allegedly indicate if a person may be a terrorist. "The system will not be triggered by nervous flyers," said James Ferryman, one of the researchers. "It is only triggered by well-specified combinations."[23] Ferryman also claimed that it was impossible to fool the technology. Critics have dubbed it the "spy in the cabin."

Designers hope the system will be available and fully operational in airlines before the year 2020. The microphones would presumably listen for keywords in passengers' conversations, much like the Echelon spy system does during telephone conversations, and is probably more functional as an intimidation tactic aimed

---

[22] *Times Online* "Airlines may be forced to fit anti-terror cameras in seats" (June 8, 2008) By Nicola Smith and Richard Woods
[23] Ibid

at preventing terrorism than it is at actually identifying someone who is about to hijack an airplane or disrupt a flight.

A spokesman for British Airways said, "While we always welcome new research and development that advances aviation security, we believe the emphasis of any new security initiatives would be better placed on preventing potential terrorists from boarding aircraft in the first place."[24]

This entire system seems like complete quackery. What if a passenger is having a bad day or if they're on their way to a funeral or a business trip they were forced to go on by their boss? What if they just hate their life but have no intention of doing any harm to anyone? Is this system going to flag them as a potential terrorist? Are we going to live in a world where we allow a computer program to supposedly determine what someone is thinking and flag them as dangerous based on their facial expressions?

This kind of system and others like it are really designed to intimidate people into conforming with the social norm and to get them to accept the idea that Big Brother is always watching them, no matter where they are, to make sure they don't misbehave. The microphones used by this system that allegedly listen for keywords spoken by terrorists is a complete joke. Are two terrorists going to say out loud to each other "OK, in five minutes let's hijack this plane?" Of course not. It is incredible that this kind of a system is even being considered and is taken seriously.

In *Nineteen Eighty-Four*, the term *facecrime* is used to describe an improper facial expression. For example, if an announcement was made that Big Brother

---

[24] Ibid

had increased food rations, if one did not show outwardly visible signs of excitement, then this was suspicious and could be a sign of resentment towards Big Brother.

Facial Recognition Cameras

Video cameras that are able to detect the identity of specifically which individuals are in their field of view have been discussed since the early 1990s, but the first systems of this kind weren't very accurate and were very expensive. As technology advanced, facial recognition systems became a reality and were installed in places like Fort Knox, casinos, shopping malls, and sporting events. Little did anyone know, but at the 2001 Super Bowl in Tampa, Florida, facial recognition cameras were used to scan for individuals seated in the crowd to locate people who had warrants out for their arrest.[25]

The system was created by Viisage who used their FaceTrac software that was developed at MIT. They input photos of criminals into the system that they obtained from local authorities and were able to find nineteen people who had been listed as targets.

ATMs are expected to possibly apply the technology to verify users, and numerous other applications will likely incorporate the technology as well. Laptop computers, for example, can be installed with software that is used to verify the user by scanning their face with the built in video camera before enabling the computer to function.

In 2005, a large shopping mall in the Netherlands installed facial recognition systems to spot suspected shop

---

[25] *Federal Computer Week* "Can a picture catch a thousand criminals?" by Dibya Sarkar (August 6, 2001)

lifters.[26] One of the first trials showed that 90% of those targeted as offenders could be spotted using the system. Feeds taken from existing security cameras were transmitted to a facial recognition database containing photographs of volunteers acting as known or suspected shoplifters. When they entered the mall and came in view of the security cameras, the system alerted security.

This same system has been used in casinos since at least 2005 to spot players banned from the establishment for counting cards or cheating.[27] (These banned players' names are added to the Black Book or the Griffin book as it is called.) In the past, security guards would flip through books containing photos of people who were banned from casinos, in order to keep those people's faces fresh in their memory so they could spot them if they came back, but now with facial recognition systems, as soon as the person walks into the door, the system will identify them and security guards will be dispatched.

Of course, you may think that by putting on a hat, glasses or a fake beard, you could fool the system, but a show on the History Channel titled *Fort Knox: Secrets Revealed* (2007) detailed some of the security measures in place to protect the gold held there, and when explaining the facial recognition systems, the security expert said that even if a person were to get facial reconstructive surgery, their system would still be able to identify them immediately.

Back as far as 1999, London, England was installing facial recognition systems to scan people as they walk on

---

[26] *LogicaCMG* "Regular Offenders can be identified by facial recognition technology" (January 2005)

[27] *The Herald* "Biometrics Helps Spot Banned Gamblers" by Tom Wilemon (May 5, 2005)

the street.[28]   London already has millions of CCTV cameras watching the streets, and they will likely all be upgraded with facial recognition software at some point in the near future. An area in London named Newham was the first neighborhood to install facial recognition cameras and used the FaceIt system developed by Visionics. The system used only 13 cameras and only 60 criminals were entered in as targets, none of which were spotted for three years, but it was just a test of the technology in its early phases in 1999.

In August of 2003, two years after the test of the system at the Super Bowl, police in Ybor City, Florida connected three dozen cameras on the streets to the FaceTrac system and entered in over 1000 photos of felons and runaways as targets. This system can also follow a target and watch them on whatever camera they come into view from, so a live person can watch their every move in real time once someone is identified.

In December 2003, the Royal Palm Middle School in Phoenix, Arizona, installed a facial recognition system on school property in an attempt to spot child molesters and other criminals.[29]   It has been rumored in early 2010, Disney began quietly looking into possibly installing facial recognition cameras in their theme parks as well.

Minnesota-based Identix Incorporated, which has contracts with the Department of Homeland Security, has been in contact with Disney regarding facial recognition systems[30] and another company called A4Vision, based in California, confirmed they had met with Disney

[28] *London Independent* "Surveillance UK: why this revolution is only the start" by Steve Connor (December 22 2005)

[29] *Video Surveillance Guide* "The history of video surveillance -- from VCR's to eyes in the sky" (March 23, 2005) by Lucy P. Roberts

[30] *Newsinitiative.org* "Walt Disney World: The Government's Tomorrowland?" by Karen Harmel (September 1, 2006)

executives to give a presentation of their facial recognition system. "They were interested," said A4Vision spokeswoman Suzanne Mattick.[31]

It's rumored that Identix has a system that can identify people using a skin print that allegedly can identify a person using only a small digital picture of their skin. It's said to be as accurate as a fingerprint scanner and can tell twins apart from each other.

Most facial recognition systems work using what is called Local Feature Analysis (LFA) which is a mathematical algorithm used to encode faces into a "face print," which is the numeric code for each person's face that is stored as a small computer file.

A leading facial recognition company, Visionics, uses what they call nodal points, which are approximately 80 different distinguishable features on the human face that are measured and written into a numerical code which represents that person's face print in the database. Visionics says that only 14 to 22 nodal points are needed for their FaceIt software to identify someone. Back in the year 2000, the system was capable of matching face prints by searching through 60 million per minute. Today these systems can probably scan through a database containing the entire population of the United States in just a few seconds.

Visionics was founded by Joseph Atick, who in 1991 was recruited by Rockefeller University in New York to create the Computational Neuroscience Laboratory where he developed his facial recognition systems. To do this, he was also given $4 million dollars in grants by the Department of Defense, particularly from DARPA, for what they called Human Identification at a Distance (or HumanID), which would become a part of the

---

[31] Ibid

Information Awareness Office. The National Security Agency paid another $4 million dollars to develop the FaceIt program. [32]

Since police often photograph and videotape protests and demonstrations as possible evidence in the event that people commit assaults or vandalism, there are now new privacy concerns for even attending public rallies because police have the ability to run video footage and photos through facial recognition software in order to identify every single person in the crowd. People may be secretly listed in police databases as "extremists" simply for attending peaceful and legitimate demonstrations. As facial recognition systems become more common, they will instantly be able to identify the names of each person in attendance of any such march or demonstration.

Operation Noble Shield

The Rockefeller funded Joseph Atick, the founder and CEO of Visionics, the pioneer and leading company in facial recognition systems, proposed that a nationwide facial recognition system be installed in every airport in America that will look for suspected terrorists who are trying to board planes. He called it Operation Noble Shield, and immediately following the September 11, 2001 attacks, Atick was contacting the media trying to promote his company in the fight against terrorism. A week and a half after the attacks, Atick testified at a special committee formed by the Secretary of Transportation, Norman Mineta, where he proposed Operation Noble Shield.

In America, at least we still have some protections

---

[32] *PR Newswire* "Federal Government Adopting Face Recognition" July 7,1997

outlined in the Bill of Rights that haven't been circumvented by fears of terrorism, and some watchdog groups do their best to resist certain Orwellian measures the government or private industry tries to impose on people. One must wonder (and fear) what will happen when oppressive dictatorships obtain this kind of technology and begin installing it on their public streets, or in private buildings to squash dissent and keep their citizens under the watchful eyes of Big Brother.

While privacy issues and Big Brother tend to be somewhat common issues in the twenty-first century, it's interesting to note that Senator Sam Ervin in the 1970s, said, "When people fear surveillance, whether it exists or not, when they grow afraid to speak their minds and hearts freely to their government or to anyone else, then we shall cease to live in a free society."[33]

Barry Steinhardt, the director of the ACLU's Technology and Liberty Program, is concerned about the large-scale implications of facial recognition systems and said, "What it tells us is that we are really on the cusp of a surveillance society where you are not going to be able to go anywhere without being subject to both surveillance and identification...I find it chilling."[34]

Verint Systems

A surveillance company called Verint systems [verifiable intelligence] has created a service that watches people shop in retail stores and monitors how long they spend in an aisle and can detect whether or not they pick

---

[33] Sykes, Charles J. – *The End of Privacy: Personal Rights in the Surveillance Society* page 162 (St. Martin's Press 1999)
[34] *CNN Talkback Live* Transcript (February 1, 2001) "Should People who are Criminals Be Under Surveillance?"

anything up off the shelf. If someone spends too much time in an aisle, the system alerts customer service and a store employee will be dispatched to that isle to ask the person if they need any help.

The system also monitors how many people come into a store, how long they spend in a store, and can calculate the ratio of customers to sales. This is not just a prototype, the Verint system has been used in stores like Home Depot and Target since at least 2006.[35]

Verint also created a service called ULTRA Customer Intelligence Analytics that data mines phone recordings for keywords. Verint says it, "Detects subtle, often counter-intuitive patterns and cause/effect relationships from recorded interactions to generate revenue opportunities."[36]

David Worthley, president of Verint Systems use to work as the chief of the FBI's telecommunications industry liaison unit which handled wire tapping. Kenneth A Minihan, the director of Verint Systems, was a director of the National Security Agency. Another big wig named Howard Safir was the former police commissioner for New York City and an executive in the DEA. Verint also receives a large amount of funding from grants given by Israel.

Aside from retail stores like Target and Home Depot using Verint systems, their equipment is also used at Dulles Airport outside of Washington, DC, and inside the US Capitol building. In August of 2002 Verint's stock was $6 per share, and by 2010, rose to more than $25.

---

[35] *CNBC* "Big Brother, Big Business" (Air Date: November 9th 2006)
[36] O'Harrow, Robert Jr. – *No Place to Hide* page 296 (Free Press 2006)

Facial Recognition Billboards

In areas of Japan, an advertising agency installed billboards that have facial recognition cameras that can identify the sex and approximate age of people who walk by and then use that information to display what they consider to be relevant products on the billboards which consist of LCD screens.[37] In Steven Spielberg's 2002 film *Minority Report*, there is a scene showing billboards using retina scanners that identify people as they walk by and not only display ads that computers have determined would be suitable for that person, but the ads talk to the people using their name, as well. "John Anderton! You could use a Guinness [beer] right about now," one says, as Tom Cruise's character walks by. In another scene he walks into a Gap clothing store and is greeted by a hologram of a woman welcoming him back and asks him, "how did those assorted tank tops work out for you?" referring to his last purchase, which was obviously in the database.

NEC, the Japanese company that designed the real life facial recognition billboards, claim that they don't store the images of people who walk by and say they are deleted after the person passes the view of the camera.[38] The company tried to downplay the Orwellian aspects of the system by comparing it to cookies that are stored on people's computers that track what items people looked at on retailer's websites in order to post recommended items for that user.

---

[37] *The London Telegraph* "'Minority Report' digital billboard 'watches consumers shop'" by Andrew Hough (March 10, 2010)
[38] *Daily News* "They're watching ... Japanese electronics company NEC develops 'Minority Report' style billboard" by Caitlin O'Connell (May 10, 2010)

Facial Recognition App on Cell Phones

Facial recognition cameras and software isn't just restricted to large and bulky mainframe computers with extensive databases. In February 2010, a Swedish company called the Astonishing Tribe released an application (an app) for cell phones that allows people to take someone's picture and then using facial recognition and face printing software, the application finds that person's Facebook or MySpace page.

The application is called the Recognizr and shortly after it was released privacy advocates were understandably spooked. Tom Gaffney, a software security expert with F-Secure, said, "This app looks like it could be a stalker's dream," and Simon Davies of Privacy International called the application an atrocious invasion of privacy and said it infinitely increased the dangers of stalking and privacy issues that already exist.[39]

Using this application, a guy can now simply take a picture of a girl that he's attracted to, whether she's in a bar, in the grocery store, or anywhere, and then within seconds pull up her Facebook page and know her name, where she lives, read all her wall posts, see all her pictures, find out who her friends are, and more. The horrific things that could be done by stalkers, criminals, blackmailers, perverts and psycho's are virtually limitless.

This is certainly not the only app of this kind. An app for the iPhone called Face Match accomplishes something similar by identifying specific individuals in photos you have uploaded to your Facebook page. The market for mobile facial recognition systems is just beginning to develop, and as the twenty-first century

---

[39] *The Sun* "Stalker Fear over Facial Recognition Phone Ap" (March 1, 2010) by Richard Moriarty

moves forward, this technology will be rapidly enhanced and could one day identify people just as easy as a human can recognize a friend in a split second after seeing them. It's not just people that these systems can identify. Google and other companies have built programs that allow users to take a photo of something with their cell phone, and the software identifies exactly what it is, and where it is geographically located. Google's application is called Google Goggles, and they are just one of several companies working on enhancing such technology.

For example, you could take a picture of a building in the middle of downtown in a major city, and the app will be able to identify it and immediately display a fact sheet on that building. Landmarks, landscapes, automobiles, practically anything could have its picture snapped, and the system will identify what it is. It's called visual search technology, and the possibilities are extremely vast. In 2009 scientists at the Smithsonian, the University of Maryland, and Columbia University were developing an app for the iPhone that could identify plant species just from taking a picture of one. [40]

Facial Recognition Software on the Internet

The facial recognition software company Face.com has developed a system that can search virtually the entire Internet in order to find photographs of a targeted individual. Once someone's picture is entered into the system, it searches through photos on social networking sites and online photo galleries finding faces that match. It functions like a typical facial recognition system by translating photos into algorithms formulated by various

---

[40] *CNN.com* "Future iPhone app may identify trees from photos" (May 4, 2009)

facial features and measurements (called nodal points), and then searches the Internet for all photos which match that algorithm. Face.com says the software is 90 percent accurate.

When this system was first developed, Face.com limited its availability but later released a software package called Photo Finder that allows anyone to search for matches over the entire Internet, including websites, online newspapers, blogs, and social networking sites.

While your Facebook photos may be set to "friends only" or "private," photos that you are tagged in which have been posted online by your friends, may not be set to private, and can easily be found by this kind of system. Are there funny but embarrassing photos of you posted somewhere on Facebook that you'd prefer your boss, parents, or children not see? Were you at a protest and possibly appear in a photo of the crowd that was posted online? Do you want your boss, neighbors, or the government knowing about what political or social movements you privately support and what events you attend? Anonymity may be a thing of the past.

Gil Hirsch, chief executive of Face.com, told *The Sunday Times*, "We have launched a service that allows developers to take our facial recognition technology and apply it immediately to their own applications."[41] What that means is practically any software company can now incorporate this Big Brother technology into cell phone apps or whatever kind of creepy and invasive programs their dark imaginations can dream up. As of September 2010 the company claimed its technology was already being used by 5,000 different developers. The genie is now out of the bottle. The company is also working on a

---

[41] *Mail Online* "The facial recognition software that will put a name to every photograph in the internet" (August 23rd 2010)

system that will search through YouTube videos in order to identify people using the same facial recognition technology.[42]

In December 2010 Facebook added facial recognition software to their website to identify people in photos after they've been uploaded.[43] Before this, people would have to physically "tag" (identify a person in a photo by linking the photo to their Facebook page). Now the system suggests who is in the photos. The beta version of this system actually worked fairly well and as the technology is refined it will be nearly impossible to remain anonymous on Facebook.

Google has an application called Picasa that in 2008 was updated to enable people to upload photos and the system automatically identifies who is in them if the person's face has already been tagged in the program. With Google's dominance in information technology and their history of Big Brother-type of applications, it shouldn't be surprising if Google develops a picture search tool that utilizes facial recognition technology. Just as the search engine can comb through millions of web pages in seconds and find an exact sentence or phrase someone posted somewhere, Google (and others) will likely develop systems that can match photos just as fast, no matter where they are posted on the Internet.

Cash Prizes Given to People Who Watch Surveillance Monitors

A company called Internet Eyes, located in Britain, actually offers cash prizes to ordinary citizens who are

---

[42] Ibid

[43] *Tecca.com* "Facebook adds facial recognition to identify friends in your photos" by Barb Dybwad (December 15, 2010)

given access to CCTV camera feeds if they see a crime being committed and are able to report it to authorities.

A businessman named Tony Morgan created the company after he learned that a large portion of security cameras watching the streets of London weren't being monitored by anyone.[44] The company initially offered a monthly prize of 1,000 pounds (approximately $1,550 US dollars)[45] for the best crime spotter of the month and then organized other payment terms for the spotters. At the time the program launched in October 2010, more than 13,000 people had signed up to watch the feeds and participate.

Charles Farrier, from the watchdog group *No CCTV*, said that the creation of Internet Eyes was a very worrying development and the government, "has put private profit above personal privacy in allowing a private company to launch its Stasi-style citizen spy game rather than defending the rights of British citizens."[46]

The system is marketed to businesses that don't have the budget for security guards to watch their security cameras 24 hours a day. Businesses pay a small fee to use the system and if someone sees what they think is a shop lifter, for example, that viewer can contact the store owner through the system which can send the owner a text message informing them of the event.

Daniel Hamilton of *Big Brother Watch* (a British watchdog organization) said, "It's astonishing to think that innocent people doing their shopping could soon be

---

[44] *The Daily Mail* "Internet game that awards points for people spotting real crimes on CCTV is branded 'snooper's paradise'" (October 5th 2009)

[45] As of January 1, 2011 Currency exchange rates flucate daily

[46] *The Daily Mail* "The CCTV vigilantes: Snoopers paid to sit at home watching store security cameras" by Jack Doyle (October 5th 2010)

spied on by an army of busybodies with an Internet connection. CCTV should be used sparingly to help solve real crimes, not to encourage this type of tawdry voyeurism."[47]

The program, which started in October of 2010, was approved by the Information Commissioner's Office.

Pre-Crime Cameras

A strange new surveillance program in the United Kingdom was implemented in 2009 that is designed to automatically identify suspicious people and prevent crime before it occurs. The program is called ISIS (Integrated Sensor Information System), which interestingly spells out *Isis,* the Egyptian goddess and mother of the sun god Horus. The London *Telegraph* explained, "When a crime looks like it is going to occur, the system will verbally warn the perpetrator and then if necessary alert the nearest police officer."[48]

The ISIS system uses what is called "computer vision technology" that analyzes security camera feeds to look for what authorities consider to be behavior that is anti-social or suspicious. The criteria for this "suspicious" behavior is said to be people wearing hooded sweatshirts, people who make sudden movements, and even "verbal aggression" that is detected by microphones placed in public places and on public transportation.

X-Ray Cameras

As if being watched, listened to, and having your

---

[47] Ibid

[48] *Telegraph* "Artificially Intelligent CCTV could prevent crimes before they happen" (September 23, 2009) by Richard Alleyne

movements monitored by artificially intelligent systems designed to supposedly determine whether you are acting hostile or not aren't Orwellian enough, leaked documents in London show that the government was looking into installing x-ray systems on lamp posts on public streets in order to see if people were concealing any weapons or explosives under their clothes.[49] There are several types of devices that can accomplish this task, such as millimeter wave machines or terahertz radiation which penetrates clothing.

In 2007 a train station in London conducted a month long test using millimeter wave scanners to look at people as they boarded trains to determine if they were concealing any weapons. A similar device was used at several other Underground (subway) stations as well. These are similar devices to the so-called naked body scanners employed at airports around the world, but they scan the entire crowd and without their knowledge.

"The real question is not whether the technology can see something under the clothing. It's how you respond to it when the technology says there's something unusual," said security expert Bob Ayers. "Do you have police strolling down each street, ready to ask people what they have under their jacket?" he wondered.[50] There is also a concern for the health risks from repeated exposure to such systems.

You may think that these "x-ray" cameras are the result of advanced twenty-first century technology, but you are wrong. A retired colonel from Taiwan's National Defense Department named Alan Yu was exposing this technology back in 1997. An article he wrote titled

---

[49] *BBC* "Could X-ray scanners work on the street?" (Monday, 29 January 2007)
[50] Ibid

Millimeter Waves and Mind Control explained, "If you want to see the future of surveillance, take a trip into the world of millimetre waves and the video cameras that are sensitive to them."[51]

He also said that in that same year, 1997, a company called Millitech expected to have millimetre-wave cameras available for around $10,000 and portable versions for $80,000. He even said that similar devices are able to see inside the human body and can detect anything that has been inserted in any orifice, such as the anal cavity, which is a common method for smuggling drugs and weapons into prisons.

Devices called T-ray scanners, or Terahertz scanners are used by the Secret Service to scan crowds when the president is making a public appearance to spot anyone who would be carrying a gun or other weapon concealed under their clothes.[52]

Some may argue that these kinds of devices will help to make people safer if they are installed on public streets, since there may be people who are carrying concealed weapons, but are we going to allow police officers to approach and detain and search anyone whenever the systems detects what it considers to be a weapon? What if a person has a concealed carry permit and is legally allowed to wear a concealed hand gun? Are they going to be tackled to the ground and beaten and tazed because the system shows they are walking down the street with a gun under their jacket even though they are allowed to?

Are people who carry a Swiss Army Knife for its convenience and functionality going to be surrounded by police and searched every time an x-ray camera sees they

---

[51] *News Post* "Millimeter Waves and Mind Control" by Alan Yu (March 1997)

[52] *The London Independent* "White rage: The rednecks out to kill Obama" by Andrew Gumbel (November 16, 2008)

have a pocket knife? In most states in America, a person is legally allowed to carry a knife as long as the blade is shorter than three inches; so what is going to happen to these ordinary law abiding citizens when they are spotted carrying a perfectly legal knife in their pocket? Are they going to be treated as criminals or terrorists? Perhaps the laws will be changed to make it illegal for people to carry an innocent pocket knife in public.

Body Scanners at Airports

After the failed Christmas Day "underwear bomber" tried to blow up a plane as it approached Detroit, Michigan on Christmas Day of 2009, Homeland Security officials immediately began clamoring for newer high-tech security measures to be implemented at airports around the country. The device touted as being able to prevent future attacks of this nature was the so-called naked body scanner that allows TSA workers to see a virtual naked image of passengers' bodies as they are being scanned by the device.

When sample photos were released showing just how detailed the images were that these machines take, many people were uneasy about what the machines revealed. In May 2010, a TSA worker in Miami, Florida was arrested for aggravated battery after he allegedly attacked one of his coworkers who was making fun of him for having a small penis after he passed through the new body scanner.[53]

Adding to the controversy over the use of these revealing scanners, the TSA had claimed that the machines could not store the naked images of people, but

---

[53] *NBC Miami* "Suspicious Package: TSA Worker Jailed After Junk Joke" by Willard Shepard and Brian Hamacher (May 7, 2010)

the Electronic Privacy Information Center uncovered documents showing that the machines do in fact have image storing capabilities, and can even send images.

EPIC obtained the technical specifications and vendor contracts through a Freedom of Information Act lawsuit, which directly contradicts the TSA's claim that the machines couldn't store the images.

In the beginning of 2010, there were about 40 machines in use at 19 different airports, and the TSA planned to install 150 more by the end of the year, and another 300 in 2011. As Thanksgiving weekend of 2010 approached, news stories started circulating about the busy travel patterns and the added security measures of the new naked body scanners now that they were installed and fully operational in airports across the country. People also began talking about how they didn't want to be subjected to the radiation believed to be given off by the scanners, not to mention the humiliation of the naked body scan, or the groping pat downs if one dared to "opt out" of the scan.

At this point in time, not every traveler had to go through the scan—only supposedly people who were chosen at random. Several attractive female celebrities made headlines for speaking about their experiences at the airports getting scanned by the new naked body scanners (called *rape scanners* by some detractors), and the publicity was not good. Former *Baywatch* babe Donna D'Errico felt that she was selected for the scan because she was hot and didn't think she was chosen at random.

She told *AOL News*, "It is my personal belief that they pulled me aside because they thought I was attractive...My boyfriend sailed through with no problems, which is rather ironic in that he fits the stereotypical 'look' of a terrorist when his beard has grown a bit. After the search, I noticed that the male agent who had pulled me out of line was smiling and whispering with two other agents and glancing at me. I was outraged."[54]

"This could, and I'm sure does, happen to other women. It isn't right to hide behind the veil of security and safety in order to take advantage of women, or even men for that matter, so that you can see them naked. It's a misuse of power and authority, and as much a personal violation as a Peeping Tom. The difference is that Peeping Toms can have charges pressed against them," D'Errico concluded.[55] The airport denied any inappropriate behavior from the TSA agents on the scene.

Reality TV star Khloé Kardashian, the younger sister of Kim Kardashian, appeared on *Lopez Tonight* during this same holiday season and happened to mention her experience with airport security as well, saying, "They basically are just raping you in public. I got asked the other day, do you want to go for a screening or get patted down. I don't want that X-Ray to see everything, honey."[56]

She continued to say "[T]he people are so aggressive, It's like, 'Chill out, you didn't find anything on me yet, calm down…' They say, 'OK, I'm going to be patting you down and I'm going to be touching the crease of your ass.'"[57] Khloé was visibly upset.

Videos then started getting posted on YouTube showing TSA agents feeling up men, women, and children as a "precaution" before letting them pass through airport security. Some people protested and

[54] *Starpulse* "Donna D'Errico 'Outraged' Over Airport Body Scan" (December 8th, 2010)
[55] Ibid.
[56] *Lopez Tonight* "Khloé Kardashian Describes TSA Pat Downs as 'Raping You in Public'" (Aired December 6th 2010)
[57] Ibid.

stripped down into Speedos or bikinis right before going through the security checkpoint to highlight how invasive and ridiculous they were. Homeland Security Secretary Janet Napolitano had been labeled *Big Sis*, as in *Big Sister*, a play on the Orwellian *Big Brother*, as a result of all the negative publicity her invasive programs were getting.

License Plate Readers

At some point in the New World Order, all vehicles will most likely be required to have a GPS tracking system installed on them in order to be authorized to drive on the roads so authorities can determine exactly where a specific vehicle is located at any given time. Until this occurs, there are other ways that Big Brother is watching your car. Since facial recognition systems can detect a specific person's face out of a crowd of tens of thousands in a split second, it should be no surprise that systems can also read the license plates on vehicles from any number of the traffic cameras or red light cameras positioned around cities.

More and more cameras are being equipped with Optical Character Recognition systems (OCR) that can read the hundreds of license plates that go whizzing by the cameras every minute. A new technology called LPR uses what is called License Plate Reader or License Plate Recognition that can read practically any license plate from any state, even with the large variations of designs and colors.

Numerous states are currently using LPR systems to spot drivers whose licenses have been suspended or revoked, or to find stole vehicles. Other ideas for the system involves finding people who have unpaid parking tickets, backed taxes, or warrants out for their arrest.

Authorities also plan to have the system keep a log on which cars pass through specific cameras and at what time. This stored information can then be used to determine if a suspect of a crime was in the area at the time it was committed.

When license plate reading systems become common place, if a person whose license is suspended for unpaid parking tickets is spotted by an LPR camera, a police officer will be immediately dispatched to pull them over and arrest them. That is, unless the government implements mandatory GPS black boxes on automobiles which would then disable a person's vehicle until the tickets were paid. These systems are already used by car dealers if people miss several payments.[58]

Police Wear Head Mounted Cameras

At the end of 2009, a police department in San Jose, California, began equipping officers with head-mounted video cameras to record their interactions with the public.[59] The officers, in this case, control when the cameras are on or off, and are supposed to turn them on every time they talk with anyone.

The devices were made by Taser International, the company that makes the infamous Taser guns often abused by police. The company paid for the first 18 units as an attempt to get the department to expand their use to all 1400 officers. The devices cost approximately $1700 each and have a $100 monthly fee per officer, which would bring the cost to $4 million dollars if the San Jose

---

[58] *Wired.com* "Hacker Disables More Than 100 Cars Remotely" by Kevin Poulsen (March 17, 2010)
[59] *KETK NBC* "San Jose police test head-mounted cameras" (December 22, 2009)

police department would implement them for all their officers.

In February 2010, nine officers in San Diego's police force began using Taser's cameras as part of another field test. "It gives real-time information on exactly what occurred at the scene. Anything that helps put the case into perspective," said San Diego Assistant Police Chief Bob Kanaski. "No more 'he said, she said.' Now it's in color."[60]

It must be noted that during numerous instances of police misconduct, civilians happen to be videotaping with a camcorder or their cell phone, and officers often order them to stop filming or even confiscate or smash their cameras to prevent any evidence from getting out and showing the officer's crimes.

Of course, the video footage and audio taken by the head mounted cameras will often only be used to support the police officer's claims of what a suspect has done or said, and it shouldn't be surprising if hard drives are sometimes "damaged" and can't have their contents retrieved when the footage would show severe officer misconduct.

In London in 2005, police shot and killed Jean Charles de Menezes who they suspected was carrying a bomb on the subway, but he was completely innocent. This was immediately following the 2005 transit bombings where three different trains and one bus were blown up, killing 52 people and injuring 700. Officers initially said that Menezes was running from police and struggled with them when they approached, and claimed that's why they killed him. Several video cameras that were in clear view of the incident were said to

[60] *Union Tribune* "Cameras change focus on crime watch" by Kristina Davis (February 24, 2010)

mysteriously have their hard drives missing, although inside sources with the security company that maintained the cameras said they were in full working order.[61]

While the police officers often record interactions with suspects, there has been a disturbing trend in police arresting citizens and charging them with felony illegal wiretapping for simply doing the same thing.[62]

If suspects or bystanders videotape interactions with police, then some police are now claiming these people are recording the interaction without two party consent—meaning the police officers don't agree to the recording—thus they claim the citizens are committing a felony illegal wire tap.[63] In most states in order for private conversations to be recorded legally, both parties must consent or it is considered an illegal wire tap. This law was designed to prevent phone conversations from being secretly recorded, and was not meant to apply to the public videotaping of an event (which happens to capture the audio too), but we have seen numerous instances where police officers charge people under this statute even though it does not apply to conversations where there is not a "reasonable expectation of privacy," such as on a public street. This has not stopped police officers around the country from unfairly charging people with "illegal wire tapping" for simply videotaping a public interaction where there was no reasonable expectation of privacy.

Police departments, and many courts, have decided

[61] *Daily Mail* "Tube CCTV: Was there a cover-up?" (August, 23 2005)

[62] *TechDirt.com* "Police And Courts Regularly Abusing Wiretapping Laws To Arrest People For Filming Cops Misbehaving In Public Places" (June 4th 2010) by Mike Masnick

[63] *The Baltimore Sun* "State police charge motorcyclist for recording stop" (May 9, 2010)

that it is OK for police to record us, but we cannot record them. This hypocritical double standard only serves to protect the Big Brother system, and restricts the rights and freedoms of honest and ordinary people. The police simply do not want people to videotape them because those videos will sometimes capture clear evidence of officer misconduct that they will not be able to deny.

Other Uses for Cameras

One use of video cameras that most of the public is unaware of is in the retail sales industry, which sometimes uses a surveillance system to photograph each costumer who comes into a store or walks onto a sales lot—and then the salesmen have to log certain information about that person—all without the customer knowing about it.[64] This system is used more to monitor the salespeople than it is to monitor the customers. The system keeps track of how many people step foot into a store, and a formula is used to determine how well the sales force is doing by cross-referencing the number of sales and the dollar amount of the invoices, with the number of people who step foot in the door.

This system is used mainly in low-traffic, high-end stores that sell items like furniture or jewelry that only get a hand full of customers who walk thought their doors each day. If the system shows that one particular salesperson has ten people walk through the door on average, and makes five sales, but another salesperson who gets ten people walking in only makes two sales, then management is going to see that his closing ratio isn't very good and will likely fire him. When commission salesmen have a bad day or a bad month

---

[64] One of these systems is eTrax by Mink Incorporated

they'll often say, "I didn't have any customers walk through the door," but this system can prove otherwise. Salesmen that this author has personally spoken with who have had to use this system at work have told me that they often have to write a brief description of what merchandise the customer was looking at, and it is then saved in a file along with that person's photograph which was taken when they tripped the sensor as they walked in the door.

If, for example, the person who walks through the door is somebody who is lost and asks for directions, then the salesman must log that entry, which is linked to that person's picture. This system also keeps track of how long each person is in the store. If a person comes in for one minute asking for directions, the system will show this and the boss won't think that their salesman couldn't close a sale. This system is also used to figure out a salesperson's average sale in dollars per walk-in.

Another Orwellian system that is used in the world of sales is a hidden camera and microphone worn by secret shoppers who companies hire to pretend to be customers who go into stores and videotape how the salesperson does with his or her presentation and closing attempts. I have personally spoken to salesmen who have been subjected to this kind of secret shopper. Since legal issues may arise from people being secretly videotaped along with an audio recording, many companies will coerce their employees into signing legal wavers that say they consent to the secret video shopper procedure which then may occur at any time.

While secret shoppers are not new and are used by a variety of industries, they were usually just people that went in and asked specific questions of salespeople and immediately upon leaving would write up a brief report on the person and answer several questions about their attitude toward the pretend customer, their product knowledge, and perhaps their personal appearance, such as what they were wearing and how clean they were. But with video cameras becoming incredibly small, these secret shopper services now have the ability to let management or a business owner view a video of the entire process himself to see and hear how the salespeople perform.

Global Positioning Systems

In the 1990s, people began hearing about GPS (Global Positioning Systems) and in the 21st century we saw the technology rapidly expand into the mainstream and become part of commonly used items such as GPS systems for navigation in vehicles, in cell phones, and even on shipments of merchandise to track its exact location as it was en route.

While many people were surprised to learn that OJ Simpson's cell phone was triangulated to discover his location as he drove in his white Bronco down the Los Angeles freeway in 1994, evading police when he was wanted for murder, today such capabilities are expected and seen as commonplace. While most of us rely on our GPS navigation systems in vehicles to guide us to our destinations and can't imagine life without them, GPS has a dark side that is exploited by Big Brother and is being used in ways that can only be described as Orwellian.

Many businesses are putting GPS systems on company vehicles, something that doesn't sit well with many of the vehicles' drivers. Are they taking too long on their lunch breaks? Did the car travel back to the employee's house before 5 o'clock? Has the vehicle traveled over 75 miles per hour? All of this and more is available to supervisors and owners who have installed GPS systems on their company's vehicles.

The wrestling superstar Hulk Hogan had a reality show called *Hogan Knows Best* that aired on VH1 from 2005 to 2007 and gave an inside look at his family and their activities. His daughter Brook was seventeen when the show first aired, and in one episode Hulk let her go on a date with some guy, but before she did, he installed a GPS tracker on her car (without her knowledge) and during the episode it showed him watching where the car was driving, making sure that she was going where she said she was. Such devices are now so small that they can be placed on people, and not just in the trunk of a car.

Placing small GPS devices on children is now becoming common, as well as friends and family locator applications for cell phones that show the exact location of your friends and family on a map by using the built in GPS transmitters in all cell phones. Some people also envision future GPS systems so small that they can be implanted inside a person's body. We may soon live in a world where it is seen as completely normal for practically anyone to see exactly where you are, anywhere in the world, at every moment of the day.

Digital Angel

The first commercially available personal GPS tracker was called the Digital Angel, and was designed by Applied Digital, the creator of the VeriChip implantable RFID chip. The Digital Angel was designed to be worn by a person like a wrist watch and was marketed for children and the elderly. Upon its release in 2000, Richard J. Sullivan, chairman of Applied Digital, boasted that his device could tap a market worth more than $70 billion dollars.[65]

The chief scientist behind the device's creation, Dr. Peter Zhou, told *World Net Daily* he believed the company's future products would be implanted into people and will be "a connection from yourself to the electronic world. It will be your guardian, protector. It will bring good things to you," and that, "We will be a

---

[65] *World Net Daily* "Digital Angel unveiled" (November 01, 2000)

hybrid of electronic intelligence and our own soul."[66]

Although the Digital Angel (called the digital beast by detractors) came out in the year 2000, it wasn't until a decade later that personal locating devices would become very well known or used.

Family Locator Apps

Most new cell phones have what they call *family locator apps* that use a cell phone's built in GPS to show exactly where other members of your family are geographically located—at all times. Verizon's website explains, "From your PC or phone, enjoy the comfort of locating family members anytime, anywhere." The app is more than just a real-time GPS locator, it allows you to receive "arrival & departure updates" for each family member and lets you schedule location updates for each family member that will alert you as to their location at any specific time you set. For example, if you wanted to know where your kids were every night at 10pm, it will alert you in case you've lost track of time and forgot to check.

An app for Sprint phones allows users to review the past locations of their children (or husbands, wives, girlfriends, or boyfriends) for the last seven days and can also be set to send you automatic notifications of a child's location at specific times on specific days. The website boasts, "You don't need to install anything on the phones you wish to locate. Sprint Family Locator uses the GPS technology already built-in to every Sprint phone, so it is compatible with every Sprint phone." The cost of the Sprint Family Locator is $5 dollars per month which

[66] *World Net Daily* "Big Brother Gets Under Your Skin" by Julie Foster (March 20, 2000)

includes tracking on up to four different phones.

'Little Buddy' Tracking Device for Children

In October 2009, a rather bulky tracking device was put on the market called the Little Buddy, which was advertised as a GPS system that parents can place in their child's backpack or lunch box so their location can be monitored on the parent's cell phone or computer. This device (and others like it) are designed for children who are too young to have cell phones which can be tracked by family locator apps.

The software for the Little Buddy allows parents to set up geographic boundaries that activate and deactivate at specific times, and if the device travels outside of those boundaries, then the parent will receive a text message or an e-mail alerting them of this. For example, a boundary around the school could be set up between 8am and 3pm and if the device (which is located in the student's back pack) leaves the school grounds before 3pm then the parent would be alerted.

The first version of the Little Buddy was rather large and bulky, and could not be placed in a child's backpack without them noticing, but as the years progress, similar devices will be extremely small and could be stashed inside a student's backpack, or even on their clothes without them even knowing.

One newscaster on the Fox News Channel joked about placing the device in her boyfriend's car so she could keep tabs on exactly where he went and when. Most people would obviously be unaware such a device was placed in their vehicle.

A commercial for the Little Buddy tracking device said, "Get peace of mind. Build trust. And be confident that your child is OK when you can't be with them."

Their claim of "building trust" is obviously doublethink, since using such a thing is a clear sign of an overbearing, controlling, or paranoid parent. The device costs less than one hundred dollars.[67]

Amber Alert GPS

Another personal GPS locator on the market that is extremely more advanced than the Little Buddy GPS tracker is called the Amber Alert GPS. It's fairly small in size, measuring 1.77" x 1.68" x .78" and is advertised as, "The world's smallest, most powerful GPS tracking device." It is marketed to parents who want to keep track of their children and can be put in their pocket or clipped onto their belt. The parents can then keep an eye on the device's location on their cell phone or computer, but this device is so much more than a GPS locator.

It costs $129.99 and the parents must pay a monthly fee ranging from ten dollars a month to forty dollars a month depending on what features they want. Some of these features include a "speed alert" that will notify parents when the GPS device exceeds a certain speed so a parent can tell if their child has gotten into a vehicle. The website even brags, "This feature is great for speeding teenagers!"[68] Do you want to know if your teenager ever drives faster than 80 miles per hour? You can easily set the device to alert you of this. You could, of course, then see exactly what street they're on.

It also has a temperature alert that will notify parents when the temperate surpasses or drops below the thresholds they designate. A feature they call

[67] *Bestbuy.com* Insignia - Little Buddy Child Tracker (Blue) Model: NS-KDTR2 SKU: 9540703
[68] https://www.amberalertgps.com/

"Breadcrumbing" allows a person to have the unit send them text messages at specific times of the day to notify them where the unit is located. You can also be notified when the device enters or leaves a specific location. The website reads, "Do you want to be notified when your child arrives at school, soccer practice, or the mall? You can with our latest feature: Destination Alert. Destination Alert allows the parent to define an area on a map, and receive notification by text and/or e-mail when the child arrives. It's easy and it gives you one more tool to keep your child safe!"

The device even has a "Voice Monitoring" feature that allows the parent to activate a microphone in the unit so they can listen in on what their child is doing. The website brags, "Even during use the child never knows that you are listening in."

The Amber Alert GPS system is named after the AMBER alert child abduction notification system that alerts local TV and radio stations if a child is believed to have been abducted. The AMBER alert system was named after a 9-year old child named Amber Hagerman who was abducted and murdered in Arlington, Texas in 1996.

Tracking the President, White House Staff, and Family Members

On CBS's *60 Minutes* in March 2010, Rahm Emanuel (President Obama's chief of staff) showed Katie Couric a security system he had in his White House office that tracked major White House players using a GPS system that showed their current location in real-time. The system keeps tabs on the President, Vice President, First Lady, family members, and others he said. The segment was brief, but it is clear that by "family members," this means Barack Obama's two kids have to wear GPS tracking bracelets probably twenty-four hours a day.

GPS Trackers at Amusement Parks

A company called SAMSys Technologies created a GPS tracking system that became available at multiple amusement parks as a way for parents to keep track of their kids. They call their device the SafeTzone System which is a GPS locator similar to a large wrist watch that can be used to keep track of the children and also enables them to buy things at the park like food and souvenirs, because it acts like an RFID debit card.

SafeTZone's website called it a "cashless spending module" and said it "eliminates the need for cash anywhere in the venue by turning each Locator into an electronic wallet. The elimination of cash will provide patrons with the freedom to utilize the venue services and make purchases at restaurants, games, attractions, and shops throughout the venue."

A press release sent out by Paramount's Great America theme park in 2004 brags that one of their parks in Santa Clara, California, began issuing the SafeTZone GPS trackers to guests so they could locate each other. The device is called the Star Watch which is a waterproof GPS system that is strapped onto people's wrists. Guests can then go to any number of "Location Stations" which show the location of others in their group. The Star Watch also allows people to send messages to other members in their group, and locate rides and restaurants in the park. The press release also noted that people would, "Receive information about Paramount's Great America's special promotions, show times and park events."

Rod Rankin, Paramount's Great America's senior vice president and general manager is quoted in the press release saying, "It's a convenient and affordable guest amenity that provides visitors the opportunity to track everyone in their group or simply find the easiest route to a favorite ride or restaurant."[69]

Paramount's Great America is owned and operated by Paramount Parks, a division of Viacom Inc, the entertainment giant that owns CBS, MTV, Nickelodeon, VH1, BET, Paramount Pictures, UPN, Spike TV, TV Land, CMT, Comedy Central, Showtime, Blockbuster, Simon & Schuster, and other media companies.

In 2004, Legoland in Denmark implemented RFID tracking of guests with devices called the "Kidspotter" which were advertised as a way to prevent children from getting lost. Leo Steiner, vice president for on-demand sales at IBM, who works with RFID, said, "Legoland will now know exactly where each customer is, how long they are spending in each area and which products are proving to be most popular."[70] Steiner sees the device as a market research tool more than a safety device.

Debbie Allen, a mother of two, told Silicon.com, "When you go to these theme parks, you tend to spend so much time trying to keep your children by your side that they get resentful and a little frustrated. If I were given the chance to feel a little more relaxed, I would jump at the opportunity; if they then used the information they had for marketing, then I really don't see the harm."[71]

---

[69] Paramount Press Release/June 24, 2004 PARAMOUNT'S GREAT AMERICA OFFERS *NEW* ELECTRONIC GUEST AMENITY AND LOCATOR SYSTEM

[70] *Silicon.com* "RFID chips on kids makes Legoland safer" (June 25, 2004)

[71] Ibid

Mobile Alarm for the Threatened

There have even been proposals for people to be forced to wear GPS monitors if they are the subject of harassment or if their life could be threatened by a dangerous ex-lover or spouse. Fifteen different districts in Holland have implemented this strategy and force people to carry such devices which can notify police with the push of a button as to the person's location so police can be dispatched to investigate.[72]

Those people are not criminals, they are the victims, and they are forced to wear GPS monitors similar to ankle bracelets worn by people on parole or house arrest.

Implantable GPS System

A patent application submitted in 2003 from a California company called Persephone, Inc., (Number 20040174258) describes their invention as a GPS device that is forcefully implanted into people and can't be removed. The title of their application is *Method and apparatus for locating and tracking persons,* which explains, "Removal of the implanted device by a runaway juvenile would likely be impossible. Even if possible, such removal would likely place the runaway at significant medical risk, which is counter to the runaway's goal of a safe escape and survival from parents or guardians."[73]

The patent application actually says that the tracking device could be implanted up a person's butt, in their rectum. The application describes the location of the

---

[72] *De Twentsche Courant Tubantia* "Mobile alarm device for threatened" (March 9, 2010)
[73] http://patft.uspto.gov/

device as being "Submuscular: for example, deep to a large muscle. Such a location is currently used for implantation of commercially available artificial urethral and anal sphincter reservoirs, which are positioned deep to the rectus abdominus muscles, within the pre-peritoneal Space of Retzius."

It gets worse. The patent application goes on to read, "Because the device is implanted in the person, it can also provide a shock, vibration, or other warning…[that] may be progressive, such that a person is subjected to a shock of increasing magnitude as he leaves a zone of confinement or enters a forbidden zone."

"The device may…include a microphone or similar device for monitoring acoustic information, thereby permitting the person to talk to a remote location."

If this isn't Orwellian enough, let me point out that the name of the company that filed this patent is called Persephone Inc, a company obviously named after Persephone, the Greek goddess that governs the underworld, or Hades (Hell).

A Mileage Tax

As cars have become more fuel efficient and hybrid and fully electronic cars have become quite popular, the number of gallons of gas that people use up in a given week has dramatically dropped, and so has the tax dollars the government rakes in from gasoline taxes. In order to compensate for this loss, some lawmakers are pushing for a new mileage tax that will tax cars based on the number of miles they drive.

The Governor of Oregon, Ted Kulongoski, was one of the first government officials to recommend a mileage tax to replace the traditional gas tax because of the loss of revenues due to more fuel efficient vehicles.[74] In 2009, he included his plans for this new tax in a transportation bill.

The governor's website outlined his reasons, saying, "As Oregonians drive less and demand more fuel-efficient vehicles, it is increasingly important that the state find a new way, other than the gas tax, to finance our transportation system."

He planned for a task force to "partner with auto manufacturers to refine technology that would enable Oregonians to pay for the transportation system based on how many miles they drive." This method would involve equipping all vehicles with GPS units that would monitor how many miles a person drove and tax them accordingly.

Oregon is certainly not the only state to consider such a proposal. The Texas Transportation Institute held a meeting in April 2009 to discuss "mileage-based user fees" and other ways to replace diminishing revenues from the gas tax. "We need to think differently about how we fund transportation," said the Texas Transportation Commission Chairwoman Deirdre Delisi.[75]

Some proposals for how the tax would be collected include a mileage check when the car has its registration renewed each year, or installing GPS systems on vehicles that would be programmed to tax people differently according to what road they were on, or if they traveled out of their state. Certain high-traffic roads, for example, would tax drivers at a higher rate, and GPS systems could enable the government to vary the tax rate depending on what county or city the vehicle was traveling in.

---

[74] Crosscut.com "Oregon will move to tax cars by the mile" By Knute Berger (December 30, 2008)
[75] *Chron.com* "Should drivers be taxed by the mile?" By Peggy Fikac (January 3, 2010)

Rental Car Company Fines Customers for Speeding

While it may not be that surprising to people that the government would install a Big Brother system to automatically fine drivers who were going over the speed limit, it was surprising to learn that in 2001 a rental car agency was fining their own customers for speeding in their rental cars. This came to light after a man named James Turner was fined $450 by the Acme-Rent-A-Car agency after the AirIQ GPS system installed on their rental cars calculated that he was speeding in their car.[76] The fine was charged directly to his credit card because the company had included language in the rental agreement explaining that the customer would consent to this, but of course, who reads the fine print on these agreements.

James Turner filed a lawsuit against the company in small claims court and also filed a complaint with the Connecticut Department of Consumer Protection.

Students Forced to Wear GPS Tracking Devices

Twenty-two students at a high school in Texas were ordered by a judge in January 2010 to carry GPS tracking devices on them in order to prevent truancy. "Bryan High students who skip school will soon be tracked 24 hours a day, seven days a week," reported KBTX, a local TV station.[77] The Orwellian program is called the Attendance

---

[76] *CNET News* "Rental-car firm exceeding the privacy limit?" by Robert Lemos (June 20, 2001)
[77] *KBTX.com* "New Program in Bryan Makes Truant Students Carry a GPS Device" (January 18, 2010) by Meredith Stanick

Improvement Management Program or AIM, and according to reports it is being used in schools, not only in Texas, but around the country.

Students who skip class are forced to appear at truancy court and then some are forced by the judge to carry the tracking devices, similar to ankle bracelets that people on parole or house arrest must wear. "Students on the program are tracked with a hand-held GPS device between the time they leave for school in the morning and the time they check in for curfew at night," reported the local news station.[78]

An official in Holland for the People's Party for Freedom and Democracy (VVD) proposed that "troublesome youth" be forced to wear GPS bracelets as well.

Tracking Cell Phone Locations

The Obama administration has argued that tracking the location of people's cell phones without a warrant is legal and should be permitted because, they say, Americans don't have a reasonable expectation of privacy concerning the whereabouts of their cell phone. U.S. Department of Justice lawyers say that "a customer's Fourth Amendment rights are not violated when the phone company reveals to the government its own records."[79]

In *Enemy of the State* (1998) Will Smith's character was tracked by a rouge group of government officials using all kinds of methods that seemed like science fiction at the time, but are actually possible. In the film, Gene

---

[78] Ibid
[79] *CNET.com* "Feds push for tracking cell phones" by Declan McCullagh (February 11, 2010)

Hackman made a statement that the National Security Agency has "been in bed with the entire telecommunications industry since the '40s," and he was right.

Not only can authorities track the real-time location of any cell phone, even when it's turned off, but they can go back and look at the records to show the location of any particular phone at anytime a phone call was made. A 2008 court order to T-Mobile in a criminal investigation says, "T-Mobile shall disclose at such intervals and times as directed by (the Department of Homeland Security), latitude and longitude data that establishes the approximate positions of the Subject Wireless Telephone, by unobtrusively initiating a signal on its network that will enable it to determine the locations of the Subject Wireless Telephone."

Kevin Bankston, an attorney for the Electronic Frontier Foundation said, "This is a critical question for privacy in the 21st century. If the courts do side with the government, that means that everywhere we go, in the real world and online, will be an open book to the government unprotected by the Fourth Amendment."[80]

Verizon Wireless keeps phone records, including cell phone locations, for 12 months according to Verizon's Vice President Drew Arena. They keep phone records for seven years.

The ACLU, the Electronic Frontier Foundation (EFF), the Center for Democracy and Technology, and other privacy advocates argue that Americans do not surrender their Fourth Amendment right when they turn on their cell phones.

Numerous attorneys have said that if such a practice is deemed illegal by a court, that the case would definitely

---

[80] Ibid

be appealed and government lawyers will fight until the practice becomes fully legal anyway.

The GPS Coordinates to Your Front Door

The census is done every ten years in America to determine how many people are living in the country and in what communities so that the appropriate number of funds and resources can be allocated to those areas. People have become familiar with the questionnaire mailed to them every ten years, asking who lives in your residence, what race they are, and several other personal questions, but as the 2010 census approached, stories began circulating that census workers were traveling door-to-door and linking the front door of each address with its GPS coordinates. Such reports turned out to be accurate.

In 2009, 140,000 people were hired as part of a $700 million dollar program to collect the GPS coordinates of every front door in America. People were obviously uncomfortable with this, especially since President Obama put his Chief of Staff, Rahm Emanuel, in charge of overseeing the census which is used to draw congressional districts. There appeared no legitimate or logical reason for such an enormous task. Why would the government need the exact GPS coordinates of every single front door in America? And why would they spend hundreds of millions of dollars doing this?

Blogger Douglas Gibbs of the *American Daily Review* wrote, "Imagine, if you will, that there are a number of people in a neighborhood that could not find the addresses they are tasked with finding. They are not locals, maybe are unable to read a map, or perhaps do not have the time to pull out a map, and they need to find you with specific GPS coordinates. Their devices would lead them to your front door with these coordinates. Imagine a crisis is afoot, and martial law is put into place. U.S. troops need to round up particular folks."[81]

He concluded, "Let's take this a step further. After all, with Barack Obama desiring to decrease the number of folks in the military, and with forces committed worldwide, we may not have sufficient military forces at home to deal with a rising national emergency. If the government decided to rely on foreign troops, perhaps United Nations personnel, most of which may not understand the street signs, much less know the lay of the land, they could use GPS devices to direct them to your front door."[82]

J.B. Williams of the *Canada Free Press*, wrote, "I can't resist the urge to question the authority and purpose behind such a BIG BROTHER initiative, when the official census itself is not due to be taken until 2010...No imagination is required to think up a whole laundry list of evil that could be done with a nationwide GPS grid of coordinate's markers painted on every private home across the country. But I was having trouble thinking up one good reason for it, even one legitimate use that would justify what must be a very expensive undertaking."[83]

Williams continued, "Why does the Obama administration need or want the latitude and longitude coordinates for every home in America? Why the rush to GPS paint every home in the next 90 days? Why must the marker be within 40 feet of every front door? For what possible purpose does the Fed need GPS coordinates for every home, and under what authority do they have the

[81] *American Daily Review* "Big Brother GPS Doorway Census" (April 27, 2009)
[82] Ibid
[83] *Canada Free Press* "Obama and ACORN GPS Marking EVERY Front Door in America?" by JB Williams (April 29, 2009)

right? Census workers, whom I asked, had the same holy-crap look on their faces that I had by then."[84]

Some bloggers even pondered whether one day the GPS coordinates could be used by Unmanned Arial Vehicles to spy on homeowners, or even blow them up with missiles if they were deemed subversive or a threat to the New World Order. The Census Bureau claimed that the GPS coordinates were needed to "ensure that all residents are counted in the right location."[85]

Remotely Disabling Automobiles

While it may seem like something out of a James Bond film, some car dealerships have been installing a device on new vehicles that allow them to remotely deactivate cars which will then prevent them from starting if people have missed their payments.

One such device was created by an Ohio company called Pay Technologies and is marketed to auto dealers as a way to disable vehicles of people who have missed their car payments. The device can also cause the car horn to honk repeatedly, and has a GPS tracker built in as well, so the location of a vehicle can been known at all times, in case they want to send a repo man to repossess the vehicle. Disabling a person's vehicle could leave a motorist stranded in a dangerous situation, or in the middle of nowhere; hazards that are apparently overlooked by the device's manufacturer.

In February of 2010, more than 100 vehicles in Austin, Texas were disabled and some had their horns honking repeatedly after a disgruntled employee of a dealership disabled the vehicles using the system in order

---

[84] Ibid
[85] US Census 2010 Overview

to get revenge on an auto dealer for firing him.[86]

"We initially dismissed it as mechanical failure," said Texas Auto Center manager Martin Garcia. "We started having a rash of up to a hundred customers at one time complaining. Some customers complained of the horns going off in the middle of the night. The only option they had was to remove the battery."[87]

After complaints started flooding in from the vehicles owners, the Texas Auto Center reset the Webtech Plus passwords for all of their employees and then gave police login entries and they traced an IP address to the suspect's Internet service provider. Police say he used a password from a fellow employee, and that his had been disabled as soon as he was fired. Austin police filed computer intrusion charges against the man.

---

[86] *Wired.com* "Hacker Disables More Than 100 Cars Remotely" by Kevin Poulsen (March 17, 2010)
[87] Ibid

Radio Frequency Identification Devices (RFID)

RFID, as many people know, stands for Radio Frequency Identification Device, and refers to a technology that encodes a unique ID number onto a tiny computer chip that can then be activated from a distance using an RFID reader which then identifies the number on the chip. It's sort of like an electronic serial number that is encoded in the RFID tag, which doesn't require any batteries, and can be extremely small and inexpensive to produce.

As with most technology, there certainly are advantages to RFIDs, such as increasing efficiency in business by minimizing errors along a supply chain. One interesting use of RFID that we may see in the future comes from Microsoft's vision of the "Home of the Future" where microwave ovens detect RFIDs in food's packaging and are automatically programmed to the correct power and time settings to cook the food properly. This home of the future would also have a refrigerator that keeps track of its contents, and when an item is not replaced in the fridge, it would automatically add it to your shopping list to order in a replacement.

Surely when RFID tags replace the standard UPC barcode, we will not have to wait in the checkout line at the grocery store for fifteen minutes and unload our groceries onto the conveyor belt, because we can just walk through a scanner with our groceries still in the cart, and they will all be scanned instantly from the RFID UPCs on each item. But not all uses for RFIDs will be so helpful to humanity.

There have been several applications filed for patents

that outline exactly what RFID tags are capable of, and it is extremely unsettling. Many devices designed and created will be promoted publicly for certain applications or benefits, but if you read the language written in their patent applications, their real Big Brother use and capabilities are discovered.

The implications of RFID tags are truly Orwellian, and their use far exceeds simply replacing UPCs on merchandise we buy at the store to make the checkout procedure faster. RFID tags operate as little tracking devices similar to, but not as powerful as, GPS systems, and have not only been forced on students at school, but have been implanted in people's hands and used for identifying them at businesses and government agencies, allowing them to enter secure areas, and even pay for drinks at fancy bars.

One patent application filed by IBM admits, "[T]he widespread use of RFID tags on merchandise such as clothing would make it possible for the locations of people, animals, and objects to be tracked on a global scale—a privacy invasion of Orwellian proportions."[88]

Documents from a company called NCR reveal they came up with the idea that RFID tags could be used for what they call "dynamic pricing" where, "RFID can be used in conjunction with electronic shelf labels to automate pricing based on the number of items on the shelf...For example...when certain popular items were in short supply (e.g., at Christmas time), the price can be automatically raised."[89]

A company called Accenture is the world's largest technology consultant firm with revenues over 20 billion dollars a year and large contracts with governments, and

---

[88] U.S. patent application # 20020116274 filed by IBM
[89] Albrecht, Katherine – *Spychips* page 79

in one of their brochures they proposed that RFID tags could be used by the government to help monitor families who had caseworkers assigned to them. The brochure reads, "[G]overnment agencies will also be looking for new ways to ensure the well-being of the people they serve. Activity-monitoring tools could give [government] caseworkers a powerful complement to home visits, while enabling them to be more vigilant about their clients' current state and potential needs."[90]

Author and consumer privacy advocate, Katherine Albrecht, writes extensively about the dangers of RFID in her 2006 book *Spychips: How Major Corporations and Government Plan to Track Your Every Purchase and Watch Your Every Move*, where she explains, "theoretically, the whereabouts of everything and everyone will be known at all times and accessible to anyone with access to the databases, authorized or otherwise. Imagine the power of being able to log onto a Google-like Internet search engine and find out all the items associated with a particular person, organization, or government entity. Then, imagine being able to find out where all those items are in real time, where they have been, and their historical relationship with other items, people, and events."[91]

In 2004, Albrecht received an e-mail from an RFID company asking her details about her biographical information, saying they were interested for "research purposes." Albrecht explains that she responded inquiring what kind of research they were conducting, and wondered why a company promoting RFID would be interested in what she, a major opponent, had to say about them. She then received another e-mail that wasn't meant

[90] Accenture brochure "Technology Comes Home" page 7
[91] Albrecht, Katherine – *Spychips* page 59

for her eyes, because the person accidentally clicked the "reply to all" button.

In the e-mail, which was meant only to be seen by people other than Albrecht, the person wrote, "I don't know what to tell this woman! 'Well, actually we're trying to see if you have a juicy past that we could use against you.'"[92] The company was obviously upset that Albrecht was raising awareness about RFID issues and they were looking to smear her and probably label her a "conspiracy theorist."

Students Forced to Wear RFID Tags

The first reports of schools forcing their students to wear RFID tags came from Japan, but not long after this, in 2005 the Brittan Elementary school in Sutter County, California implemented a system which forced students to wear ID badges embedded with RFID tracking tags. Every time the students entered or left a classroom, a sensor installed at the door way would log this, and would determine whether a student had skipped class. The school soon made headlines around the country and an immediate backlash caused them to abandon the system.

The RFID system was put in place without any parental knowledge, and the reason for it was said that it helped keep the students "safe" and simplified attendance-taking.

One concerned parent asked, "Are we trying to bring them up with respect and trust, or tell them that you can't trust anyone, you are always going to be monitored and

someone is always going to be watching you?"[93]   The
Electronic Frontier Foundation and the American Civil
Liberties Union (ACLU) also stood up for the students
and denounced the system.

The company behind the technology, InCom, agreed
to pay the school royalties from future sales if their
product was implemented in other schools.[94]

Soon afterward, State Representative Lois Kolkhorst
(R-Brenham) of Texas introduced an amendment that
would not allow schools to track students using RFID
without parental approval.   "I will not allow that to
happen in school districts unless parents approve it," she
said.   "I will not have our children treated like parolees
from the Texas prison system."[95]

A preschool in Richmond, California, implemented a
system in 2010, where young students now wear jerseys
that contain RFID tags which identify them and are used
for taking attendance and tracking the whereabouts of the
children throughout the school.   The program cost
$50,000 and was paid for by a federal grant.[96]   In the
coming years, the use of RFID trackers on students may
become a standard fixture, and despite some resistance,
the practice is spreading.

VeriChip / Positive ID

The VeriChip is the "world's first implantable RFID

---

[93] *Associate Press* "Parents Protest Student Computer ID Tags"
(February 10, 2005) by Lisa Leff

[94] Ibid

[95] *Brenham Banner-Press* "Kolkhorst's amendment bans schools
from electronically tracking students" by Arhur Hahn (March 14,
2005)

[96] *The Associated Press* "California students get tracking devices"
(August 18, 2010)

tag," as the manufacturer so proudly brags as they promote what may be one of the world's most controversial products. In 2004, the chip's manufacturer, Applied Digital, received approval from the FDA [Food and Drug Administration] to market the device in America for the purposes they had outlined regarding a personal identification tag that is implanted under the skin.[97] Similar devices had been implanted into pets and livestock in the previous years in order to identify them, but the FDA's ruling opened the door for implanting humans on a wide scale.

At first, Applied Digital tried to market the VeriChip only as a way for hospitals and emergency workers to access people's medical records in case they were discovered unconscious, so they could identify the person and view their medical history to learn what may have happened so they would know how to treat the person, but secretly the company was hoping and planning for their device to replace traditional ID and credit cards. Some reports had stated that the company was in talks with MasterCard shortly after the FDA approved the device for human implantation, and many people started seeing what was likely in the works for the implantable device.

In May of 2002, an entire family concerned with terrorism became the "first family ever to be implanted with microchips" as a cleverly packaged publicity stunt promoting the so-called safety benefits of implantable RFIDs.[98] One news report which featured interviews with the family quoted one of them saying, "the VeriChip could be a lifesaver."

In April 2004, a nightclub in Spain began offering

[97] *Associated Press* "FDA approves computer chip for humans" (October 13, 2004)
[98] *BBC* "US family gets health implants" (May 11, 2002)

chip implants to their customers which were linked to their credit cards and drivers license so they could enter the club without their wallet or purse. Other night clubs followed, including Bar Soba in Glasgow, Scotland. Harvard Medical School's chief information officer, Dr. John Halamka, had the chip implanted in himself in December 2004, and the trend continued.

In 2005, 160 security officials in Mexico, including the Mexican Attorney General, had received the chips as a security measure for accessing certain buildings and rooms.[99] In April 2005, the Chief of Police in Bergen County, New Jersey, Jack Schmidig, received the VeriChip, marking the first time in history a U.S. official received the implant.[100]

In 2005, a video surveillance company responsible for installing video cameras on public streets in Cincinnati, Ohio, had several of their employees get implanted with the VeriChip in order to access secure areas.[101] In June 2006, the Governor of Wisconsin, Jim Doyle, signed a bill into law making it illegal for companies to require people to be implanted with the VeriChip or similar RFID device.[102]

A company called Ben's Car Audio posted a promotional video on the Internet showing a prototype of a device they installed on a car that used an RFID implanted in the owner's hand (Benjamin Thompson) to

[99] *Associated Press* "Mexican Attorney General personally goes high-tech for security" by Will Weissert (July 14, 2005)
[100] *All Business* "Bergen County Chief Of Police Jack Schmidig Leads Regional Roll-Out of VeriChip by Receiving a VeriChip" (April 22, 2005)
[101] *World Net Daily* "Employees get microchip implants" (Feb 10, 2006)
[102] *Associated Press* "Bill forbids mandatory microchip implant" by Ryan J. Foley (April 25, 2006)

unlock his car door and start the car without needing any keys. Ben went on to admit that the implantable chips were, "a little out of the ordinary, so there probably aren't going to be very many people that want to do that," so his company offers key chains with RFID tags on them for people who don't want one implanted in their hand.[103]

In 2008, SEGA videogame developer Yu Suzuki even said that he may incorporate implantable RFID tags into videogames one day, saying it would be cool, "like the Matrix." It has also been proposed that all immigrants entering the country on Visas be implanted with the chips.[104]

In November 2009, the VeriChip Corporation acquired a credit monitoring and anti-identity theft company named Steel Vault. The merged company is called PositiveID, and this acquisition confirmed what a lot of people had anticipated for years—in that the VeriChip company would move to enable its implantable RFID technology to be used as an electronic form of ID and purchasing method—not just a way to transmit medical records as they had been previously claiming.

PositiveID CEO Scott Silverman said, "PositiveID will be the first company of its kind to combine a successful identity security business with one of the world's first personal health records through our Health Link business. PositiveID will address some of the most important issues affecting our society today with our identification tools and technologies for consumers and businesses."[105]

---

[103] *YouTube* "RFID started and unlocked car"

[104] *LiveScience.com* "Proposal to Implant Tracking Chips in Immigrants" by Bill Christensen (May 31, 2006)

[105] *Bnet.com* "VeriChip Buys Steel Vault, Creating Micro-Implant Health Record/Credit Score Empire" by Jim Edwards (November 11, 2009)

Religious Implications

Most people have heard of the mark of the beast, which is what Christians believe will be some kind of device forced onto society by a world dictator called the Antichrist who claims to be God and the Messiah. It is often thought of as some kind of an electronic currency that may take the form of an implantable RFID microchip or tattoo on the hand which will replace cash, checks, and debit cards, and can then track and trace every purchase every person makes anywhere in the world. The last book in the Bible, titled the *Book of Revelation,* which was written approximately around 68 AD to 95 AD, makes a chilling reference to such a device. The Bible reads, "And he causeth all, both small and great, rich and poor, free and bond, to receive a mark in their right hand, or in their foreheads, and that no man might buy or sell, save he that had the mark or the name of the beast, or the number of his name."[106]

While *Big Brother: The Orwellian Nightmare Come True* is not a religious book, it certainly can't be overlooked that RFID or similar technology has religious implications for a large percentage of Christians who see the development of such devices as Bible prophecy unfolding. Even for those who do not believe in the religious implications of this technology, it is obvious that many are still concerned with RFID tags replacing paper currency and debit or credit cards as the primary method of economic transactions.

See this author's previous book, *The Resistance Manifesto,* for detailed information regarding the theological implications and interpretations of the mark of the beast and Big Brother technology.

---

[106] *The Bible*: Revelation 13:16-18

More Privacy Issues with RFID

There are many more privacy concerns with RFID tags other than replacing paper currency or debit cards as the primary method of payment for purchases. With more and more companies basically forcing their employees to wear ID badges with RFID chips in them, the Big Brother potential is virtually limitless. With each employee's every move monitored and databased, algorithms could be set up to determine whether an employee is spending too much time in the break room, or even the bathroom, since sensors will detect and monitor when they enter and leave any room in the office. Did the employees use their RFID tags to activate the soap dispenser in the bathroom before they exited? The system could easily monitor this. The tags could also easily monitor how much time each employee spends in proximity with other employees.

Companies may set time limits for how long a person may interact with someone in a different department. They may calculate that someone from accounting only needs to talk with someone in the sales department for ten minutes per day, and if the system detects that these two people from the two different departments are in proximity for 30 minutes per day, then the superiors will determine that they are wasting company time gossiping, instead of quickly handling work issues. Is an employee not spending enough time at their own desk? The system can monitor this, and efficiency reports will be drafted to determine the average amount of time an employee is expected to spend at their desk, in the break room, in other cubicles or offices, and in the bathroom.

It's highly likely that RFIDs and EPCs (Electronic Product Codes) will completely replace the traditional UPC barcode we are all familiar with that is found on the package of virtually every item we buy. So it's also highly likely that RFID tags will be on everything sold, and perhaps not only on the packaging, but built into the product itself. This way a simple scanner could determine exactly what a person is carrying on them, including what their waistline or bra size is. Someone's trash could be scanned to see exactly what items or packaging is being thrown away without even having to touch the trash itself.

There has been talk of a so-called *Internet of Things* which is a plan for a unique number to be given to every single thing, similar to a serial number, allowing each specific item to be tracked with regards to exactly where it has been, who has been in possession of it, for how long, etc. An RFID tag that can simply hold a measly 128 bits can hold a number large enough so that a different number could be assigned to every single item in the world. (For example: 128 bits can store a number with 38 zeros after it, i.e., 100,000,000,000,000,000, 000,000,000,000,000,000,000.)

If and when this *Internet of Things* database is created and all purchases are done electronically and without cash, will parents of children under eighteen have access to their child's purchase history? Of course they will, and the parent would be able to see if they bought condoms, or spent too much money at the arcade. Parents could also see exactly what clothes their daughter buys to see if they're dressing too slutty.

Of course, people will say that the technology has its benefits, such as if an adult buys a case of beer for someone under twenty one, and then that kid gets caught, then a quick scan of the beer can will show who purchased it and when. Kids will, of course, create technology that instantly destroys or erases the RFID tags on products for this very reason, but the cops could also do a check on the kid's parents, or older siblings to see what their purchasing history was, and if they purchased a case of beer earlier that night, then they would obviously be implicated anyway.

If cash becomes difficult or impossible to use, and is replaced by RFID tags like the VeriChip, and all purchases are done electronically and linked to the individual purchasing them, then it's possible that certain groups of people will be forbidden to even purchase certain products. For example, someone collecting welfare may not be allowed to buy certain "luxury" items like chocolate candy or brand name soda, because the system has determined that these items cost too much and since the government is paying for them, they may simply not allow them to be bought.

When RFIDs become standard in drivers licenses, will it be possible for authorities to scan crowds of people at certain protests to determine exactly who is in the crowd? Even if it's not, then facial recognition systems would be able to determine who attends such events by identifying every single person in attendance.

If practically everyone is using RFID tags for financial transactions, and someone has a warrant out for their arrest, then their chip will be flagged, and possibly deactivated, so they couldn't even use it. There will also be unforeseen computer glitches and even power outages that will cripple people's ability to buy anything and make them wish they hadn't abandoned the use of cash.

RFIDs on Medication

Attaching RFID tags to all kinds of products, and even people, is certainly cause for concern, but we may one day find tiny RFID tags attached to individual pills that can be swallowed, which are designed to determine whether or not someone has taken their medication.

A necklace called the MagneTrace was built by the

Georgia Institute of Technology and monitors which pills people swallow and transmits the information to a smart phone or a computer. It was said that the device can remind patients if they forget to take their medication, and can tell doctors, caregivers, or family members, what pills a person has been taking and when.

Maysam Ghovanloo, an engineer working on the device says that it can't be tricked by someone holding a pill close to the necklace attempting to trigger its sensor because the algorithms it uses can detect whether or not the pills pass through the esophagus, as opposed to being placed near the necklace. "We wanted it to be very difficult to cheat," says Ghovanloo.[107]

Multiple other companies are working on similar technology that embeds microchips inside pills, making them "smart-pills," as they say. One company, Novartis AG, is planning to have the technology approved and available sometime around 2013.[108]

These kinds of "smart-chips" are activated by the stomach acid after they've been swallowed and then transmit their data to a Smartphone or over the Internet to a nurse or doctor so people's dosage can be monitored, along with the exact time the pills were taken. The computer chips can be added to existing pills and use Bluetooth technology.

Trever Mundel, who is in charge of developing the technology, admitted this would create massive privacy issues, saying "The regulators all like the concept and have been very encouraging. But...they want to

[107] *Technology Review* "Monitoring Pill Popping A magnetic sensor system could increase drug compliance" By Anna Davison (March 12, 2008)
[108] *Reuters* "Look out, your medicine is watching you" by Ben Hirschler (November 8, 2010)

understand how we are going to solve the data privacy issues."[109]

Using these kinds of pills, there is no need for a person to have to wear any kind of RFID reader around their neck or chest like the model developed by MagneTrace.

Will certain children be forced to take medication because they have a lot of energy and are said to have Attention Deficit Disorder or Attention Deficit Hyper Active Disorder? Or will some adults be forced to take certain prescriptions because they are deemed "paranoid," because they believe in certain "conspiracy theories" about the government or Big Brother?

RFID Vehicle Registration Tags

A company called TransCore has created a system using RFID tags that stick on windshields that would allow the government to detect whether people have proper insurance, registration, or unpaid parking tickets. The system is called EVR, short for Electronic Vehicle Registration, and the company hopes to make the system a standard feature on cars.

A brochure from TansCore reads, "eGo makes possible the introduction of electronic vehicle registration applications, which enable public agencies to automatically detect and screen, via RFID, motor vehicles for compliance with federal and state registration regulations and to correspondingly automate enforcement actions and violation processing for non-compliant vehicles."[110] This plan involves installing RFID readers

---

[109] Ibid.

[110] Electronic Toll and Electronic Vehicle Registration brochure from TransCore.

at various points on roads throughout cities to detect tags attached to vehicles. These devices will probably be made obsolete by more advanced government mandated GPS black boxes.

Mind-Reading Machines

Tom Cruise starred in *Minority Report* which was released in 2002, where he played a police officer who would arrest people for what was called "pre-crime" which meant crimes that they were going to commit in the future. Pre-crime was detected by a small group of people (called Precogs) who have the ability to see into the future. Of course, this is only science fiction, but the idea of punishing someone for a crime they may commit in the future is something that society may soon have to deal with. This actual "pre-crime" isn't detected by psychic human beings who see visions of the future, but instead is the result of high-tech equipment that is said to be able to detect whether or not an individual is thinking about committing a crime or has any dangerous intent.

These systems were originally designed to screen airport passengers in order to supposedly prevent terrorists from getting on board a plane by literally reading their minds to determine whether or not ticket holders are thinking any evil thoughts. An article in the *Associated Press*, published in January 2010 explains, "As far-fetched as that sounds, systems that aim to get inside an evildoer's head are among the proposals floated by security experts thinking beyond the X-ray machines and metal detectors used on millions of passengers and bags each year."[111]

The interest in such systems gained momentum immediately after the so-called "underwear bomber" was caught on a plane headed for Detroit, Michigan on

---

[111] *Associated Press* "Mind Reading Systems Could Change Air Security" (January 8, 2010) by Michael Tarm

Christmas Day in 2009. This man had packed explosives in his underwear and they were not detected by any security measures, and after he boarded the plane, he attempted to ignite the device, but failed.

Immediately after the failed "underwear" attack, President Barack Obama urged Homeland Security to develop better screening technology, saying "In the never-ending race to protect our country, we have to stay one step ahead of a nimble adversary."[112]

Others jumped on the bandwagon saying that new technology and security measures must be implemented. Philip Baum, editor of the magazine *Aviation Security International*, said, "Regulators need to accept that the current approach is outdated...It may have responded to the threats of the 1960s, but it doesn't respond to the threats of the 21st century."[113]

One type of device is the WeCU system which is used at airports in Israel. (WeCU means "We See You," as in Big Brother sees you.) This system involves showing passengers different images on a screen that are associated with certain terrorist groups and then measures several signs on the person, such as their eye movements, increased heart rate or breathing, or any nervous twitches. The system's creators claim to have developed ways to measure people's reactions to determine whether they are affiliated with any of the symbols that are shown to them on the screen. "One by one, you can screen out from the flow of people those with specific malicious intent," said Ehud Givon, CEO of WeCU Technologies.

Another system looked at by the Department of Homeland Security is called the Future Attribute Screening Technology, or FAST, and works like a

---

[112] Ibid
[113] Ibid

polygraph that scans people's pupil dilation, facial movements, and other measurements to detect deception. The system also detects a person's fidgeting or nervous ticks.

Robert Burns, a project manager for FAST, insists the system can detect the difference between people who are simply stressed out or upset because they may be late for a flight, and those people who are harboring ill will. The Department of Homeland Security says the system uses a range of "innovative physiological and behavioral technologies" to pick up "indications of malintent [malicious intentions] or the intent or desire to cause harm."[114]

"We are running at about 78 percent accuracy on mal-intent detection, and 80 percent on deception," said John Verrico, a Department of Homeland Security spokesman.[115] In a Homeland Security video showing the system in action, targeted subjects are asked questions such as "are you attempting to smuggle an explosive device" or "are you from the local area?"

Another system called MALINTENT [Malicious Intentions] is also being tested by the Department of Homeland Security and is designed to detect whether a person might be harboring criminal intent based on their minute facial muscle moments which the system uses allegedly as evidence of emotional state, mood, and intention.

Unlike traditional lie detectors, these new systems don't require people to be hooked up to anything and take all of their measurements and operate without any physical contact with the person. These devices and

---

[114] *London Telegraph* "New airport screening 'could read minds'" by Catherine Elsworth (September 23, 2008)
[115] Ibid

others are planned to be used at airports, border check points, and at special events that have heightened security. Designers plan to create a system that can scan people as they stand in line or walk through the airport.

The Russian based Psychotechnology Research Institute has developed a program they call Mindreader 2.0 that they say can determine how a person's subconscious mind feels about certain photos, and can detect whether people have a positive feeling or a negative feeling about them. The system uses what is called Semantic Stimuli Response Measurements Technology, or SSRM Tek, that supposedly detects a person's involuntary response to subliminal messages.

It has been reported that the Department of Homeland Security has visited the Institute to learn more about the technology to determine whether it may be of use for screening passengers before they board an airline. The Psychotechnology Research Institute began working with the US defense contractor SRS Technologies and in May 2009, the Department of Homeland Security paid for testing of the Mindreader 2.0 system.[116]

The Mindreader 2.0 system flashes a quick image on a screen so fast that a person doesn't consciously recognize it, and then they are asked to press a button rating their feeling either favorably or unfavorably. If the image is of Osama bin Laden, for example, and they press the favorable button, then they are flagged as a potential terrorist.

The head of the Institute, Elena Rusalkina, is the widow of Igor Smirnov, who is considered the father of psychotronic weapons in Russia. The Soviet military

---

[116] *Wired Magazine* "The Weird Russian Mind-Control Research Behind a DHS Contract" By Sharon Weinberger (September 20, 2007)

used some of Smirnov's subliminal mind control methods during the Soviet Union's war in Afghanistan in the 1980s by using subliminal sounds to affect the Mujahideen. Smirnov also consulted with the FBI during the 1993 standoff at the Branch Davidian compound in Waco, Texas, and it is rumored that he and the FBI planned, or did use, some kind of subliminal device on David Koresh and his followers. If you think that these devices are Orwellian, they actually get much, much worse.

In January 2009, the TV newsmagazine *60 Minutes* aired a segment titled "Mind Reading" that showed new technology being developed at Carnage Mellon University that can literally read your mind. The segment featured neuro scientist Marcel Just and his college Tom Mitchell who had developed one of these systems. Marcel Just didn't want to call it mind reading, and insisted it was "thought identification" instead.

One of the *60 Minutes* producers sat in the machine and was shown ten different objects to think about, such as a hammer, screw driver, and apartment, and the computer scanned her brain and was able to determine exactly which objects she was thinking about, and in what order. The device is called a Functional MRI machine, or fMRI. After the demonstration, Lesley Stahl, the anchor for the segment, was visibly disturbed. This same scanner can detect whether a person is feeling kindness, hypocrisy, or even love.

The segment continued to show scientists in Berlin, Germany, at the Bernstein Center, who were conducting tests where whey would scan people's brains as they were choosing whether to add or subtract two numbers they were given, and the computer was able to identify what they decided.

"I always tell my students that there is no more

science fiction anymore. All the science fiction I read in high school, we're doing," said Paul Root Wolpe, director of the Center for Ethics at Emery University in Atlanta. He goes on to say, "Throughout history, we could never actually coerce someone to reveal information. Torture doesn't work that well, persuasion doesn't work that well...the right to keep one's thoughts locked up in their brain is among the most fundamental rights to being human." He then raised issues about who would be legally allowed to use this technology, whether the government could soon force people to use it, or even if parents could subject their children to it when they suspect they are lying about something.

This technology is not just in its testing phase in laboratories at Universities. A company called No Lie MRI advertises their services using fMRI which they say "provides unbiased methods for the detection of deception and other information stored in the brain."[117]

There is also talk of a device that can potentially shine a beam of light or radio waves onto a person's head and can then detect their internal brainwaves as a result. Such a device could obviously be used without a person's knowledge or consent, unlike the fMRI machines that require people to lie down and sit still in order to be scanned.

John Dylan-Haynes, of the Bernstein Center for Computational Neuroscience in Berlin, Germany, is testing a program that can detect in your mind where you've physically been. This device is not theoretical, and has already been built. He demonstrates the system by showing scenes from inside different houses, and then says, "Now I would put you in a scanner and I would show you some of these scenes that you've seen, and

---

[117] http://noliemri.com/index.htm

some of them you haven't seen...and right at this moment, we would be able to tell from your brain activity that you've already seen this environment before." Haynes explains that this technology could soon be used to determine if someone was a burglar in a house or had attended an Al-Qaeda training camp before.

When Paul Root Wolpe, the ethics professor from Emery University, was asked if this device would violate the Fifth Amendment which says you don't have to incriminate yourself, he explained that the Fifth Amendment says you don't have to testify in court about what you did or didn't do, but it doesn't protect you from blood samples or DNA samples that may be taken from you and incriminate you, and so in the same way these brain scans may be allowed by courts and ruled that they do not to violate your Fifth Amendment rights.

This kind of research is not only isolated to a single lab or university. In March 2010, a story hit the news wires telling how British scientists from University College London discovered that they could identify brain activity linked to different memories using fMRI technology, and could identify thought patterns and literally read people's minds and determine whether they had seen a particular film or not, just by looking at their brain scan.[118]

In one study, scientists showed ten people three different short films and when later scanned, the scientists were able to determine which film each person had seen by identifying patterns in the brain associated with each film. These patterns are called episodic memories, which mean they are memories of autobiographical events, such as things you've personally seen or heard, as opposed to

---

[118] *Digital Journal* "Scientists: Brain scans can effectively read your mind" (March 12, 2010) by Elliot Meszaros

memories formed based on being told something, for example.

If all of this sounds like it is still decades away from being used in criminal court cases, you are wrong. A woman in India was convicted of murder in 2008 because of a brain scan. An article in the *New York Times* explained, "India has become the first country to convict someone of a crime relying on evidence from this controversial machine: a brain scanner that produces images of the human mind in action and is said to reveal signs that a suspect remembers details of the crime in question."[119]

In June of 2008, a judge in India allowed a brain scan to be used as evidence that the suspect had "experiential knowledge" about the crime that only the killer would know. The suspect was sentenced to life in prison.

"I find this both interesting and disturbing," said Henry T. Greely, a bioethicist at Stanford Law School. "We keep looking for a magic, technological solution to lie detection. Maybe we'll have it someday, but we need to demand the highest standards of proof before we ruin people's lives based on its application."[120]

The specific brain scan that was used in this case involves hooking people up to electrodes and then they are read specific details of the crime scene, and according to the research, certain parts of the brain light up when a memory is stimulated, leading authorities to believe that whatever caused the jump in brain activity was the result of the person having actually personally witnessed what was read to them first hand. This technology obviously has its critics since it is very new and hasn't undergone

---

[119] *New York Times* "India's Novel Use of Brain Scans in Courts Is Debated" By Anand Giridharadas (September 14, 2008)
[120] Ibid

extensive testing.

Even one of the first developers of this electroencephalogram-based (EEG) lie detection technology was shocked that a court in India had used the program as evidence when the technology was so new. "Technologies which are neither seriously peer-reviewed nor independently replicated are not, in my opinion, credible," said Dr. Rosenfeld, a neuroscientist at Northwestern University. "The fact that an advanced and sophisticated democratic society such as India would actually convict persons based on an unproven technology is even more incredible," he concluded.[121]

Other scientists hail the technology as a revolutionary evidence gathering procedure paralleling, or perhaps, being more important than DNA. Keith Ashcroft, who is considered an expert witness in Britain, said, "According to the cases that have been presented to me, BEOS [Brain Electrical Oscillations Signature] has clearly demonstrated its utility in providing admissible evidence that has been used to assist in the conviction of defendants in court."[122]

Henry T. Greely, from Stanford admitted that if and when this technology becomes commonplace, that there will be serious implications on personal privacy, as well as the First, Fourth, Fifth, Sixth, Seventh and 14th Amendments to the U.S. Constitution, but said, "the potential benefits to society of such a technology, if used well, could be at least equally large."

Will these devices or others like them become common in courtrooms, schools, or businesses? Will we one day live in a society where everything people say will be subjected to be verified by a mind-reading machine?

---

[121] Ibid
[122] Ibid

We will soon find out.

The Defense Advanced Research Projects Agency (DARPA), which develops new technology for the US military, included $4 million dollars in their 2009-2010 budget for a program named *Silent Talk*, which aims to "allow user-to-user communication on the battlefield without the use of vocalized speech through analysis of neural signals."[123]

Another $4 million dollars was given to the University of California to investigate "synthetic telepathy" which entails creating a device that can detect brain waves that have speech encoded into them in order to literally read the mind of the person using it to determine exactly what they are thinking.[124]

Not even in the dystopian world found in Orwell's book did Big Brother have the ability to read people's minds. "With all their cleverness they had never mastered the secret of finding out what another human being was thinking."[125] —*Nineteen Eighty Four*

Artificial Nose to Smell Terrorists' Fear

Aside from advanced systems that read facial expressions, iris dilation, heart rate, breathing patterns and body language, authorities are also attempting to construct devices that can literally smell a person's fear in their quest to perfect mind-reading machines. The Department of Homeland Security advertised that they were looking for specialists who could design systems that would smell "deceptive individuals." The technology is based on the

---

[123] *Wired Magazine* "Pentagon Preps Soldier Telepathy Push" Katie Drummond (May 14, 2009)
[124] Ibid
[125] Orwell, George –*Nineteen Eighty Four* page 148

idea that a person's body odors change according to their mood.

Researchers at the Massachusetts Institute of Technology (MIT) are trying to create an artificial nose that can smell adrenaline, which researchers believe is given off in higher amounts from someone who has a guilty conscience.

Homeland Security is also working on collecting a "smell bank" that holds scents collected from crime scenes which they believe will be able to identify specific individuals the same way as DNA.

Professor Kenneth Furton at Florida International University in Miami, is working on technology he says could soon identify criminals by matching scent molecules taken from crime scenes to a "smell bank," that contains the scents of people, much like a fingerprint database. He pointed out that scientists can already determine a person's race, age, and environment based on their scent, and in some cases, what they had for their last meal. Scientists are also looking to identify odors that signify if a person is depressed, or has a disease.

Honda's Mind Reader

The car manufacturer, Honda Motor Corporation, has designed a device that reads a person's brain waves and can control a robot from the user's thoughts. At a press conference in Japan in 2009, the company unveiled an updated version of a robot they called Asimo, which walks on two legs and is controlled by a person wearing their strange mind-reading head gear. The device is considered a brain-machine interface which was developed by a joint venture between Honda and the Advanced Telecommunications Research Institute International and the Shimadzu corporation.

The device looks like a bicycle helmet covered with electrical components and uses what is called electroencephalography (EEG) and near-infrared spectroscopy (NIRS) to measure brain activity. One may wonder why Honda would be interested in such technology, since it wouldn't seem to have any benefit to the automobile industry. It seems Honda is looking to expand their business and one day build robots that help around the home. They also think it would be cool to use such technology to allow people to open their car trunk or change the air-conditioning setting just by thinking about it, because apparently, they think that pushing a button is just too difficult.

"When your hands are full doing the dishes, you could have a robot give you a hand watering the plants [just by thinking]," said Tatsuya Okabe, a scientist at the Honda Research Institute.[126]

The 2009 version of the Asimo robot and this mind-reading system was actually quite pathetic. A video clip on the Internet shows a person wearing the helmet and moving the robot around, but at the time, it was very primitive. Of course, researchers are hoping to make dramatic advances in the coming years.

When asked if the device could one day be used to drive a car, Yasuhisa Arai, the director of Honda's R&D department responded, "I don't want to deny the possibility, but there are many challenges. Practical uses are still way into the future."

Another Japanese company that makes robotic toys, Rolling Robots, is also planning on creating toys and other gadgets with mind-reading sensors by the year 2020 that they hope can be used to send text messages and

---

[126] *Business Week* "From Honda, a Mind-Reading Robot" (March 31, 2009) by Ian Rowley

operate other electronics. [127]

Video Game Interfaces

Videogame manufacturers are hoping to one day replace the joystick or gamepad with mind-reading devices that players wear on their heads which will control the video game character by the person's thoughts. One manufacturer, NeuroSky, has designed a primitive device called the Darth Vader game, but say other more sophisticated games are in the works.

Some people strangely say these devices could increase mental focus and actually help kids with attention deficit hyperactivity disorder, autism or mood disorders. Of course, playing more video games is the last thing that these kids need, but this is a good marketing strategy for videogame companies.

"It fulfills the fantasy of telekinesis," said Tan Le, co-founder and president of San Francisco-based Emotiv, another designer producing similar devices they hope will be used on the Nintendo Wii, Sony PlayStation and Microsoft Xbox.

Another company called CyberLearning has been selling what they call SmartBrain Technologies systems for the PlayStation and Xbox. The device uses EEG and EMG-based biofeedback and costs about $600. The company has sold more than 1,500 systems between 2005 and 2009, and also plans on marketing their products to children with behavior disorders.

"Our biggest struggle is to find the target market," said co-founder Lindsay Greco. "We're finding that parents are using this to improve their own recall and

---

[127] *Physorg.com* "Japan eyes 'mind-reading' devices, robots by 2020" (April 22, 2010)

focus. We have executives who use it to improve their memory, even their golf."[128]

The God Helmet

Orwellian devices aren't only being built that can read people's minds, but similar devices may be used to manipulate people's brainwaves to give them intoxicating feelings like they get from drugs, alcohol, or adrenaline rushes like skydiving.

A strange invention dubbed the "God helmet," which is a modified snowmobile helmet, stimulates the brain with magnetic fields in order to give the person wearing it a "spiritual experience." The "God helmet" was created by Michael Persinger who designed it to be used in research for what is called neurotheology, which is the study of neurology's connections to spirituality. People who use the device have reported feeling as if there was another being in the room with them, and even sensed what they say is the presence of God.[129]

It's likely that such devices will one day be commercially available for personal use and could become a substitute for people doing drugs who are looking for a high. Of course, these devices open the door to all kinds of dangers, such as brain damage from long term exposure, or even psychological addiction to the device. They will likely become extremely small in the future and could be placed on the head and covered up by a person's hair and not be noticed by others so they could be worn anywhere. Some people may get such a high from these devices that it could be similar to heroin

---

[128] *Associated Press* "'Mind-Reading' Device Could Revolutionize Video Games" (April 30, 2007)
[129] *BBC Two* "God on the Brain" (April 17, 2005)

or cocaine, and abuse of the technology could severely disrupt individual's lives.

One also wonders if this technology will be able to permanently alter areas of the brain, and if it could be mandated as part of a rehabilitation program for prisoners in order to alter their thought patterns or attitudes.

Neural Interfaces

While it's interesting that devices can be worn on a person's head that measure brain waves and can be used to control robots, videogames, or read a person's mind and detect memories, a much more invasive method of using a person's thoughts to control external machines or computers is found in what are called neural interfaces, which are devices that are connected directly to the human brain. Neural interfaces, sometimes called brain implants, or a brain machine interface (BMI) are electronic systems that are literally, physically wired into the human brain through surgery.

In July 2001, someone with access to the Department of Neurobiology at Hebrew University in Jerusalem, Israel, used a hidden camera to videotape bizarre and cruel tests that were being done on monkeys to implant them with neural interfaces. The footage shows several monkeys secured in restraining devices with their skull caps removed, and you can clearly see their brains protruding out of the top of their heads with neural interfaces attached. The video is extremely horrific to watch. It's in color and can be found on YouTube if you search for "hidden camera monkey brain experiments." The person narrating the video mentions a Dr. Zohari, who they identify as the project manager of the experiments.

A strange neurophysiologist at Yale University, named Dr. Jose Delgado, carried out similar experiments in the 1960s that involved implanting electrodes in the brains of animals and he was able to remotely induce a wide range of emotions and physical movements in them. Videos are available on YouTube that show Delgado's team demonstrating a cat equipped with a neural interface that enabled them to cause the animal to get angry and start hissing with the push of a button. Another video shows a bull with a neural interface implanted in its brain that's charging straight at a man and when the researcher sends a signal to the receiver, the animal stops immediately.[130]

In his book *Physical Control of the Mind*, published in 1971, Dr. Delgado wrote, "The technology for nonsensory communication between brains and computers through the intact skin is already at our fingertips, and its consequences are difficult to predict. In the past the progress of civilization has tremendously magnified the power of our senses, muscles, and skills. Now we are adding a new dimension: the direct interface between brains and machines."

He said that it was, "already possible to induce a large variety of responses, from motor effects to emotional reactions and intellectual manifestations, by direct electrical stimulation of the brain."

"Also, several investigators have learned to identify patterns of electrical activity (which a computer could also recognize) localized in specific areas of the brain and related to determined phenomena such as perception of smells or visual perception of edges and movements. We are advancing rapidly in the pattern recognition of electrical correlates of behavior and in the methodology for two-way radio communication between brain and computers."[131]

In his writings, Delgado acknowledged people expressed fears that this new technology was a threat to possible unwanted and unethical remote control of the

---

[130] *YouTube* "Mind Control - Bull & Cat Tests in the 60's"

[131] Delgado, Jose – *Physical Control of the Mind* page 95 - 96

thoughts of people by others, but wrote that he believed the dangers are outweighed by the expected clinical and scientific benefits.

Ray Kurzweil, who is seen as a prominent futurist believed to be able to accurately forecast approaching technological developments in the coming decades wrote, "Improving our lives through neural implants on the mental level, and nanotechnology-enhanced bodies on the physical level, will be popular and compelling."[132] Kurzweil believes that around the year 2099, neural interfaces will be implanted into almost everyone, and that, "humans who do not utilize such implants [will be] unable to meaningfully participate in dialogues with those who do."[133]

What he means is that humans will have their brains wired into the Internet and will become a species of cyborgs who have merged with computers.

Brain Gate

A neural interface called Brain Gate was one of the first devices used on humans and was developed in 2003, by a company called Cyberkinetics along with the Department of Neuroscience at Brown University in Providence, Rhode Island. The device was designed to allow people paralyzed from spinal cord injuries to use the neural interface to operate computers or electronic wheelchairs with their thoughts.

The first version of the device used 96 different electrodes to sense different neurons firing in specific areas of the brain and transferred those signals to a computer. In 2010, the company's website said that three

---

[132] Kurzweil, Ray - *The Age of Intelligent Machines* page 146-147
[133] Kurzweil, Ray - *The Age of Intelligent Machines* page 234

different people have had the device installed, the first of which was a 25-year-old paralyzed man named Matt Nagle who can be seen in videos on the Internet using Brain Gate to move a mouse around a computer screen.

An article on CNN's website mentioned the possibilities of such devices turning the population into cyborgs, saying, "Beyond alleviating the effects of severe disabilities, normal functioning humans could also benefit from 'upgrades' to improve intelligence, sensory awareness or simply to counter the effects of aging."[134] The article also quoted Microsoft founder Bill Gates as saying that one of his Microsoft colleagues is anticipating cybernetic enhancements, and that he's ready to be "plugged in." Gates said that he personally would not want to be implanted with such things.

Military Applications

The US military has show interest in neural interfaces and various documents and budgets explain some of their proposed Orwellian uses. One report commissioned by the Office of Defense Research and Engineering titled *Human Performance* explained, "The most successful implementation of invasive interfaces has occurred in medical applications in which nerve signals are used as the mechanism for information transfer. Adversarial actions using this approach to implement enhanced, specialized sensory functions could be possible in limited form now, and with developing capability in the future."[135]

---

[134] *CNN.com* "Brain Chip Heralds Chip neuro tech dawn" (July 17, 2006)
[135] *Human Performance* Pentagon report on brain–computer interfaces (March 2008) page 77

Documents dating back to 1996 from the Department of Defense show that plans were being drawn up to use neural interfaces on soldiers and the civilian population as well. One document discussing technology the military hoped to have in place by the year 2025, titled *Information Operations: A New War-Fighting Capability* reads, "The implanted microscopic brain chip performs two functions. First, it links the individual to the IIC [Information Integration Center] creating a seamless interface between the user and the information resources. In essence, the chip relays the processed information from the IIC [Information Integration Center] to the user, second the chip creates a computer generated mental visualization based upon the user's request."[136]

The documents claim the devices would help increase security, saying, "An implanted microscopic chip does not require security measures to verify whether the right person is connected to the IIC [Information Integration Center], whereas a room, helmet, or sunglasses requires additional time-consuming access control mechanisms to verify an individual's identity and level of control within the Cyber Situation."[137]

The document foresaw resistance to such ideas, saying, "Implanting 'things' in people raises ethical and public relations issues. While these concerns may be founded on today's thinking, in 2025 they may not be as alarming" and goes on to say, "The civilian populace will likely accept any implanted microscopic chips that allow military members to defend vital national interests."[138]

---

[136] *Information Operations: A New War-Fighting Capability* (Volume 3 of *Air Force 2025*) page 35

[137] *Information Operations A New War-Fighting Capability* (Volume 3 of *Air Force 2025*) page 35

[138] *Information Operations A New War-Fighting Capability* (Volume 3 of *Air Force 2025*) page 36

Aside from military applications, the documents say that neural interfaces could be used to upload information into people's minds and make them feel like they are playing a virtual reality video game. It reads, "This capability will have extraordinary commercial applications from medical advances. These advances will help restore patients with damaged neural, audio, and visual systems as well as enable them to achieve the ultimate virtual reality trip."[139]

The *Human Performance* document produced for the Pentagon in 2008, acknowledges the "evils" of using these devices and admits, "one can consider the potential that an adversary might use invasive interfaces in military applications. An extreme example would be remote guidance or control of a human being." It continues to list examples of experiments that were able to remotely control animals as if they were remote controlled toys, saying, "There has been non-medical research into remote monitoring or control of animals (rats, sharks, pigeons, etc.) [53, 54, 55] with applications in research or law enforcement, with related strong interest in the popular press."[140]

Intel Planning Neural Interfaces to Surf Internet

An article in *Computerworld* magazine published in 2009, discussed how computer giant Intel thinks that by the year 2020 we won't need to use a keyboard or a mouse to control computers, cell phones, or televisions

---

[139] *Information Operations A New War-Fighting Capability* (Volume 3 of *Air Force 2025*) page 25

[140] *Human Performance* Pentagon report on brain–computer interfaces (March 2008) page 70

anymore, and will instead use neural interfaces. The article stated, "Big Brother won't be planting chips in your brain against your will. Researchers expect that consumers will want the freedom they will gain by using the implant."[141]

Andrew Chien, the vice president of research and director of future technologies at Intel Labs said, "There are a lot of things that have to be done first but I think [implanting chips into human brains] is well within the scope of possibility."

Another Intel research scientist named Dean Pomerleau told *Computerworld* that "We're trying to prove you can do interesting things with brain waves. Eventually people may be willing to be more committed...to brain implants. Imagine being able to surf the Web with the power of your thoughts."

They are using fMRI technology at Carnegie Mellon University and the University of Pittsburgh to map thought patterns and have found that different people's brain patterns are similar when they think similar thoughts, allowing scientists to develop ways to detect the thoughts of different people using the same method.

Intel's Dean Pomerleau said they will soon be able to build a brainwave sensor that people can wear on their head and will be connected to a computer. The next step, he said, is to implant neural interfaces into people's brains.

Wireless Neural Interface

Most neural interfaces consist of devices implanted into the human brain and have wires protruding out of the

---

[141] *Computerworld* "Intel: Chips in brains will control computers by 2020" by Sharon Gaudin (November 19, 2009)

person's (or animal's) skull which lead to a computer, but one British scientist is developing a wireless chip that can be injected into the skull with a large hypodermic needle, and can then communicate wirelessly to a computer.

The chip is being developed by Dr. Jon Spratley who designed a prototype while earning his PhD at Birmingham University. "We are just trying to help people with severe communication problems or motor neurone disease—like Dr Stephen Hawking or Christopher Reeve," he said.[142]

"It's an area that is being heavily researched in America but so far all the tests have involved wired sensors. This prototype uses wireless technology to remove the risk of infection and that's the real drive of our work."

Dr. Spratley hopes the device can be used by quadriplegic people, enabling them to operate computers, electric wheel chairs, or even bionic arms or legs. "If they can imagine using a limb, even if they can't move it, you can tap into that signal. Then you just have to imagine moving the muscle and the leg will move, the brain will train itself," he said.

Dr. Spratley is looking for funding to start human trials.

Depression Implant

If you think it's strange that companies have developed technology that can wire a human brain into a computer in order to detect brain waves, the technology gets even more sinister. In 2005, the Food and Drug

---

[142] *Daily Mail* "All in the mind: The 'telepathy' chip that lets you turn on the TV using the power of thought" by David Derbyshire (September 3, 2009)

Administration (FDA) approved a neural interface system to treat depression.[143] The device is wired into the brain and stimulates the Vagus Nerve in order to make people feel happier.

The manufacturer of this horrific device is a company called Cyberonics which has sold a similar brain implant that reduces seizures in people with epilepsy. The depression implant costs about $20,000, including surgical and hospital expenses, according to Cyberonics chief executive, Skip Cummins. The company has also been conducting various studies hoping the device will be approved to treat anxiety, bulimia, and other chronic disorders.[144]

Dangers of Neural Interfaces

Hidden beneath the lofty goals of helping paralyzed people gain more mobility and independence lies a dark underbelly of disastrous consequences arising from the widespread use of neural interfaces. Detecting and reading brainwaves is one thing, but neural interfaces have already shown that they can also do the opposite, and actually manipulate brainwaves as well. Futurists like Ray Kurzweil anxiously anticipate a world where these devices are as common as cell phones, and envision enhancing human perception, memory, and cognitive abilities. But this technology, perhaps more than any other, contains disastrous consequences that are often overlooked by transhumanist dreamers.

It's not an unfounded fear to wonder if a neural interface that physically jacks people's minds into a

---

[143] *Reuters* "US OKs Cyberonics depression implant-shares soar" (February 3, 2005)
[144] http://us.cyberonics.com/en

centralized computer system could then possibly literally control people's thoughts once they are plugged in. While this may seem far-fetched, as I have already uncovered, the military has proposed that such devices could take people on the "ultimate virtual reality trip" and implants that make people "feel better" have already been created. These devices may lead to mass mind control, quite literally.

In 1993, Sylvester Stallone and Sandra Bullock starred in a science fiction film taking place in the future called *Demolition Man,* which included a scene where prisoners were connected to neural interfaces that reprogrammed their minds in order to rehabilitate them and change their attitudes and behaviors.

The *CBS Evening News* once aired a segment discussing high-tech methods for keeping tabs on prisoners and included an interview with a specialist who said, "one thing we could implant could be a subliminal implant. In other words, basically messages being piped into the subconscious constantly. 'Do the right thing. Do what's required of you. Be a good citizen. Don't disobey the law.'"[145]

The infamous mark of the beast spoken about in the Bible, which predicts that a global dictator will force the entire earth's population to take a "mark" on their hand or forehead or else they won't be able to buy or sell anything, is often believed to be a Radio Frequency Identification Device (RFID) or some kind of device that replaces cash and checks as methods of doing financial transactions. But some speculate that the "mark of the beast" is actually a neural interface they believe will cause everyone who has one to literally lose control of their own mind, and then be completely controlled by an

---

[145] Shown in *9/11 The Road To Tyranny* by Alex Jones (2001)

artificial intelligence system or whoever is in charge of the neural interface mainframe.

The topic of the mark of the beast is beyond the scope of this book, but the possibility of neural interfaces literally controlling people's minds is a very real and dangerous scenario that we seem to be rapidly approaching.

Psychotronic Weapons

Paranoid people have often feared that the government was able to read their minds with some kind of advanced technology, which is now actually real (**See Mind-Reading Machines**), but what is perhaps even more insidious, is technology that is able to project thoughts into people's heads simply through radio waves. While neural interfaces need to be wired directly into the brain of a person and involve extensive and invasive surgery, technology that can beam thoughts and voices into people's heads doesn't require any physical contact with the person, and can easily be done without their knowledge. While this may seem far-fetched, as you read further, you will find that the US Air Force has actually patented such technology.

The term *psychotronic weapons* refers to weapons that affect the mind, mainly through radio waves, and aside from beaming voices or subliminal messages into people's heads, psychotronic weapons can affect people's moods and concentration, and can even cause sudden sickness or death.

In 1980, a Lieutenant Colonel in the US Army named Michael Aquino coauthored a paper titled *From PSYOP to MindWar* that suggested using psychotronic weapons against American citizens to alter the brainwaves of the public on a mass scale, thus altering their mood.

Aquino wrote, "Infrasound vibration (up to 20Hz) can subliminally influence brain activity to align itself to delta, theta, alpha, or beta wave patterns, inclining an audience toward everything from alertness to passivity. Infrasound could be used tactically, as ELF-waves endure for great distances; and it could be used in conjunction

with media broadcasts as well."[146]

So basically what Lieutenant Colonel Aquino wrote was that the government should target American citizens with radio waves to either cause them to get anxious or lethargic, depending on the goals of the government at the time. So, if, for example, there was a massive protest planned for a specific city or even across the country, the government could use the MindWar strategy of transmitting infrasound to cause people to feel lazy and lethargic, thus massively declining the number of protesters because many people simply wouldn't feel like going. They could also use other frequencies of radio waves to give the target audience an overwhelming feeling of anxiety, if they choose, and perhaps cause massive rioting.

Many researchers point to HAARP (High Frequency Active Auroral Research Program) as being capable of broadcasting such ELF waves and infrasound on a mass scale, and being capable of focusing it on a specific location. While it is denied that HAARP can be used as a weapon, what is not disputed are Aquino's own words in his publicly available report *From PSYOP to MindWar*, where he openly advocated using psychotronic weapons on an unsuspecting population.

Radio Frequency Hearing Effect

An article published in the *Washington Post* in 2007 discusses the existence of technology that can beam voices into people's heads, and begins by saying there is, "a community of people who believe the government is beaming voices into their minds. They may be crazy, but the Pentagon has pursued a weapon that can do just

---

[146] Aquino, Michael – *From PSYOP to MindWar* p. 10

that."[147]

The article continues to discuss people on the Internet who think that they have been targeted by the government and used as test subjects or harassed using what is called the Radio Frequency Hearing Effect, which is very real. So real, in fact, that on October 22, 2002 patent number 6,470,214 was awarded to the technology which is designed to, "induce a thermal-acoustic signal in the bone/tissue material of the head that replicates the input audio signal and is conducted by the bone/tissue structure of the head to the inner ear where it is demodulated by the normal processes of the cochlea and converted to nerve signals which are sent to the brain, thereby enabling intelligible speech to be perceived by the brain." The patent was awarded to the United States Air Force who first filed for it in 1996.[148]

A man named Donald Friedman, who believes he is a victim of this technology (called a targeted individual, or a TI), has dedicated his time and energy to exposing the government's misuse of psychotronic weapons and has filed multiple Freedom of Information Requests to obtain documents proving it. One such document was released in 1998 by the US Army titled *Bioeffects of Selected Nonlethal Weapons* which discusses weapons that can beam voices into people's heads, give them fevers, and even cause epileptic seizures.

One of Friedman's requests was responded to with a motion for an enlargement of time, which is a legal request to delay the release of a document. The request to delay the document's release was made by the Secret Service which read, *"Plaintiff's FOIA request is for*

---

[147] *Washington Post* "Mind Games" by Sharon Weinberger (January 14, 2007)
[148] http://patft.uspto.gov/ patent number 6,470,214

document [sic] concerning directed energy technology that is very sensitive. Some of this documents [sic] pertain to research conducted by divisions within defendant agency that is used to carry out its mandate to protect very high government officials. In fact, in one case, the documents… could not be mailed but had to be hand carried interstate."[149]

An article in *Wired* magazine discussed Friedman and his claims, and admitted, "It's very easy to poke fun at people like Friedman. On the other hand, it does show that if a non-lethal device ever was developed which could cause symptoms associated with madness, it would be completely deniable. The device would completely destroy the target's credibility, neatly ensuring it remained covert. The military utility would be low, but it might be very handy for some three-letter agencies," (meaning the CIA, FBI, NSA, etc.)[150]

Dr. Robert O. Becker, who has been nominated for the Noble prize for his work in bio-electromagnetism, wrote that such devices have an, "obvious application in covert operations designed to drive a target crazy with voices."[151]

Aside from the patent awarded in 2002 to the US government for the Radio Frequency Hearing Effect, another patent (#4,877,027) was filed over a decade earlier in 1988 for an invention known as a "microwave voice device." The abstract for this patent reads:

Sound is induced in the head of a person by radiating the head with microwaves in the range of 100 megahertz to

---

[149] *Wired.com* "Secret Directed-Energy Tech Protecting the President?" (November 14, 2008) by David Hambling
[150] *Wired.com* "Telepathic Ray Guns' and Vaporized Shoes" (March 24, 2008) by David Hambling
[151] *Anomaly Magazine* "Guided by Voices" (February 1, 2008)

10,000 megahertz that are modulated with a particular waveform. The waveform consists of frequency modulated bursts. Each burst is made up of ten to twenty uniformly spaced pulses grouped tightly together. The burst width is between 500 nanoseconds and 100 microseconds. The pulse width is in the range of 10 nanoseconds to 1 microsecond. The bursts are frequency modulated by the audio input to create the sensation of hearing in the person whose head is irradiated.

An article published in the December 1980 issue of *Military Review* titled "The New Mental Battlefield," explained that the Soviet Union had built and used these kinds of weapons against political dissenters to cause illness or death with no evidence of foul play.[152] The author of the article, Colonel John B. Alexander, is considered the "founding father" of such weapons in America. A 1993 issue of *Defense News* reported that U.S. military officials were obtaining some of this Soviet "mind-control technology."[153]

The US Army has fully functioning devices that utilize this technology and call it a Voice to Skull (V2K) device and is classified as a non-lethal weapon. Some people suspect that these kinds of weapons were used in the assassinations of John F. Kennedy, Robert F. Kennedy, John Lennon, and others, meaning they believe Lee Harvey Oswald, Sirhan Sirhan, and Mark Chapman, (the shooters) had psychotronic weapons used on them to brainwash them and urge them to kill.

It's a fact that the MK-ULTRA program which began in the 1950s experimented heavily with mind control and

---

[152] *Military Review* "The New Mental Battlefield" (December 1980 issue) by Colonel John B. Alexander
[153] *Defense News* "U.S. Explores Russian Mind-Control Technology" by Barbara Opall (January 11-17, 1993)

brainwashing techniques, and such activities were considered conspiracy theories until the early 1970s when documents were released under the Freedom of Information Act and the extent of the horrors of this program were seen. One of the main goals of the MK-ULTRA experiments was to create technology and methods to turn an ordinary person into a mind-controlled assassin who would carry out any order given to them regardless of the consequences or danger.

Silent Subliminal Presentation System

When most people think of subliminal messages, they think of messages recorded backwards on rock albums from the 1970s, a method called backmasking, or messages mixed in with music so you can't noticeably hear them, but are believed to be noticed by the subconscious mind. While backmasking (using backwards messages) is really just a publicity stunt used by numerous musicians and not an actual subliminal message, the existence and use of subliminal messages is a very real scientific practice.

Below is information about another Orwellian patent awarded for a device that generates subliminal messages that don't need to be masked with music.

Inventor: Lowery; Oliver M. (Norcross, GA)
Patent # 5,159,703 awarded on October 27, 1992

The Abstract:

A silent communications system in which nonaural carriers, in the very low or very high audio frequency range or in the adjacent ultrasonic frequency spectrum, are amplitude or frequency modulated with the desired intelligence and propagated acoustically or vibrationally, for inducement into the brain, typically through the use of loudspeakers, earphones or piezoelectric transducers. The modulated carriers may be transmitted directly in real time or may be conveniently recorded and stored on mechanical, magnetic or optical media for delayed or repeated transmission to the listener.

The patent makes it clear that, "The 'silent' recordings are inaudible to the user or by others present and are therefore very effective for use during periods of sleep or when in the presence of others. Additionally, the basic requirements of subliminal stimulation are met. That is, the affirmations are efficiently transmitted to the ear and, while undetected by the conscious mind, are perceived by and efficiently decoded by the subconscious mind."

The patent goes on to read:

OBJECTS OF THE INVENTION

Accordingly, several objects and advantages of my invention are:

(a) to provide a technique for producing a subliminal presentation which is inaudible to the listeners(s), yet is perceived and demodulated (decoded) by the ear for use by the subconscious mind.

(b) to provide a technique for transmitting inaudible subliminal information to the listener(s) at a constant, high level of signal strength and on a clear band of frequencies.

(c) to provide a technique for producing inaudible

subliminal presentations to which music or other "foreground" programming may be added, if desired.

Other Subliminal Messages

An article titled *Secret Voices* published in a 1979 edition of *TIME* magazine reported that approximately 50 different department stores in the US and Canada were playing subliminal messages with the music systems hoping to reduce shoplifting from customers and theft from employees. One undisclosed East Coast chain claimed that their theft had dropped by 37% after using the system. [154]

The following year, in 1980, the *Wall Street Journal* published an article investigating systems that broadcast subliminal messages in stores that say things like, "I am honest. I will not steal." The article reported that after a New Orleans supermarket started using subliminal messages, their loss dropped to the lowest on record. [155] They also reported that shortages from cashiers dramatically dropped as well.

In 1984, a hearing in the US House of Representatives titled *Subliminal Communication Technology* investigated the use of subliminal messages and subliminal advertising in public places. [156]

In 1978 when a serial killer calling himself BTK

---

[154] *Time Magazine* "Secret Voices: Messages that Manipulate" (September 10, 1979)

[155] *Wall Street Journal* "Words Whispered to Subconscious Supposedly Deter Thefts, Fainting" by Neil Maxwell (November 25, 1980)

[156] Subliminal Communication Technology, Hearing before the Committee on Science and Technology, U.S. House of Representatives, Ninety-eighth Congress, Second Session, No. 105, August 6, 1984

(Bind, Torture, Kill) came to the attention of police in
Wichita, Kansas, a local TV station (under the direction
of the police) broadcast a subliminal message hoping to
influence the killer, urging him to turn himself in. In a
broadcast about the murders, the station included a
message saying, "Now call the chief," although the
attempt was unsuccessful.[157]

In 2004 dozens of electronic slot machines in Canada
were found to display subliminal messages that some felt
encouraged people to gamble more.[158] The machines
would flash a quick picture of a winning hand on the
screen, although the company, Konami, said the images
were caused from an error in the software. The machines
were ordered to be fixed.

It's interesting how the power of suggestion works.
Subliminal messages are not necessarily "brain washing"
techniques, but rather function as the name entails, by
"suggesting" something, thus causing a thought to arise in
a person's mind. Everyone is familiar with pulling up to a
fast food restaurant's drive through menu and after you're
done placing your order, you are often asked if you want
two apple pies or chocolate cookies for $1.99. They
know that just by suggesting this, they will spark a desire
in a measurable percentage of customers and dramatically
increase their sales.

Project Blue Beam

While governments have perpetuated countless
hoaxes, disinformation campaigns, and false flag terrorist

---

[157] *KAKA.com* "BTK Back: A subliminal message was sent to BTK
in 1978" (February 10, 2005)
[158] *PC World Magazine* "Slot-Machine Maker Asked to Halt
Subliminal Messages" by Marc L. Songini (March 2, 2007)

attacks in order to manipulate large populations of people—no plan is perhaps more grandiose than the idea of faking an appearance by God himself. There have been several times in recent history that the American government has proposed the idea of staging the appearance of God, who would then appear to speak to people and urge them to participate in an insurgency. This "supernatural" event can be done through a combination of holographic projections and sophisticated sound systems.

In February of 1999, the *Washington Post* reported on one of these plans, explaining that during the first Gulf War, the United States had actually considered projecting a huge holographic image of God in the sky over Baghdad.[159] This plan included the use of a 5-15 KHz acoustic beam that would make it seem like God was talking to the Iraqi people and would urge them to turn on their leader Saddam Hussein, sparking a revolution.

A similar plan was considered under Project Mongoose, a series of CIA operations against Cuba designed to overthrow Fidel Castro. Officials discussed having a submarine surface in the Havana harbor and project a huge Jesus-like figure onto the clouds that would then appear to speak and tell the Cuban people to overthrow "Godless Communism."[160]

This technology has been called Project Blue Beam, and could be used to either stage a "supernatural" visitation from "God," or even one from aliens arriving from outer space. In 1987, President Ronald Reagan

---

[159] *Washington Post* "When Seeing and Hearing Isn't Believing" by William M. Arkin (February 1, 1999)
[160] "Alleged Assassination Plots Involving Foreign Leaders," An Interim Report of the Select Committee to Study Governmental Operations with respect to Intelligence Activities, United States Senate, November 20, 1975.

made a very clear reference to aliens from outer space invading earth and causing all the nations of the world to unite and stop fighting each other. He actually said this at a United Nations meeting and video of the statement can be found online. "In our obsession with antagonism of the moment, we often forget how much unites all the members of humanity. Perhaps we need some outside, universal threat to make us recognize this common bond. I occasionally think how quickly our differences worldwide would vanish if we were facing an alien threat from outside this world."[161]

Some wonder whether this comment was said as a primer for a possible use of Project Blue Beam during the Cold War in order to frighten the Russians.

Leaders throughout history, dating back to ancient times, have claimed to have the power of God, or to speak on behalf of God in order to control their people and maintain their power and authority. Therefore, it should come as no surprise that government officials involved in covert operations would try to use Big Brother technology to take on the appearance of God himself.

"God is power [and] we are the priests of power."[162]
—Emmanuel Goldstein, the 'bad guy' in *Nineteen Eighty-Four*

Sonic Nausea Systems

While using the radio frequency hearing effect and other psychotronic weapons may be limited to those with expensive and complicated technology, a widely available and inexpensive device that uses ultra sonic waves to

---

[161] Speech at the Forty-Second UN General Assembly of the United Nations (September 21, 1987)
[162] Orwell, George – *Nineteen Eighty-Four* page 235

induce headaches and nausea can be purchased on the Internet or in catalogs selling law enforcement products. The *Shomer-Tech* catalog sells such a device called the Sonic Nausea System for only $29.99. The online catalog reads, "Hiding this device in your inconsiderate neighbor's house might put an end to their late-night parties. The abusive bureaucrat's office, the executive lunchroom... the possibilities are endless for that small portion of inventive payback."[163]

Another more advanced version is also sold, called the Super Sonic Nausea system which is advertised to, "disrupt speeches, demonstrations, crowd dynamics, etc. This device has been used to 'influence' more of these than you might expect. Deployed near the podium, you might just have a case of an increasingly un-impressive speaker with diminished sharpness and lacking concentration, or perhaps is even unable to complete his presentation. Or, loitering youths on your property might be enticed to move along with no confrontations necessary."

This "Super Sonic Nausea system" is said to be a "rarely-available government model" and is produced by a company called DSG Laboratories. This version sells for only $99.99. Just imagine for a minute what kind of similar devices are in existence but are not made commercially available. Such devices are extremely small and portable, and could easily be covertly used to inflict discomfort on any number of people, in any number of situations, without anyone even having a clue.

---

[163] http://www.shomer-tec.com/product/sonic-nausea-266.cfm

Information Technology

In *Nineteen Eighty-Four* the main character, Winston Smith, works at the Ministry of Truth, (a propaganda department) and his job is to go through old books and newspapers and delete information that the government doesn't want people to have access to anymore. Winston also changes "facts" in books and newspapers and reprints them to reflect the changes as if they were still in their original form. Big Brother has complete control over all information available to the people, both in the present, and from the past.

As you likely know, the mainstream media in our society has been tightly controlled for decades in order to shape the majority of information that reaches the population to keep people focused on what the establishment desires, and also at the same time, to prevent people from discovering issues that the establishment desires to keep private. Such a practice was fairly easy until the Internet became an environment where independent journalists and countless "alternative" news sites and bloggers were able to gain large followings of people and can operate with practically zero budget, yet reach millions of people just like the mainstream news does.

This has created a fairly large amount of competition for the mainstream establishment media, and has damaged their long held monopoly of information. Of course, they are not going to sit idly by and lose their grip on the flow of information, so they were forced to come up with new strategies in order to minimize the effect that independent blogs and news sites have on the population.

In 2006, a report from the Joint Special Operations

University titled *Blogs and Military Information Strategy* outlined a plan that would allow the government to underhandedly combat the popularity of independent bloggers and journalists. "Hiring a block of bloggers to verbally attack a specific person or promote a specific message may be worth considering," read the report.[164]

It also suggested the government hack the blogs of journalists whose writings threaten the world view that the establishment is trying to promote and then change articles to make them say ridiculous things to ruin the credibility of those journalists.

It reads, "[T]he enemy blog might be used covertly as a vehicle for friendly information operations. Hacking the site and subtly changing the messages and data—merely a few words or phrases—may be sufficient to begin destroying the blogger's credibility with the audience. Better yet, if the blogger happens to be passing enemy communications and logistics data, the information content could be corrupted."[165]

A Harvard law professor named Cass Sunstein was appointed by President Obama to head the Office of Information and Regulatory Affairs, and just like most high level kingpins in any president's administration; his Orwellian goals seem too strange to be true. Sunstein published a white paper in January 2008 titled *Conspiracy Theories* where he proposed that the government "might ban conspiracy theorizing" and could "impose some kind of tax, financial or otherwise, on those who disseminate such theories."[166] The "conspiracy theories" Sunstein is

---

[164] *Blogs and Military Information Strategy* page 20 by James Kinniburgh and Dororthy Denning
[165] *Blogs and Military Information Strategy* page 21 by James Kinniburgh and Dororthy Denning
[166] Sunstein, Cass R. "Conspiracy Theories" Harvard University - Harvard Law School (January 15, 2008) page 14

looking to attack, aren't conspiracy theories at all, but rather evidence and editorials that expose information that is damaging to the establishment, such as information about the true nature of the 9/11 attacks, the War in Iraq, and any number of other issues ranging from the Bilderberg group, Bohemian Grove, Skull and Bones, and other secretive establishment organizations.

In an article Sunstein wrote for the *Journal of Political Philosophy*, he also outlined a plan for the government to infiltrate "conspiracy" websites in order to undermine them by posting absurd comments on articles and social networks. He also suggested that government operatives infiltrate meetings held by "conspiracy theorists" in order to "(break) up the hard core of extremists who supply conspiracy theories."[167]

Sunstein said the government needed to, "Enlist nongovernmental officials in the effort to rebut the [conspiracy] theories. It might ensure that credible independent experts offer the rebuttal, rather than government officials themselves. There is a tradeoff between credibility and control, however. The price of credibility is that government cannot be seen to control the independent experts."[168]

It was also suggested that "government agents (and their allies) might enter chat rooms, online social networks, or even real-space groups and attempt to undermine percolating conspiracy theories by raising doubts about their factual premises, causal logic or

---

[167] Sunstein, Cass R. & Vermeule, Adrian "Conspiracy Theories: Causes and Cures," 17 *Journal of Political Philosophy* 202 (2008) page 15

[168] Sunstein, Cass R. & Vermeule, Adrian "Conspiracy Theories: Causes and Cures," 17 *Journal of Political Philosophy* 202 (2008) page 20

implications for political action."[169]   By "real-space groups" he means that agents should attend political protests and meetings in order to cause trouble, attempting to discredit the group while pretending to support their cause.

Sunstein has also called for making websites liable for comments posted in response to articles which would basically shut down any website that the government targeted with their online trolls. (A troll is a term used to identify someone online who posts comments on articles, blogs, or videos to derail the focus and to cause trouble rather than engage in a discussion about the topic at hand.) Sunstein's book, *On Rumors: How Falsehoods Spread, Why We Believe Them, What Can Be Done* was criticized by some as a blueprint for online censorship.

It's important to highlight that these ideas are not just the dreams of an obscure intellectual college professor. Cass Sunstein was appointed to a high level position in the Obama administration (the administrator of the head the Office of Information and Regulatory Affairs).

Sunstein is also vehemently against the right for people to own guns. In a lecture he gave at the University of Chicago Law School on October 27, 2007 he said, "The Supreme Court has never suggested that the Second Amendment protects an individual right to have guns."[170] Such a statement is completely false and a lie, and is another example of doublethink by an establishment insider. He continued his lecture predicting that the Second Amendment would be repealed, and the right to own guns will be a thing of the past. Sunstein is certainly not alone with his Orwellian dreams of trying to prevent

---

[169] Sunstein, Cass R. & Vermeule, Adrian "Conspiracy Theories: Causes and Cures," 17 *Journal of Political Philosophy* 202 (2008) page 22
[170] *YouTube* "Cass Sunstein Predicts Repealing Right To Bear Arms"

alternative political views from becoming a consensus. His goals of censorship and disrupting alternative media are shared by many in the establishment, both on the left, and on the right.

In 2006, the United States Central Command, (CENTCOM, a division of the Department of Defense) hired people to engage "bloggers who are posting inaccurate or untrue information, as well as bloggers who are posting incomplete information," about the so-called war on terror. [171]

As part of government's Information Operations, the Pentagon had people setup websites designed to look like foreign news websites, whose only purpose was to publish military propaganda and make it seem like it was news. [172] Israel also has teams of people who work to flood websites with messages to support Zionists crimes and try to deflect blame onto others. [173]

In January 2009, the US Air Force announced a "counter-blog" response plan aimed at finding and reacting to material from bloggers who have "negative opinions about the US government and the Air Force." [174] The plan outlines a twelve-point "counter blogging" flow-chart that describes how they can handle "misguided" online writers by posting comments designed to derail the discussion causing it to drift off topic.

A leading think tank in the UK called Demos published a report in August 2010 titled *The Power of*

---

[171] *The Raw Story* "Raw obtains CENTCOM e-mail to bloggers" (October 16, 2006)

[172] *USA Today* "Pentagon launches foreign news websites" (April 30, 2008) by Peter Eisler

[173] *HAARETZ* "Israel recruits 'army of bloggers' to combat anti-Zionist Web sites" (June 19, 2009) by Cnaan Liphshiz

[174] *Politico.com* "Air Force Releases 'Counter-Blog' Marching Orders" By Noah Shachtman (January 6, 2009)

Unreason that suggested government agents should infiltrate websites in an attempt to discredit ideas that the 9/11 attacks in America and the 7/7 bombings in London were "inside jobs." The report explained that these online agents needed to increase trust in government and that the government needed to "fight back by infiltrating Internet sites to dispute these theories."[175]

Jamie Bartlett, the author of the report, essentially called people who discuss "conspiracy theories" and false flag terrorism "extremists" who make stories up. The Demos think tank logo incorporates an obvious all-seeing eye as the letter "o" in their name which can be seen on their official website http://www.demos.co.uk.

Demos was co-founded in 1993 by Communist Martin Jacques, who was the editor of *Marxism Today*, the journal of The Communist Party of Great Britain. The other co-founder was Geoff Mulgan who was closely affiliated with Prime Minister Tony Blair.

Carnivore

Anyone with average intelligence knows that Internet service providers (and the government) keep databases on practically every website each individual user visits, what files you download, what links you click, and can access every e-mail you've ever sent. Some may be surprised at just how simple this is, and how long this has been possible. The all-encompassing system designed for this task was originally called Carnivore and was created by the FBI during the Clinton administration as the Internet became widely used by the public.

The public inevitably found out about Carnivore and

---

[175] *The Independent* "Secret services 'must be made more transparent'" By Rachel Shields (August 29, 2010)

its capabilities so the FBI later changed its name to DCS1000, which stands for Digital Collection System. This system can easily monitor a specific individual's Internet usage in real time, as well as go back and see the exact history of all Internet searches and websites they've visited, what comments they've posted on articles or social networking sites, and what files they've downloaded. It is reasonable to assume that this same system can secretly access any computer's hard drive if the computer is connected to the Internet, and the contents of that person's hard drive can be copied and analyzed, all without having physical access to the computer. The built-in webcams and microphones in laptops can also be remotely activated by authorities as well, and can be used to watch and listen to you without your knowledge. Of course, these activities are illegal without a warrant, but that is why they are highly classified. Anyone who denies that such tasks are easily carried out, is simply in denial, or has no clue about what modern technology is capable of.

"As for sending a letter through the mail, it was out of the question. By a routine that was not even secret, all letters were opened in transit."[176] —*Nineteen Eighty-Four*

Have you downloaded music or movies illegally on torrents or file sharing networks? It's usually just the large downloaders that get busted, but if Big Brother is watching you for some other reason, then you may just "coincidentally" find yourself getting arrested or sued for pirating intellectual property.

Internet service provider Earthlink has resisted the government's attempts to monitor Internet traffic through their systems, and admitted that the FBI has forced the company to allow them to tap into their system. Robert

---

[176] Orwell, George – *Nineteen Eighty-Four* page 97

Corn-Revere, a lawyer for Earthlink said at a hearing, "We believed it would enable the government to acquire more information than the law permits, not just about the person who was the target of the investigation, but potentially about a large number of other subscribers who had nothing at all to do with the investigation...Over time, the cumulative effect of widespread surveillance for law enforcement, intelligence, and other investigatory purposes could change the climate and fabric of society in fundamental ways."[177]

In a world where George Orwell's 1984 nightmare has come true, we would expect that practically all of our communications are intercepted, monitored, analyzed, and stored indefinitely by Big Brother. Echelon and Carnivore are the two most well-known mechanisms for conducting this kind of surveillance, but for decades most of the information concerning these systems has been kept highly secret. If and when the details and capabilities of these systems are made public, it would be chilling to learn just how far-reaching they are.

In the post-9/11 world when security has become big business, many private companies are developing Big Brother technology that may rival similar government systems in hopes of identifying "troubled" people before they may "do something crazy."

At a military tech conference at the International First Responder-Military Symposium in the Town of Hamburg, New York in September 2010, one company showed off a system that's capable of listening to phone calls, reading emails, as well as people's posts on social networking

---

[177] Robert Corn-Revere "Testimony on Carnivore and the Fourth Amendment" Federal Document Clearing House Congressional Testimony (July 24, 2000)

sites and other areas of the Internet for what was described as "resentment towards the government."[178]

Professor Mathieu Guidere of the University of Geneva, Switzerland, explained that, "The computer system detects resentment in conversations through measurements in decibels and other voice biometrics. It detects obsessiveness with the individual going back to the same topic over and over, measuring crescendos."[179]

A similar data mining system is used on emails to detect what are allegedly patterns of fixation on specified subjects and any data that involves radicalization or ideological arguments. When demonstrating the system, Guidere invoked the memory of the September 11, 2001 attacks, saying that it can detect signs "pointing to a potential terrorist."

The system demonstrated at the conference could review about 10,000 voice or other electronic transmissions in an hour, a capacity that would soon increase to 100,000 per hour and beyond, touted the designers.

The system was even promoted as some kind of emotional stability tester that could be used to screen potential employees, war veterans, law enforcement officials, and practically anyone else unfortunate enough to be subjected to the device. "By recording the voice of the patient, the program can rate negativity and positivity with depression and other emotional disorders," said Guidere, who is working with Dr. Newton Howard, the director of MIT's Mind Machine Project, a program dedicated to building artificially intelligent machines.[180]
(*See Artificial Intelligence*)

---

[178] *Buffalo News* "Technology identifies troubled individuals" by Lou Michel (September 26, 2010)
[179] Ibid.
[180] Ibid.

Telcom Immunity

It was revealed that major telecommunication companies secretly cooperated with the Bush administration to illegally wiretap phone calls of American citizens allegedly to help fight the war on terror. It turns out that the National Security Agency had entire rooms built within the major telecommunication companies in order to tap into their networks and communication hubs. The problem was, this was against the law, and while it was initially denied by the Bush administration and telecommunication executives, the large-scale wire tapping was later fully revealed.

Citizens clamored for legal action to be taken, but the Bush administration passed a law giving retroactive immunity to all of the telecom companies involved in the illegal wiretapping.[181] The message the government sent to private industries was basically that they could break the law and not worry about any legal ramifications because the government would just grant them immunity if they were ever busted.

During his presidential campaign, Barack Obama denounced the legislation granting them immunity, but when the time came to vote for the immunity, he voted to support it.[182]

Reading Your E-mails Without a Warrant

Internet giant Yahoo has battled with the government over whether or not e-mails were protected by the

---

[181] *Cnet News* "Senate endorses retroactive FISA immunity for warrantless wiretapping" (July 9, 2008) by Declan McCullagh
[182] *The New York Times* "Obama Voters Protest His Switch on Telecom Immunity" by James Risen (July 2, 2008)

Constitution's requirement that a search warrant be required in order for the government to read them. To many people's surprise, it is perfectly legal for the government to read your e-mails without a warrant after they are 180 days old, but the government began pushing to read e-mails without a warrant that were not that old if the e-mails had already been read by the person receiving them. For some reason, the government insisted then, that the Fourth Amendment to the Constitution didn't apply because the e-mail had already been read.

Yahoo disagreed and refused to turn over customer e-mails to the feds that were less than 180 days old, saying it required a warrant. Google, the Electronic Frontier Foundation, the Center for Democracy & Technology and other groups also told a federal judge presiding over the case that accessing e-mail less than 180 days old requires a valid warrant under the Fourth Amendment, regardless of whether it has been read.

"The government says the Fourth Amendment does not protect these e-mails," explains Kevin Bankston, an Electronic Frontier Foundation lawyer. "What we're talking about is archives of our personal correspondence that they would need a warrant to get from your computer but not from the server."[183]

The 1986 Stored Communications Act defines electronic storage as "(A) any temporary, intermediate storage of a wire or electronic communication incidental to the electronic transmission thereof; and (B) any storage of such communication by an electronic communication service for purposes of backup protection of such communication."

The government insists that the storage of previously

[183] *Wired.com* "Yahoo, Feds Battle Over E-Mail Privacy" by David Kravets (April 14, 2010)

opened e-mails does not qualify for protection, because the e-mails are not in "electronic storage" which they say enables them to read them without a warrant.

The Cybersecurity Act

The Cybersecurity Act is a bill that if passed would give the President of the United States the power to declare a "cybersecurity emergency" and shut down or limit Internet traffic in any "critical" information network "in the interest of national security."

If the president wanted too, he could basically force major websites to be shut down for a duration of time in the immediate aftermath of a major terrorist attack or a pandemic, and even cause the visitors of those websites to be forwarded to a specific government page which would then display government propaganda with one-sided information about what had just occurred, and what actions should be taken, such as coerced evacuations or inoculations. This ability is similar to the Emergency Broadcast System installed on television networks that enables local, state, and national authorities to take over all major broadcast networks and cable channels to then broadcast a message to all viewers simultaneously on all channels.

This bill was introduced by Senator Jay Rockefeller, the great-grandson of John D. Rockefeller, nephew of banker David Rockefeller, a family that has long been a part of the secret establishment. When discussing how "dangerous" the Internet was to national security and why he felt the Cybersecurity Act was important, Jay Rockefeller stated, "It really almost makes you ask the question, would it have been better if we had never invented the Internet."

The so-called Einstein Security Shield is reported to

use NSA technology and according to the declassified summary is designed to look for indicators of cyber attacks by digging into all Internet communications, including the contents of e-mails.[184]

Hackers sent a virus to attack Iran's new nuclear power plant in 2010; doing so much damage that it set their nuclear program back allegedly by two years.[185] In all likelihood it was an attack orchestrated by Israel to delay Iran's nuclear program for their own self-interest. Many see cyber-security programs as power grabs by governments to more easily regulate and monitor global Internet traffic.

Some believe that Julian Assange, the famed editor of the WikiLeaks whistleblower website, was an unknowing patsy of billionaire George Soros, who people believe was funding WikiLeaks in order to create a compelling reason to pass the Cyber Security Act in order to further secure the Internet. While there is rampant speculation surrounding Julian Assange and WikiLeaks regarding their funding and the goals, Julian Assange is most likely a true activist-hacker and info-warrior who believes that he is just bringing the world the secret information the military doesn't want people to know about concerning the true nature of the war in Iraq and the global war on terrorism

As a result of the famous publishing of 250,000 cables (documents) in 2010, Julian Assange and the WikiLeaks supporters found themselves in a difficult dilemma, as well as the target of various conspiracy theories. They stole and leaked classified information to the public, but once that was done, then obviously the

---

[184] *Wall Street Journal* "Details of 'Einstein' Cyber Shield Disclosed by White House" By Siobhan Gorman (March 2, 2010)
[185] *Jerusalem Post* "Stuxnet virus set back Iran's nuclear program by 2 years" by Yaakov Katz (December 15th 2010)

security was strengthened, making it impossible to do the same thing in the future. But some short-sighted conspiracy theorists claim WikiLeaks *only* released the 250,000 cables so the government could clamp down on cyber security, following in line with the Hegelian Dialectic of problem-reaction-solution. While this was undoubtedly a side-effect of the leaking of the classified info, it certainly was not the intention of Assange.

Cyber security measures implemented by the government will always serve as a cover to gain a more intimate look at the personal communications of everyone.

CNN's Fake Cyber Attack Broadcast

In February of 2010, CNN aired a one hour simulation of the aftermath of a cyber attack on America. The broadcast consisted of a boardroom of high-level officials, including (former) Secretary of Homeland Security Michael Chertoff, Director of National Intelligence John Negroponte, former Director of the CIA John McLaughlin, Bill Clinton's former press secretary Joe Lockhart, and other high-powered and well-known government officials. The group sat around and pretended to have a real discussion about how the government would deal with a cyber attack that had just shut down the Internet and electrical grids across the country.

The opening screen of the broadcast explained, "Cyber ShockWave will provide an unprecedented look at how the government would develop a real-time response to a large-scale cyber crisis affecting much of the nation." The event took place at the Mandarin Oriental Hotel in Washington, D.C. on February 16, 2010. When breaking to, and coming back from commercials, CNN showed a screen saying, "we were warned," which is what they titled their broadcast.

CNN's Wolf Blitzer hosted the event and began by saying, "What you're about to see is not real, but the threat is very real, indeed. You're about to get an unprecedented look at how the US government would deal with a massive cyber shockwave." He went on to describe the program as a cyber war game scenario.

Clips of this war game can likely be found on YouTube and show the panelists pretending to react to an actual cyber attack that just hit America. What's fascinating about this broadcast is the seriousness and the seeming authenticity of the panelists. If you had not noticed the word "simulation" posted in the corner of the screen, or had just listened to the broadcast, you would swear they were responding to an actual attack that just occurred.

It's fascinating that these high-powered government officials were simply playing make-believe, but all of them seemed like they could be nominated for an Academy Award for their performances. They appeared scared and were coming up with scenarios off the top of their head about what needed to be done to respond to the "attack." What their fake concern shows is just how good of actors these people are. They looked, and sounded, no different during this session of make-believe, than they did during press conferences or during regular interviews. These powerful panelists on this war game were some of the best liars that have ever lived, and their simulation shows how easily they can look the American people in the eye and seem extremely concerned about an event, simply by acting. It was surely no coincidence that this fear-mongering simulation was broadcast at the same time the Obama administration was trying to get support for the Cybersecurity Act which grants sweeping powers to the government over the Internet.

The Way You Type Can Identify You

Some computer scientists believe that they can actually identify a person's age, sex, and culture just from analyzing the way they type depending on their speed and rhythm. This seems like pseudoscience of course, but Professor Roy Maxion, associate professor at Newcastle University, has been researching these claims and a former Police detective Phil Butler, head of Newcastle University's Cybercrime and Computer Security department, believes the system could be used to track online criminals and pedophiles.

"Roy's research has the potential to be a fantastic tool to aid intelligence gathering for crime fighting agencies, in particular serious and organized crime and for those tracking down pedophiles," Butler said.[186]

"If children are talking to each other on Windows Live or MSN Messenger, we are looking at ways of providing the chat room moderators with the technology to be able to see whether an adult is on there by the way they type," he explained.

The basis of this technology is that each individual has identifying patterns to the way they type, and once that pattern is identified, then a program could be installed to look for that pattern to see if it shows up in a chat room.

Your Laptop is Listening to You

In 2006 it was reported that Google had discussed

---

[186] *The Telegraph* "Typing technique could trap pedophiles" (March 27, 2010)

using the microphone that is built into all laptop computers to listen to the user and their environment and analyze the audio for keywords which would then be used to place specific advertisements on web pages that reflected conversations the microphone was picking up.[187] The lengthy user agreement that people agree to through implied consent when they log on to Google.com would include legal language that would allow this.

If this system were in place, for example, if you were talking a lot about working out or hiking when you're around your computer, the system would identify these keywords as being frequently discussed topics and would then choose specific advertisements to display as a result. It was also discussed that this system would choose advertisements based on what television or radio shows were detected that are playing in the background.[188] If the system detected cooking shows, your ads would be for food and kitchen related items. If you were watching football, then it would detect this and tailor the advertising accordingly.

The Onion, a popular parody and satire news site, produced a video that looked like a news segment about what they described as new software for Google's cell phone that would use voice recognition software to listen to people's conversations, and then play relevant advertisements during that conversation.[189] The writers of this sketch obviously had read the reports of Google's discussion about using the built-in microphones to listen to people and chose to satirize the idea.

---

[187] *The Register* "Google developing eavesdropping software: Audio 'fingerprint' for content-relevant ads" (September 3, 2006)
[188] Ibid
[189] *YouTube.com/TheOnion* "New Google Phone Service Whispers Targeted Ads Directly Into Users' Ears"

Google Street View

Another Orwellian feature implemented by the Internet giant Google is their Street View feature that was launched in May 2007 and provides panoramic views from nearly every street in America and other countries around the world. Online travel map programs, such as Yahoo Maps and Google Maps, have been a favorite of many people since search engines began, but Google's Street View function allows users to choose any address in the country, and then shows them a 360 degree view of that area as it looks from the street.

For example, you can type in your address on the Google Maps page (or using your cell phone) and then select the "Street View" function, and you can then view your own house as if you are standing on the street right in front of it. You can then change the direction and position of the camera, and simulate traveling down your street as if you are in a virtual reality game. Users can even zoom in.

This Street View map was created from a fleet of cars that had special 360 degree cameras placed on the top, and then they drove down practically every street in America as the cameras captured photos of the entire journey. Later, Google used smaller vehicles and even snowmobiles to capture images of pedestrian areas, alleys, and narrow streets, and then added them to the Street View.

This feature caused some resistance by people who were upset about this invasion of their privacy, and the Department of Homeland Security even delayed the publication of certain street views in Washington, DC because they were worried that images may have been taken of some security-sensitive areas. The Department of Defense wouldn't let Google capture images of US

BIG BROTHER

Military bases and had them remove certain locations from the database.

There are entire websites that contain funny and embarrassing photos that the Google Street View cameras have picked up, such as people coming out of strip clubs, passed out drunk in their yard, and women sunbathing. While some of these photos are amusing, they also illustrate just how far-reaching the eyes of Big Brother are.

Years after the Street View feature was available, it was revealed that the same cars which drove around taking the photos had also intercepted information from unsecured Wi-Fi hotspots from businesses and people's homes. *PC World* explained, "It simply intercepted the unencrypted data that businesses and individuals beamed through the air willy-nilly. The data was left in the middle of the street so to speak, and Google gathered it as it drove through collecting photographs."[190] Google said it was an accident and they did not plan on using the information gathered.

Social Networking Sites

Social media, or social networking sites, quickly changed the landscape of society as Facebook and Twitter rapidly gained popularity shortly after their creation. MySpace and Facebook allowed people to quickly set up their own webpage for free, and exchange photos, status updates, and messages with their friends and family, but such social media also has its downfalls. Facebook and MySpace allowed people for the first time to easily open up their entire life to the Internet, and practically anyone

---

[190] *PC World* "Google Wi-Fi Data Capture Unethical, But Not Illegal" (June 12, 2010) by Tony Bradley

with a computer. Their name, birthdates, interests, friends, family members, school, place of employment, photos, and more are often published openly for the world to see.

Such media has caused many people to become extremely self absorbed and have turned themselves into their own idol, along with their fan base of "friends" that regularly comment on their status updates or photos. Many people love the attention they get from posting a status update on any dumb thought they had that they feel is clever, and oftentimes there is no shortage of "friends" to post their comments, which are equally worthless.

Girls often like to post pretty (and slutty) photos of themselves and bathe in the attention from people's comments as countless guys who are on their friends list tell them how beautiful they are. What is even more bizarre, is that many, if not most of the "friends" on their page, aren't really friends at all, but just acquaintances, and many are people they've just met once or twice and don't really associate with in real life. Facebook has become a cyber stalker's dream come true. Before MySpace and Facebook, if a guy was interested in a girl he met at a party or through friends, he would have to ask for her phone number face to face in order to communicate with her again in the future, but now it is commonplace for people to look others up on Facebook, and then send them a "friend request" which allows them to access that person's personal information, photos, status updates, and friends list.

You don't even need to know a person's full name to find them online. For example, if a guy meets a girl at a party and is interested in her (or interested in stalking her) all he does is go to the page of a person he's already friends with that he knows is friends with the girl he is interested in, and then scrolls through that person's friends list until he finds the girl he's stalking. This is easy since people are listed with their picture, as well as their first and last name. This is not looked at as creepy at all by most girls, but instead has become a normal part of our culture.

These social networking sites also have broad implications on personal relationships, as well. In the past, if two people were in a relationship or were married, then communication with ex boyfriends, ex girlfriends, or others who harbored a secret crush on an individual, was largely limited. But now, since practically everyone has a Facebook page, if an old high school friend who secretly had a crush on someone for years, perhaps decades, that person can now look up their crush on Facebook and establish communication with them, all without that person's significant other or spouse being aware of it. (Not to mention that person will also have instant access to information such as where their crush lives, where they work, names, photos, and ages of their kids, as well as a link to their love interest's spouse's page where they can then peer into their life as well.)

Also, in the past, when showing our family and friends photos of our life or things we've done, they had to all sit down around a table and everyone would look through the photos and talk about them, but now most photos are posted on Facebook and are widely available to the entire world. Photos of people's kids, homes, friends, and more are all just a click away. Even photos taken by other people are shown once you are tagged in them.

As you are probably familiar with, people even link up their current dating partner or spouse on their Facebook page, and then anyone can click on the link and see who that person is in a relationship with, and then view all of their photos and learn all about them from the details of their life that are posted on their page. There is even a Facebook app for cell phones that allows people to see the physical location of their friends based on the GPS systems in their phones.[191] A feature on Twitter called Twitter Tracker also allows users to identify their location when they post their Tweets (messages).[192]

There have been numerous instances of people's homes being burglarized while they were out of town because they posted a status update telling the world that they were going on vacation, and how long they would be gone. These were not complete strangers who burglarized people's homes, it was people on their "friends" list who saw their status updates and knew they would be gone.[193] As you probably know, most people will accept a "friend request" from just about anybody, no matter how little they know them. Just look at the number of "friends" that some people have on Facebook, especially attractive girls. Beautiful girls often have four or five hundred, sometimes close to a thousand "friends" on Facebook or MySpace because most guys will track them down and find their page after meeting them only once and send them a friend request so they can voyeuristically peer into their life. Most girls feel bad about declining a friend request, so most people accept them all, no matter how little they know the person.

In 2009 a group of young teenagers were arrested in Los Angeles, California for burglarizing various celebrities' homes, including Paris Hilton's, Lindsay Lohan's, and others. The group was called the Bling Ring

---

[191] *The Times* "The Facebook tool which turns your mobile into a snoop" (April 1, 2008) by Adam Sherwin
[192] *Metro* "Twitter is watching you... New technology tells the world where you're tweeting from" (March 12, 2010) by Joanne McCabe
[193] *News Channel 8* Arlington, VA "Facebook Status Updates Linked to Burglaries" (March 25, 2010) producer: Markham Evans

by the media, and was said to have watched their celebrity targets on Facebook and Twitter to determine when they were going to be out of town, so they could then break into their houses.[194] When the celebrities posted a status update or a Tweet saying they were traveling somewhere for an event or a vacation, the Bling Ring knew their home would most likely be unoccupied. The group stole several million dollars worth of jewelry and clothes from the celebrity homes before getting caught.

Facebook and MySpace Own the Photos You Post

The media frenzy surrounding Eliot Spitzer's high class hooker scandal in 2008 brought something else to light other than the governor's scandalous sex life. What you post on social networking sites is available for the world to see. Photographs of Ashey Dupre (his alleged high-class call girl) were immediately published around the world, including pictures of her family members, all of which were taken from her MySpace page. Her lawyer threatened to sue media outlets for publishing the photos, claiming she owns the copyright to them, but let's take a closer look at what you sign away when you use MySpace or Facebook.

By simply using these websites, you agree to their Terms of Service, but who really reads that boring stuff anyway? Maybe you should. Let's look at Myspace.com first. When you post your personal and family photos on your page, you are automatically entering into a licensing agreement with MySpace and its affiliates to use your photos in any way they like. Not only can they use them, but they can edit or modify them, as well. Keep in mind

---

[194] *London Guardian* "Bling ring on trial for Hollywood celebrity burglaries" (January 17, 2010) by Paul Harris

that MySpace is owned by News Corporation, so people are basically giving Rupert Murdoch and his media empire, including Fox News, the New York Post, and dozens of other media outlets, permission to do whatever they want with their photos.

The Terms of Service that you agree to by using the website reads, "By displaying or publishing ("posting") any Content on or through the MySpace Services, you hereby grant to MySpace a limited license to use, modify, delete from, add to, publicly perform, publicly display, reproduce, and distribute such Content solely on or through the MySpace Services, including without limitation distributing part or all of the MySpace Website in any media formats and through any media channels."[195]

Section 6.2 of the agreement says, "MySpace is not required to pay you for the use on the MySpace Services of the Content that you post," and that the content which they now control is, "sublicensable (so that MySpace is able to use its affiliates, subcontractors and other partners such as Internet content delivery networks and wireless carriers to provide the MySpace Services), and worldwide (because the Internet and the MySpace Services are global in reach)."

Did you understand that? You are granting them and their "affiliates, subcontractors and other partners" use of your material, all without paying you. And you thought they were *your* photos. If you have a problem with this, and post a blog about it on your MySpace page, or send out a bulletin to all your friends warning them, then MySpace can remove your bulletin or blog, and delete your account. The Terms of Service state, "MySpace reserves the right, in its sole discretion, to reject, refuse to post or remove any posting (including private messages)

---

[195] http://www.myspace.com/index.cfm?fuseaction=misc.terms

by you, or to deny, restrict, suspend, or terminate your access to all or any part of the MySpace Services at any time, for any or no reason, with or without prior notice or explanation, and without liability."

Facebook is no different. At one time, when you would delete your account, any rights that they claimed to your content would expire, but they later updated their Terms of Service so you automatically grant them the rights (without any compensation) to any photo or anything else you post on Facebook, forever.

It reads, "You hereby grant Facebook an irrevocable, perpetual, non-exclusive, transferable, fully paid, worldwide license (with the right to sublicense) to (a) use, copy, publish, stream, store, retain, publicly perform or display, transmit, scan, reformat, modify, edit, frame, translate, excerpt, adapt, create derivative works and distribute (through multiple tiers), any User Content you (i) Post on or in connection with the Facebook Service or the promotion thereof subject only to your privacy settings or (ii) enable a user to Post, including by offering a Share Link on your website and (b) to use your name, likeness and image for any purpose, including commercial or advertising, each of (a) and (b) on or in connection with the Facebook Service or the promotion thereof."

So if you or any of your friends or family members are ever swept up in any kind of scandal, then don't be surprised if within hours, personal photos of you or your friends or family find their way onto the cover of the *New York Post*, and are plastered all over celebrity news shows and mainstream media networks. Since you are also giving them a free license to "use your name, likeness, and image for any purpose" they could also sell your photos which could find their way onto a billboard advertising a product you'd rather not have any affiliation with.

Police on Facebook

Police in multiple cities around the country have been setting up fake accounts on Facebook using photos of attractive girls as the supposed user and then sending friend requests to students to look at their photos to see if there are any pictures of people under the age of twenty-one who can be seen holding alcoholic drinks.

One such instance that made news happened in Wisconsin in 2009 when 19-year-old Adam Bauer, a student at the University of Wisconsin-La Crosse, received a friend request from police posing as an attractive girl that resulted in him being charged with underage drinking. "She was a good-looking girl. I usually don't accept friends I don't know, but I randomly accepted this one for some reason," he said.[196]

Shortly after he accepted the friend request from the unknown attractive girl, Bauer was confronted by police who had a photo of him from Facebook showing him holding a beer. He was then ticketed for underage drinking. At least eight students at UW Lacrosse were targeted in the same manor including one of Bauer's friends. "I just can't believe it. I feel like I'm in a science fiction movie, like they are always watching. When does it end?" Bauer said after his court appearance.[197]

The students said that they were being safe and partying at home and insisted that nobody was driving afterwards. La Crosse police officer Al Iverson said, "Law enforcement has to evolve with technology. It has to happen. It is a necessity—not just for underage drinking."

---

[196] *La Crosse Tribune* "Facebook friend turns into Big Brother" (November 19, 2009) by KJ Lang
[197] Ibid

This is certainly not an isolated incident of Big Brother watching Facebook. In January 2008, several teenagers were arrested in Illinois for underage drinking after a sheriff's deputy found photos of them partying that were posted on Facebook.[198]

In February 2006, a 16-year-old boy in Colorado was arrested for juvenile possession of a firearm after police saw pictures that he had posted of himself posing with guns on MySpace.[199]

One student in Miami, Florida was arrested and charged with inciting panic after he posted a police sketch of a rape suspect as his profile picture on Facebook.[200] While certainly this was an untasteful and juvenile attempt at a joke, it certainly didn't incite a panic.

In August 2006, a student at the University of Illinois was arrested for urinating in public while another student was able to escape. The student that was originally arrested said he didn't know the name of the one who ran away, but police were able to get his name from other witnesses (who were not urinating) but were in the same group. The arresting officer then used Facebook to discover that the two students were friends, and then came back and charged the first student who was originally arrested for urinating in public with obstruction of justice because he had lied to police and said he didn't know the other student.[201]

In February 2007, eleven high school students at a

---

[198] *WLS-TV Chicago ABC 7* "Authorities make string of underage drinking arrests from Facebook photos" (January 14, 2008)

[199] *Rocky Mountain News* "Boy who posed with guns convicted" (April 5, 2006) by Sue Lindsay

[200] *The Miami Student* "Student arrested for inducing panic with Facebook picture" (February 9, 2006) by Graham Wolfe

[201] *Daily Ilini.com* "Student arrested after police Facebook him" (August 1, 2006) Kiyoshi Martinez

Catholic school in Canada were suspended for posting negative comments about their principle on Facebook.[202] There also have been numerous reports of people being fired from their jobs after complaining about their boss or their employer in their status updates.[203]

Facebook Sells Your Personal Information

Social networking sites are a gold mine of information for advertisers and marketers. People list their favorite music, movies, TV shows, and activities on their page, and most people think this is just to inform their "friends" of what they like, but Facebook shares people's information with "third parties," which means advertisers and marketers.[204]

Aside from getting information listed in everyone's profile, Facebook can also data mine status updates and search for keywords that are frequently used in people's postings. Does the word *party* come up a lot of times in someone's status update? Or the word *dog*, or *jogging*? Advertisers love access to this information since they can see into your life and learn what's important to you.

Facebook has been around in its present form since 2006, and has stored practically every piece of information users have typed onto their profiles, including years worth of status updates, all of which can be sold to whoever Facebook wants. Facebook founder Mark Zuckerberg became a billionaire from Facebook, which is free for its millions of users, so how do you think the

---

[202] *CBC News* "11 Ontario students suspended for cyber-bullying" (February 12, 2007)
[203] *NBC Bay Area* "Fired Over Facebook Status" (March 6, 2009) by P.K. LO
[204] *Fox 5 DC* "Facebook to Share Your Info for Money" (April, 27 2010)

website generates so much money? In a transcript released in May 2010 of Zuckerberg chatting with a friend about the personal information people were posting on Facebook, Zuckerberg called the people "dumb fucks."[205]

Twitter

The "tweets" (messages) posted on Twitter have been compared to graffiti scribbled in bathroom stalls, meaning it's utterly worthless, but somehow Twitter became a social phenomena in 2009 after word spread that Ashton Kutcher and Oprah were having a contest to see who could reach one million followers first. This caused word of Twitter to enter the mainstream media, and immediately every news station and television show included Twitter on its list of things you should connect with them on. (Twitter.com/MarkDice for example)

The only real reason for someone to have a Twitter account is if they are a celebrity or a public figure who has a fan base that want to keep up to date with what they're doing, something that can more easily be done on Facebook since people can see others' photos and videos as well, but somehow Twitter caught on and became very trendy in 2009. If you look at the tweets (twitter's terminology for a message posted), one can see how useless Twitter really is, with most tweets consisting of worthless messages describing how someone's lunch was or saying that it's a beautiful day, but for some reason the Library of Congress decided to create an archive of every Twitter message ever posted.

The Library of Congress's blogger Matt Raymond

---

[205] *The Register* "Facebook founder called trusting users dumb f*cks" (May 14, 2010) by Andrew Orlowski

thought this was a great idea, saying, "I'm no Ph.D. but it boggles my mind to think what we might be able to learn about ourselves and the world around us from this wealth of data. And I'm certain we'll learn things that none of us now can even possibly conceive."[206] Twitter said that they would soon post every single Tweet dating back to the first one on March 21, 2006.

Twitter gives an interesting look into the minds of its users by listing what it calls "trending topics," which are the top keywords or phrases that people post in their messages. "Tweets and other short-form updates create a history of commentary that can provide valuable insights into what's happened and how people have reacted," wrote Dylan Casey, Google's product manager for real-time search. "Want to know how the news broke about health care legislation in Congress, what people were saying about Justice Paul Stevens' retirement or what people were tweeting during your own marathon run? These are the kinds of things you can explore with the new updates mode."[207]

Cell Phones are Bugs

While it has been fairly well known that Echelon can detect and record practically anyone's phone conversation and has archives of countless hours of phone calls, it was surprising to learn in 2006 that law enforcement and intelligence agencies can activate the microphone on someone's cell phone and use it as a directional bug, *even when the phone is turned off,* and can then listen to

---

[206] *Wired.com* "Library of Congress Archives Twitter History, While Google Searches It" (April 14, 2010) by Ryan Singel
[207] Ibid

conversations in the surrounding areas.[208]

The power can be off, but then with the push of a button, someone can secretly activate the microphone, and the phone will still appear to be off. This can easily be done without probable cause, and without a warrant. The only way to prevent this is to take the battery out of your phone. The microphone and webcam on your computer can be used the same way and activated remotely without your knowledge.

One might think that this technology is only something that is available to intelligence agencies such as the NSA, CIA, or the FBI, but what is even more chilling is that there are numerous websites offering such services to anyone for a small fee. Such services also allow a person to receive files of all the person's recorded phone calls, and the person doing the spying can even get a call on their own phone every time the targeted person uses their phone so they can listen in to their conversations in real time.

This is highly illegal, but these companies are offshore, or simply offer software that allows you to do it yourself.[209] They use a disclaimer saying it's illegal to do it to anyone's phone without their knowledge or consent, but we all know they are just covering themselves legally, and are fully aware that their systems are used without the victims' knowledge.

These commercially available illegal snooping systems have practically the same capability as the FBI does, and can activate the microphone in your cell phone when it's turned off to listen to anything in the surrounding area. The person using these illegal snooping

---

[208] *CNET.com* "FBI taps cell phone mic as eavesdropping tool" by Declan McCullagh and Anne Broache (December 1, 2006)
[209] *WAVY-TV NBC*

services can also intercept all text messages, voice mails, and can listen to your phone calls in real time because they get an alert anytime your phone has a call connected.

Cell Phone Photos

As cell phones have become miniature personal computers, complete with Internet access and digital cameras, many people obviously use their phone to take photos which they later post online to Facebook or other websites. What most people are not familiar with is that every photo you take with your phone can actually be viewed and downloaded by your cell phone carrier or anyone who has access to their system.

This became clear in 2005 when a hacker was able to obtain photos taken on cell phone cameras by numerous celebrities, including Demi Moore, Ashton Kutcher, Nicole Richie, and Paris Hilton.[210] This hacker did not have access to these celebrities' phones themselves, but was able to download the photos through the Internet.

So unlike photos taken from traditional digital cameras, the ones taken by your cell phone camera are available for anyone to see who has the ability or the authority to snatch them wirelessly.

Voice Synthesizers

Another scary aspect of advancing technology are voice synthesizers that can take samples of someone's voice, and then allow someone else to speak into a microphone, and then the computer will output exactly what that person said, with the same voice inflections, but

---

[210] *Security Focus* "Hacker penetrates T-Mobile systems" by Kevin Poulsen (January 11, 2005)

in the person's voice who has been chosen to be synthesized. They can basically fake anyone's voice and make it seem like it's someone else talking. Back in the 1990s, the Department of Defense had a system that could accomplish this. In a demonstration in 1999, the voice of General Carl W. Steiner of the U.S. Special Operations Command was made to say, "Gentlemen! We have called you together to inform you that we are going to overthrow the United States government."[211]

The implications of voice synthesizers are enormous. Imagine if someone took voice samples of you and then using the system, called your boss and told him the most offensive, crazy things, in order to get you fired. Your boss isn't going to suspect that it's a computer voice synthesizer. He's going to just think you lost your mind, or decided to tell him what you really think. What if someone synthesized your boss's voice and called you asking for important company information such as passwords or sales figures; information you would never give out to anyone except your boss, of course. What if a competitor or a thief used this system to impersonate your boss in order to get this valuable information?

Such crimes will undoubtedly become a reality and will have to be dealt with when this technology becomes widely available. You may think that caller ID would prevent this from occurring on some phones, but I'm sorry to inform you that simple systems known as caller ID spoofers can cause any name and phone number to show up on the person's phone who is receiving a call to make it look like someone else is calling you.[212] It doesn't take an electrical engineer to build a home-made

---

[211] *The Washington Post* "When Seeing and Hearing Isn't Believing" (February 1, 1999) by William M. Arkin
[212] *Associated Press* "Spoof services undermine Caller ID" (March 13, 2006)

caller ID spoofer, because there are simple apps for popular smart phones like the Droid and the iPhone that can be used on phones that have been jailbroken which means the limitations placed by the phone's manufacturer or cell carrier are eliminated, allowing the phone to run unapproved apps and do other things that most phones can't do. This voids your phone's warranty and can cause problems for your phone, but some people like the freedom of having jailbroken phones.

I have personally had someone demonstrate his (jailbroken) Droid phone's caller ID spoofer to me and after he called my phone, making a different number appear on my caller ID, he went on to tell me how he used the app to call two different friends of his and left obnoxious voicemails on each of their phones, making it look like the people had called each other, both leaving the insulting voicemails for each other, so naturally, both of them thought the other person called them since their phone number showed up on the caller ID for the obnoxious voicemail. Most cell phones won't allow these kinds of apps in their app store for obvious reasons because you can imagine the kind of havoc that they can cause.

It's only a matter of time before visual synthesizers are able to easily create fake video footage as well, possibly in real-time. Many people were surprised when the 1994 film *Forest Gump* made it look like Tom Hanks' character was shaking the hand of President John F. Kennedy, when he'd been dead for decades when *Forest Gump* was filmed. In the following years this same technology was used to produce new commercials selling various products with celebrity pitchmen who had been dead for years. People seemed to be disturbed by these commercials and this practice rapidly diminished, but the technology continued to advance.

Technology had advanced so much from the making of *Forest Gump* in 1994, when the sequel of *Tron* was released in 2010, audiences learned that the lead actor Jeff Bridges had his face digitally morphed to make him look like he was 35 years old again, just like he was at the time the original film was released in 1982, even though now he was in his 60's. Not only that, but the studio also digitally placed his new younger face on a completely different actor's body for the entire film!

It was also around this same time that a news story surfaced explaining that George Lucas (writer and producer of the *Star Wars* franchise) was buying the rights to dead actors so he can use their likeness in future films by digitally bringing them back from the dead.[213]

This news prompted actors to begin outlining their wishes regarding their likeness in any future films they may appear in after they are dead. It is now common for actors to list restrictions in their wills regarding this kind of resurrection technology in order to prevent their estate, family members, or any film studios from using their likeness in a future film they wouldn't agree with.

"There were huge printing shops with their sub-editors, their typography experts, and their elaborately equipped studios for the faking of photographs. There was the teleprograms sections with its engineers, its producers, and its teams of actors especially chosen for their skill in imitating voices."[214] —*Nineteen Eighty-Four*

Supermarket Club Cards

You probably have one, or several, supermarket

---

[213] *NBCBayArea.com* "George Lucas Wants to Resuscitate Dead Actors Using Computers" (December 7, 2010)
[214] Orwell, George – *Nineteen Eighty-Four* page 37

"club" cards or "membership cards" that many grocery stores give out to their customers for free that allow you discounts on many different items. As you know, these cards aren't typical membership cards like a Costco card that you have to pay for, but are instead offered to every customer for free, and are scanned at the register when you pay, often saving you a few dollars. When you filled out the application to get your card, most of them asked for your full name, address, birth date, and phone number.

Most people forget they gave that information to the store and don't realize the store is creating a huge database of your purchasing history, even if you pay with cash. This information is sold to telemarketers or advertising agencies that can then have an intimate look at what kinds of products you're interested in. People even fear that this information is, or one day will be, sold to health insurance companies and can be used to justify premium increases based on what kinds of food a person consistently buys and how often they buy it. Such fears are not completely unwarranted.

There is a way around this (at least for now there is) by simply filling out a fake name, address and telephone number on the applications for these club cards. It's been my personal experience that they don't check your driver's license to see if the name and address match with the application, so you can do this if it makes you feel more comfortable. You would of course have to make all your purchases in cash because if you use your debit card, credit card, or even an old fashioned check, then your name will be linked to the items and the bank can sell this information to health providers or anyone else. Cash, of course, will most likely be phased out and replaced entirely by an electronic currency in the future, or cash purchases may require you to swipe your driver's license or government issued ID card, so even if you pay with cash, everything you purchase will still be linked to you. If you are naive and think your friendly local supermarket isn't keeping tabs on everything you buy, you are wrong. In March 2010, the purchasing history from a grocery store was used to track down people who purchased salami that was feared to be contaminated with salmonella.[215] In this case, the database of customers could have saved people the aggravation of possibly getting sick from salmonella, but it also illustrates the reach of Big Brother in the most unexpected places. Big Brother is watching what you eat.

Data Mining

Data mining is the process of searching for patterns in massive amounts of data. There are several major companies that compile enormous amounts of data on people and sell this information to advertisers and marketers. It is truly staggering to learn the amount of data these companies have on people, and what that data is used for. Many of these databases have records of people's marital status, ages of their children, income, value of their home and cars, as well as their occupation, religion, ethnicity, and even social security numbers and medical information. These lists have been sold to marketers and advertisers for decades so they can target specific types of people for their products, but after the 9/11 terrorist attacks, the government began using commercial databases like ChoicePoint, LexusNexus, Acxiom, and others to search for links between suspected terrorists.

To give you an idea of just how large these data

---

[215] *Associated Press* "CDC uses shopper-card data to trace salmonella" (May 10, 2010)

mining companies are, in February 2008, ChoicePoint was purchased by Reed Elsevier in a cash deal for $3.6 billion dollars.   ChoicePoint has more than 17 billion records of individuals and businesses, which it sells to an estimated 100,000 different clients, including 7,000 federal, state and local law enforcement agencies.[216] When one learns that these companies do more than simply maintain a database of details about people, it can be truly worrisome what their systems are capable of doing.

ChoicePoint has a system they call NORA (Non-Obvious Relationship Awareness) that can find relationships between people in ways you couldn't imagine. In 1994 the MGM casino in Las Vegas started using the NORA system to find out whether or not any high-rollers had ties to the dealers or employees that could be used in cheating or otherwise scamming the casino. The system could also detect whether people kicked out of the casino for card counting or cheating had any personal ties to employees who may have been in on the scam.

The NORA system can display a chart or list of people's relationships to others that are not noticeable on the surface. For example, if a dealer at the casino had a brother who was roommates with someone who won big at that dealer's table, the system would know and the dealer would be suspected of helping that person win and be in on the scam. The system can determine whether people frequently go to the same restaurant, attend the same church, have mutual friends, etc.

The Direct Marketing List Source is a document consisting of 1600 pages that contains information such as people's names, ages, addresses, what books they buy,

---

[216] http://epic.org/privacy/choicepoint/

magazines they subscribe to, what they buy online, etc. It also has a list called the Gay America Megafile with almost 700,000 names of people that the database has identified as being homosexual. The list is considered the Bible of mailing lists.

Data mines can calculate how much a bachelor usually spends on a weekend out, and where, and can determine whether or not he enters into a relationship or if he has gotten married. Marketers then know what other products they can market to him due to his changing lifestyle.

A company called Elensys obtained prescription records from pharmacies and then sent out material to those customers targeting them depending on what ailments they had or what medication they were taking. After this was made public, CVS pharmacy purchased full page ads in major newspapers apologizing for selling their customer's private information.[217]

Another major company in this field, Axciom, has a service they call InfoBase TeleSource, which is a system that companies with toll free telephone numbers use to identify the names and other information about people who call in. Even people who block their caller ID or people who have unlisted numbers are still identified by this system.[218] If someone calls in to an 800 number asking about a particular product, the person answering the phone has information pop up on their screen such as the person's name, address, and even what kind of home they live in, the cars the person owns, and whether they are a member of a health club or a gym.

A special airing originally in 2006 on CNBC called

---

[217] *The Washington Post* "CVS Also Cuts Ties to Marketing Service" (February 19, 1998)

[218] *The Washington Post* "Unlisted Numbers not Protected from Marketers" (December 19,1999) by Robert O'Harrow, Jr.

Big Brother, Big Business showed a fancy restaurant in New York using a similar system to identify people when they called in to make reservations, and allows the staff to create profiles for customers that include information such as when their birthday is, or if they were a "difficult" customer in the past.

In 1998, a company called Image Data began purchasing drivers license pictures from the DMV and using them in the private sector. They designed a system for retail stores that would display people's pictures on a screen when they swiped their credit card so the clerk could confirm that it was the person, and not someone else using the card.[219] Image Data had received $1.5 million dollars from the Secret Service to develop the project.[220] When it was discovered that the DMV offices were selling people's pictures and personal information to a private company, some DMVs were pressured to stop this practice.

Shortly after the 9/11 attacks, the government started its own data mining operation they called the MATRIX, [Multistate Anti-Terrorism Information Exchange Program] that used a variety of commercial and government databases to search for links between suspects or to identify any unusual behavior such as strange purchases or money transfers. The MATRIX system could do a search for all the people who have blond hair, are six feet tall, drive a black convertible, who work as an accountant, and who live in a particular zip code. The MATRIX program was shut down in June 2005 after funding was cut, largely as a result of concerns

---

[219] *The Washington Post* "Posing a Privacy Problem? Driver's-License Photos used in Anti-Fraud Database" (January 22, 1999) Robert O'Harrow, Jr.
[220] *The Washington Post* "U.S. Helped Fund Photo Database of Driver Ids" (Feb 18,1999) Robert O'Harrow, Jr

over privacy, but it is likely the technology was absorbed into other government agencies.

Another element used by casinos to maximize their profits is a system called a "Total Rewards" card used by Harrah's casinos that track players' winnings and losses, and combined with other information about the person, the casino has calculated a "pain point" that they determine is the maximum amount a person is willing to lose which may leave them with a negative feeling about the casino causing them never to return. If a player's pain point is approaching because their losses are mounting, then that person will be approached by a staff member and offered a free dinner to make them feel better about their experience at the casino, causing them to likely return and not leave feeling like they had wasted all of their money. The people offered the free dinner have no idea they are specifically chosen for this reason, and just think the casino gives away random dinners to anyone.

Through data mining, the Canadian Tire company has determined that people who purchase carbon-monoxide detectors, birdseed, and pads for the bottom of chair legs rarely miss a payment on a credit card. "If you show us what you buy, we can tell you who you are, maybe even better than you know yourself," said a former Canadian Tire executive.[221] Cable and satellite TV companies know what shows are watched in your home, and digital recording services like Ti-Vo and AT&T's U-verse know what shows you record. If your name is on the cable bill, then you are linked in a database to the shows that are watched and recorded. What you watch on television on a regular basis says a lot about you, and marketing companies like to know these things.

[221] *Newser.com* "Your Credit Card is Spying on You" (April 7, 2010) by Kevin Spak

If you choose to use mainly cash for your day to day purchases of food, clothes, gas, etc, are these artificially intelligent systems and complex algorithms going to flag you for being suspicious? The government doesn't like people who pay cash, since they are more difficult to monitor, so this alone could flag you for closer analysis. The system will know you use cash for most purchases, because it will see a lack of purchases using a debit card or credit card. It may not know *what* you spend that cash on, but it surely notices if you cash your paychecks or withdraw large amounts of cash from your account on a regular basis, and this is seen as suspicious.

If a person is a political activist or a journalist who is causing trouble for the establishment or a particular president, could that person then be flagged for an audit in attempts to disrupt or discourage his activity? Could he be listed as a trouble maker so the next time he is pulled over for going five miles an hour over the speed limit, the officer will see that he is a "trouble maker" and give him the ticket instead of let him off with a warning?

Could these systems falsely list you as dangerous because of your political affiliations so when a future potential employer does a background check on you, the report lists you as a subversive person or an "extremist?" What if the employer disagrees with your political views or activism that shows up listed in your background check and chooses not to hire you because of this? You would have no way of knowing why they actually decided to hire someone else. If you return too many items to stores in order to get a refund, you may be identified as a "returnaholic," and may be flagged as someone who buys a product to use it for a while and then returns it.[222]

---

[222] *Economizer* "Returnaholics cost retailers billions of dollars a year" (May 18, 2010) by Mitch Lipka

Did you purchase a blow up doll as a joke for a friend's bachelor party? Your name might then be added to certain mailing lists and you could now start receiving junk mail from sex shops or escort services.

There are numerous publicly available websites that disclose all kinds of information about people, sometimes for free, and others for only a small fee. These services offer people's address, phone numbers, birthdates, criminal history, and much more. One service has a slogan saying they are "not your grandma's phone book." Some available features include an e-mail lookup which allows you to enter in someone's e-mail address and then the website searches through a massive list of websites to see if any accounts were opened from that e-mail, and then lists them. A person's Facebook page, and even Amazon.com and other online retailers such as Target.com can show up as having accounts linked to a person's e-mail address.

If you pay a small monthly fee on some of these services you can get photos of the people as well and see what they've been posting online and get other information such as their income and credit score. Most of these services also offer what is called a reverse telephone directory, which allows you to enter in a person's phone number and it will then reveal the name and address of the person who has that number.

A Michigan University academic named Arthur R. Miller published a book back in 1971 titled *The Assault on Privacy* where he wrote, "The new information technologies seem to have given birth to a new social virus—'data-mania.' We must begin to realize what it means to live in a society that treats information as an economically desirable commodity and a source of power."

During a special interview on *CNBC* titled "Inside

the Mind of Google," the company's CEO Eric Schmidt was asked about privacy concerns involving the information age and Google's domination of the Internet, to which he answered, "If you have something that you don't want anyone to know, maybe you shouldn't be doing it in the first place."

Web Bugs in Microsoft Word Documents

It was discovered that Microsoft Word documents, as well as Excel spreadsheets and PowerPoint slide show files, can be embedded with tracking tags called Web Bugs that gather information about who opens the documents and when.

The Web Bugs were discovered by Richard Smith, the chief technology officer at the Privacy Foundation. "What this means basically is that if an author of a document for whatever reason cares about who is reading it, he can bug it and then monitor it," Smith said. "They can find out the IP address and host name of whoever is reading the document."[223]

There are numerous ways that this tracking method can be used, such as embedding the bugs into company documents so they can be tracked to see who is reading them and can trace back the electronic trail if a document was leaked to the press, for example. The person who embedded the Web Bug can also track how often a particular file is opened. If someone cuts a portion of text from a document that is being tracked, and pastes it into a new document, then unbeknownst to them, the Web Bug is also transferred and continues its tracking capabilities. There is also talk of similar tracking bugs being placed in

---

[223] *CNET News* "Word documents susceptible to 'Web bug' infestation" (August 30, 2000) by Paul Festa and Cecily Barnes

other file formats as well, such as MP3 files or video files. Once a Web Bug is placed in a document (or other file), it transmits information over the Internet to the person who planted it so they can monitor the file. Since practically every computer is almost always online, this is extremely simple.

Cryptome.com, a hacker and whistleblower site created by John Young and Deborah Natsios in 1996, was taken off the web briefly in February 2010 as a punishment after they posted a secret handbook written by Microsoft that was meant only for law enforcement that educated them about certain Big Brother capabilities the software giant built into their products.[224]

The document, titled *Microsoft Online Services Global Criminal Compliance Handbook,* is only 22 pages long and was described by PC World magazine as a "data-hunting guide for dummies" that shows law enforcement how to access the vast information Microsoft stores about people when they use products like Hotmail, Windows Live Messenger, MSN, Microsoft Office Live, Xbox Live, and others.

Someone who knows how to maneuver through these systems can access all kinds of personal information such as user names and passwords, along with web browsing history, etc. Xbox Live, an online gaming platform for the Xbox 360 game console, stores a user's full name, credit card information, phone number, email address, and more. There have actually been several Xbox video game systems recovered by police after they were able to track down the stolen Xbox after the thief logged on to Xbox Live, the online gaming community. In one instance police tracked the thief's IP address and then were able to

---

[224] *PCWorld* "Microsoft's Spy Guide: What You Need to Know" By Brennon Slattery (Feb 25, 2010)

trace back which store their Live unit was purchased at, and then found a person's name in the store's computer linked to that item, and police went to the address and discovered the stolen Xbox 360.[225]

Tracking Documents You Print

While it should be common knowledge that the government and computer savvy hackers can track a person's Internet usage and search through the contents of a person's hard drive, most people would never imagine that a simple document printed from their computer could be traced back to them, especially if it were something like a page of text that had no personal information on it.

Laser printers are no longer expensive units only used by large companies for high page count documents and rapid printing. Laser printers have become common in households due to their quality and dramatically lower prices than in the past. But what nobody really knows is that most manufactures secretly designed a feature into laser printers and photocopiers that encode the printer's serial number onto each page that is printed by using a series of tiny dots that most people can't even see with the naked eye. Of course, consumers are not told of this process, and printer manufacturers like to keep quiet about it.

Peter Crean, a senior researcher at Xerox, admitted his company's laser printers, copiers, and multifunction workstations, all secretly put the serial number of each machine coded in little yellow dots on every printout that can't be seen by the naked eye. "It's a trail back to you,

---

[225] *PlayFeed* (GearLive.com) "Xbox Live Helps Recover Stolen Xbox 360" (September 18, 2006)

like a license plate," Crean said. [226]

The reason for the secret encoding is said to assist in fighting counterfeit money and fraudulent documents, and is a method that has been used since the 1980s. "The industry absolutely has been extraordinarily helpful [to law enforcement]," says Lorelei Pagano, a counterfeiting specialist with the US Secret Service, the agency in charge of tracking counterfeiters. [227]

Peter Crean of Xerox said the government worked with the company to develop the technology in the 1980s because of fears that their advanced copiers could easily be used to print counterfeit money.

It's likely that the Secret Service or other government agencies can use the Carnivore system to send out pings searching for a specific printer serial number that can be detected if the printer is installed on a computer that is connected to the Internet. Of course, when a printer is purchased, the serial number is linked to the person's credit card or checking account who bought it. While it may be tough to argue that this technology isn't good for catching counterfeiters, what else could it be used for?

What if a government whistle blower prints out sensitive and damaging documents and anonymously (or so he thinks) sends them to the media? He could then, without even suspecting it, be linked to the documents. Did you design and print out some inflammatory leaflets about a powerful senator or congressperson and put them on people's doors in your community? These flyers could be traced back to you.

---

[226] *PC World* "Government Uses Color Laser Printer Technology to Track Documents" (November 22, 2004) by Jason Tuohey
[227] Ibid

Radiation Intelligence

People may think that if a computer isn't connected to the Internet that their data is secure, but they are wrong again. Computer monitors, including LCD screens, give off a measurable amount of radiation that can be detected using what is called radiation intelligence (RINT) or Van Eck phreaking. A Dutch computer scientist named Wim van Eck discovered this in 1985 and published the first paper on the subject, hence the term Van Eck phreaking. In computer hacking, the term "phreaking" is a slang term referring to hacking or experimenting with telecommunication systems, often in underhanded ways.

Some people thought that Van Eck phreaking could only be used on older tube monitors, and not newer LCD flat screens, but in April 2004, a research team at the University of Cambridge in the United Kingdom showed that LCD monitors were also vulnerable to electromagnetic eavesdropping. The team built equipment capable of doing this at the university lab for less than $2000.[228]

Van Eck phreaking was used to test the security of electronic voting systems in Brazil in 2009 and was found to be able to monitor the voting machines, thus compromising the secrecy of the voting process.[229]

---

[228] Kuhn, M.G. "Electromagnetic Eavesdropping Risks of Flat-Panel Displays" *4th Workshop on Privacy Enhancing Technologies*: 23–25 (2004)
[229] *Tech Dirt* "Brazil E-Voting Machines Not Hacked... But Van Eck Phreaking Allowed Hacker To Record Votes" (November 23, 2009)

Keyboard Loggers and Backdoors

Commercially available software programs called keyboard loggers can easily be installed on someone's computer which then can capture and record everything the person does, including what they type in a word processor, their e-mails, and even bank passwords and login information for other sensitive accounts. Such programs are often used by suspicious spouses who want to find evidence of their significant other cheating, but more sinister motives such as stealing people's passwords or business data are also reasons people install the software on others' computers.

Such software also often creates a secret backdoor allowing people to access a person's computer, and their files without them knowing. In 1999, NetBus software was used to plant child pornography on the computer of a professor at Lund University in Sweden. Thousands of images were found by the system administrators, and of course, they assumed that the professor had downloaded them himself. The professor was fired and charged with possession of child pornography but later acquitted after authorities had learned that NetBus had been installed on his computer allowing someone to control it without his knowledge or consent.[230] The man was reported to have suffered severe psychological damage from the incident, which is completely understandable. After all, if such disgusting material was discovered on your computer and you were charged with possession of child pornography but knew you didn't have anything to do with it, you would certainly have a difficult time defending yourself and clearing your name from being attached to such a deplorable act.

---

[230] http://www.expressen.se/1.153215

In Neil Strauss's 2005 bestselling book, *The Game*, which is a memoir of his time hanging out with pickup artists and guys who were teaching seminars on how to meet girls, he said that he discovered someone had put a keyboard logger on his computer and suspected it was one of his roommates who had started his own rival seminar company. Such businesses can be fairly lucrative and Strauss's roommate wanted to corner the market and learn what his competition was doing.

Photocopier Hard Drives

A story airing on *CBS News* in April 2010 showed a warehouse in New Jersey that was described as having 6,000 used photocopiers that were for sale, and almost every one of them had a hard drive that recorded every single document that was photocopied on each machine during its existence. Apparently all digital copiers built since 2002 contain hard drives which can store tens of thousands of images.

Think of the kinds of documents that people copy. Bank statements, credit card statements, income tax forms, birth certificates, and more. All of which are stored on the machine's hard drive without your knowledge or consent.

The *CBS News* segment equipped a man with a hidden camera and sent him off shopping to buy a used copier from one of dozens of large warehouses that are in the used copier business. He bought three different copiers for around $300 each. After all the contents of the hard drives were examined, it was revealed that one machine came from the sex crimes division from the police department in Buffalo, New York. Some documents on the hard drive were copies of domestic violence disputes and lists of sex offenders. Other documents were lists of targets in a drug investigation. On another machine they found 95 pages of pay stubs complete with people's names, addresses, and social security numbers.

The third machine, they discovered, came from a health insurance company, and they were able to print out hundreds of pages of confidential medical records including people's prescriptions, blood test results, and a cancer diagnosis.

Ordering a Pizza in the Future

A funny, yet disturbing, video can be found on YouTube if you search for "ordering a pizza in the future" that depicts someone calling a fictitious pizza place to order a pizza and discovers just how all-knowing Big Brother is. When a man calls into the restaurant, the person on the other end of the phone picks up and already knows who he is, where he lives, and the last time he called. When the customer orders two double meat pizzas he is informed that there will be an additional $20 charge on his bill because the computer system has access to his health records and shows that he has high blood pressure and high cholesterol. The screen then shows the man's bill includes the $20 "health surcharge" because his health insurance provider now knows he's ordering a fatty pizza.

The man is also informed of an added $15 "delivery surcharge" to cover the added risk to their delivery driver for delivering to an orange zone which signified a high crime neighborhood. When the customer surprisingly asks to clarify that he lives in an orange zone, the order-taker acknowledges a recent change in status due to a robbery near his home that the computer database shows.

When the customer starts complaining about his $67 bill for two pizzas, the woman on the line pulls up his recent purchase of two tickets to Hawaii and hassles him about it, saying he shouldn't complain about spending that much money on two pizzas because he just spent $800 on plane tickets for a vacation.

He then changes his order to a vegetarian pizza to save money since he won't have to pay the extra $20 health surcharge, and the order taker says it's a good choice and will be good for his waist line as she pulls up a screen of "recent purchases" and shows that the man just bought a new pair of jeans with a 42 inch waistline.

The video is great satire showing just how invasive Big Brother can be, and how with everything we do being stored in databases, the information can easily be sold to practically anyone and used in ways we would prefer it not be. There have been reports years ago that certain pizza delivery restaurants were checking people's names who ordered pizzas to see if they had any warrants out for their arrest when they paid with a credit card over the phone. If a warrant was listed, instead of having a pizza delivery driver show up to the house, the police would arrive to arrest the person.

Orwellian Government Programs

While the "alphabet agencies" (CIA, NSA, FBI, ATF, etc.) have access to incredible Big Brother technology and countless commercial and government databases, there are also creepy Orwellian projects that have been secretly created and funded by elements within the government for the purpose of maintaining the power of the ruling elite.

Many of these programs used (and continue to use) underhanded and often illegal methods to accomplish their goals which range from controlling the mainstream media to covertly trying to smear, intimidate, blackmail, or even assassinate people who pose a threat to the establishment.

Often Orwellian goals are defended by the government claiming that such measures are needed to keep people safe from criminals or terrorists, but it is often the very people working for these programs who are the criminals. Immediately after the September 11th attacks of 2001, the government fear-mongering began and was used as a justification for subverting the Constitution of the United States and implementing the long-awaited Orwellian dreams of the establishment. Any resistance to the new tyrannical, invasive, and unconstitutional measures was attacked as being unpatriotic. Officials would continuously say that we needed to give up some of our freedoms in order to keep people safe from terrorists, which were said to lurk around every corner.

Thomas Jefferson famously stated, "Those who

would give up essential liberty to purchase a little temporary safety deserve neither liberty nor safety." Jefferson obviously knew the strategy of tyrannical leaders and how they use fear-mongering as a justification to increase their power and trample over their population.

Operation Mockingbird

A major system that Big Brother uses to control the population is the mainstream media. This amazing propaganda machine has the ability to shape the culture and the mindset of a nation by the information the owners choose to broadcast on a daily basis. The character Howard Beal famously ranted about the power of television in the 1976 film *Network*, telling his audience, "This tube can make or break presidents, popes, prime ministers...This tube is the most awesome God-damned force in the whole godless world, and woe is us if it ever falls into the hands of the wrong people."

Intelligent people have varying degrees of awareness that the US government is in bed with the mainstream media, and anyone who monitors the news media with discerning eyes can often easily identify specific stories and strategies that are being used to persuade and intimidate the population. As enlightened people know, the mainstream media operates both as a propaganda arm for the establishment, as well as a gate-keeper that prevents certain information from being disseminated to the masses.

The evidence for these charges is massive and irrefutable. The most damning of which comes from the findings of a Senate Select Committee in 1975 that investigated the American government's covert influence over the mainstream media, including broadcast news, newspapers, and magazines. The committee, called the

Church Committee, published its findings in 1976 and uncovered what was called Operation Mockingbird, which involved the CIA secretly paying editors of major media institutions and popular journalists to act as gate-keepers and propagandists for the establishment.

"The invention of print, however, made it easier to manipulate public opinion, and the film and radio carried the process further."[231] —*Nineteen Eighty-Four*

In 1948 an espionage and counter-intelligence branch within the CIA was created for the purpose of "propaganda, economic warfare; preventive direct action, including sabotage, anti-sabotage, demolition and evacuation measures; subversion against hostile states, including assistance to underground resistance groups, and support of indigenous anti-Communist elements in threatened countries of the free world."[232]

Later that year Operation Mockingbird was established to influence the domestic and foreign media. Philip Graham, the owner of *The Washington Post,* was recruited to help run the project within the industry and develop a network of assets who would go along with the program. After 1953, the network had influence over twenty-five different newspapers and wire agencies. The Mockingbird program also involved all major television stations.

Thomas Braden, who was the head of the International Organizations Division of the CIA, played a substantial role in Operation Mockingbird and later revealed, "If the director of the CIA wanted to extend a present, say, to someone in Europe—a Labour leader— suppose he just thought, this man can use fifty thousand

[231] Orwell, George – *Nineteen Eighty-Four* page 181-182
[232] Wise, David and Ross, Thomas - *Invisible Government* (Random House 1964)

dollars, he's working well and doing a good job—he could hand it to him and never have to account to anybody... There was simply no limit to the money it could spend and no limit to the people it could hire and no limit to the activities it could decide were necessary to conduct the war—the secret war...It was multinational."[233]

According to the Church Committee's report, which was published in 1976, "The CIA currently maintains a network of several hundred individuals around the world who provide intelligence for the CIA and at times attempt to influence opinion through the use of covert propaganda. These individuals provide the CIA with direct access to a large number of newspapers and periodicals, scores of press services and news agencies, radio and television stations, commercial book publishers, and other foreign media outlets."[234]

The committee also concluded that the cost of the program was approximately $265 million a year, which when adjusted for inflation as of 2010 means that in today's dollars the program was spending an astounding one billion dollars a year.

One year after the Church Committee released its findings, *Rolling Stone* magazine published an article on Operation Mockingbird and named various prominent journalists who they alleged to be involved with it. Some of these included Ben Bradlee, who wrote for *Newsweek*, Stewart Alsop who wrote for the *New York Herald Tribune*, James Reston (*New York Times*), Charles Douglas Jackson (*Time Magazine*), Walter Pincus (*Washington Post*), William C. Baggs (*The Miami News*),

[233] Thomas Braden, interview included in the Granada Television program, *World in Action: The Rise and Fall of the CIA* (1975)
[234] *Final Report of the Select Committee to Study Government Operations With Respect to Intelligence Activities* (April 1976)

and others.

In 2007, a large amount of CIA documents called the "Family Jewels" were declassified and released by the National Security Archive, which revealed that the CIA had routinely wiretapped Washington-based news reporters and committed other shady and illegal practices. The targets of these wiretaps were most likely seen as threats to the establishment and were not playing along with the propaganda and gate-keeping efforts within the media establishment, so the CIA wanted to keep a close eye on them and gather information on their sources and future stories.

As with nearly every other case of rampant institutional corruption in government agencies, the CIA claims to have ended Operation Mockingbird and their influence over the media—another claim that is laughable. The power of the mass media to control society is too great for the establishment not to do everything they can to harness it for their own benefit.

The man credited with being the father of public relations is named Edward Bernays, who was a master of social engineering, propaganda, and shaping public opinion early in the twentieth century. He was also the nephew of the famous psychologist Sigmund Freud. In 1928 Bernays published a book titled *Propaganda* that described his methods for shaping public opinion and people's attitudes and behaviors. A quick glance over several of the excerpts from *Propaganda* reveals just how powerful the control of information is to a government.

Bernays wrote, "Those who manipulate the unseen mechanism of society constitute an invisible government which is the true ruling power of our country. We are governed, our minds are molded, our tastes formed, our ideas suggested, largely by men we have never heard of. This is a logical result of the way in which our democratic society is organized. Vast numbers of human beings must cooperate in this manner if they are to live together as a smoothly functioning society. In almost every act of our lives whether in the sphere of politics or business in our social conduct or our ethical thinking, we are dominated by the relatively small number of persons who understand the mental processes and social patterns of the masses. It is they who pull the wires that control the public mind."[235]

This is strikingly parallel to what George Orwell wrote in *Nineteen Eighty-Four* when he said, "All the beliefs, habits, tastes, emotions, mental attitudes that characterize our time are really designed to sustain the mystique of the Party and prevent the true nature of present-day society from being perceived."[236]

Bernays can be largely credited with making cigarette smoking socially acceptable, and appear to be cool. In 1929 he was hired by the American Tobacco Company, which was one of the original 12 companies comprising the Dow Jones Industrial Average, in order to help promote smoking. The way he did this was by hiring a group of attractive female models to march in the New York City parade and planned to have them light up cigarettes to shatter the taboo of women smoking in public. Bernays also contacted the press saying that the women would light up "Torches of Freedom" in support of women's rights. The next day, the *New York Times* ran an article headlined, "Group of Girls Puff at Cigarettes as a Gesture of Freedom."[237]

Bernays was also the man responsible for diamond rings being synonymous with marriage and love. The De Beers diamond company hired him to shape the public's

---

[235] Bernays, Edward – *Propaganda* page 9
[236] Orwell, George – *Nineteen Eighty-Four* page 187
[237] *New York Times* "Group of Girls Puff at Cigarettes as a Gesture of Freedom" (April 1, 1929)

mind into associating a diamond ring with love. Before this, women's wedding rings were primarily a simple gold band, but Bernays was able to use propaganda to convince both men and women, that if a man is to propose to a woman, he needs to do so with a large diamond ring.

Bernays sat on the board of the U.S. Committee on Public Information (CPI), which was a government agency set up specifically to influence public opinion in support of America's role in World War I and to help sell the war to the public.

Only a complete moron would think that government agencies don't continue to massively influence the mainstream media today. Even those who expect such manipulation are often surprised to learn the extent of it and its power.

COINTEL PRO

A truly Orwellian scheme conducted by the FBI admittedly between 1956 and 1971 is COINTELPRO (an acronym for Counter Intelligence Program) which illegally investigated and disrupted political organizations, religious organizations, civil liberty groups, anti-war groups and others that were deemed problematic by the establishment. COINTELPRO and the illegal and sinister activities carried out by the program are fully admitted by the FBI, although after its discovery they claimed that they stopped using such tactics. Common sense says otherwise.

The original program targeted people and groups seen as "subversive" or that threatened the establishment's hold on power. Martin Luther King Jr. and other leaders in the civil rights movement and those associated with the NAACP (the National Association for the Advancement of Colored People), and the Southern

Poverty Law Center were targeted, as well as groups protesting the Vietnam War, including many college students. J. Edgar Hoover, who was the head of the FBI at the time, had ordered agents to "expose, disrupt, misdirect, discredit, or otherwise neutralize" the leaders and activities of such groups.[238] It's important to understand that most of the groups and the targets of COINTELPRO were not doing anything threatening, criminal, or dangerous, and were only trying to change society for the better by encouraging civil rights or protesting the Vietnam War. But this is not what the establishment wanted.

Agents involved in the program did a lot of illegal, underhanded, and dirty tricks to disrupt their targets; including mailing fraudulent letters to leaders of organizations claiming to be from someone else with accusations that someone's wife was cheating on them. Illegal wire taps, spreading false and slanderous rumors about people, frame-ups, vandalism, and worse were all common and are still methods used today by elite law enforcement and intelligence agents to disrupt, discourage or discredit their targets.

The PATRIOT ACT

"The consciousness of being at war, and therefore in danger, makes the handing-over of all power to a small caste seem the natural, unavoidable condition of survival."[239] —*Nineteen Eighty-Four*

In response to the September 11th 2001 terrorist attacks on America, Congress quickly passed the

[238] http://www.pbs.org/hueypnewton/actions/actions_cointelpro.html
[239] Orwell, George – *Nineteen Eighty-Four* page 170

PATRIOT ACT on October 26, 2001, which granted the government a wide range of unconstitutional powers so officials could allegedly prevent further terrorist attacks. Any resistance to the bill was countered with claims that those people were un-American or wanted to help the terrorists. The very name for the bill, the "Patriot Act" was chosen to give the impression that if you were a patriotic American who loved his country, then you should support the bill. (Full title: *The Uniting and Strengthening America by Providing Appropriate Tools Required to Intercept and Obstruct Terrorism Act of 2001,* which was designed to spell, "USA PATRIOT Act")

The bill passed 98-1 in the Senate, and 356-66 in the House of Representatives. Senator Russ Feingold of Wisconsin was the only United States Senator to vote against the bill because he saw some of the provisions stripped civil liberties guaranteed by the Constitution.

Feingold said, "Of course, there is no doubt that if we lived in a police state, it would be easier to catch terrorists. If we lived in a country that allowed the police to search your home at any time for any reason; if we lived in a country that allowed the government to open your mail, eavesdrop on your phone conversations, or intercept your e-mail communications; if we lived in a country that allowed the government to hold people in jail indefinitely based on what they write or think, or based on mere suspicion that they are up to no good, then the government would no doubt discover and arrest more terrorists. But that probably would not be a country in which we would want to live."[240]

The bill is 342 pages long with 1,016 sections and

---

[240] http://www.quotesstar.com/quotes/f/feingold-showed-that-a-politician-206442 html

amended over 15 federal statutes, and contains numerous Executive Orders, regulations, and new policies aimed at "fighting terrorism." Many of these new powers allowed the government to engage in secret surveillance, and even commit "sneak and peeks" which means that a person's house can be searched without his knowledge, while that person is not even served with a search warrant (or aware the search took place) until months later. If a neighbor happens to see a sneak and peak going on and starts asking questions, then that person can be placed under a gag order and legally cannot mention anything to anybody about what they saw.

The Patriot Act even allowed for people to be detained for months without even being charged with a crime, a clear violation of the Sixth Amendment. In the first year after it was signed into law, more than 1,000 non citizens were secretly detained without being charged and their identities were not released. Thousands more were placed under surveillance.

"In the vast majority of cases there was no trial, no report of the arrest. People simply disappeared."[241]
—*Nineteen Eighty-Four*
In a speech to a Senate Judiciary Committee on December 6, 2001, John Ashcroft (the Attorney General at the time), tried to demonize people who voiced opposition or disagreement with the powers granted by the Patriot Act saying, "to those who scare peace-loving people with phantoms of lost liberty; my message is this: Your tactics only aid terrorists—for they erode our national unity and diminish our resolve. They give ammunition to America's enemies, and pause to America's friends. They encourage people of good will to remain silent in the face of evil."

---

[241] Orwell, George – *Nineteen Eighty-Four* page 17

Ashcroft's claim is in stark contrast to what Thomas Jefferson said about liberty, when he said that people who give up freedom in order to gain security will have neither freedom nor security.

In section 802 of the Patriot Act under the *Definition of Domestic Terrorism*, the language defines the new meaning of the term "domestic terrorist." It reads:

> `(5) the term `domestic terrorism' means activities that—
>> `(A) involve acts dangerous to human life that are a violation of the criminal laws of the United States or of any State;
>> `(B) appear to be intended—
>>> `(i) to intimidate or coerce a civilian population;
>>> `(ii) to influence the policy of a government by intimidation or coercion; or
>>> `(iii) to affect the conduct of a government by mass destruction, assassination, or kidnapping;

While everyone would agree that kidnapping, assassination or mass destruction would certainly be terrorism, "intimidating" the civilian population or attempting to influence policy of the government by "coercion or intimidation" could be applied to ordinary political rhetoric. It has been said by critics of the Patriot Act that the Bush administration was guilty of intimidating the population by fabricating and exaggerating threats that led to the Iraq War. Others argue the Patriot Act was a power grab by the government and there were already provisions in place to investigate and prevent terrorist attacks, and capture the perpetrators.

Constitutional Protections Eliminated by the Patriot Act

First Amendment

Freedom of religion, speech, assembly, and the press.

Fourth Amendment

Freedom from unreasonable searches and seizures.

Fifth Amendment

No person to be deprived of life, liberty or property without due process of law.

Sixth Amendment

Right to a speedy public trial by an impartial jury, right to be informed of the facts of the accusation, right to confront witnesses and have the assistance of counsel.

Eighth Amendment

No excessive bail or cruel and unusual punishment shall be imposed.

Fourteenth Amendment

All persons (citizens and noncitizens) within the US are entitled to due process and the equal protection of the laws.

Information Awareness Office

The Information Awareness Office (IAO) was an intelligence-based office within the United States government that was created in January 2002, by the Defense Advanced Research Projects Agency (DARPA) to work on surveillance and information technology to discover and track "terrorists." It was started under the direction of John Poindexter, who was the former National Security Advisor for President Reagan.

Poindexter wanted the system to analyze people's travel patterns, money transactions, and even unusual medical activities such as treatment for anthrax sores, which could mean that someone was cooking up the poison themselves. Poindexter himself has a shady past, and during the Iran-Contra hearings he responded to questions 184 times saying he didn't remember the details.

The logo for the IAO cannot get any more Orwellian, and consists of a pyramid with an all-seeing eye on the top, similar to the one on the back of the one dollar bill, with a beam of light shining out of it and covering the entire globe which is shown in the foreground. The office originally used the term Total Information Awareness as its goal, but was later changed to Terrorism Information Awareness to sound less Orwellian.

When news was first uncovered about the Information Awareness Office and its goals of creating huge databases from personal information of every person in the United States, including e-mails, phone records, and medical records, all without a search warrant, civil libertarians expressed concern.[242]

The office also called for a massive biometric program including facial recognition systems and cameras that can identify people by the way they walk. A special data mining system was also implemented for the IAO which they called Evidence Extraction and Link Discovery that can find relationships "among people, organizations, places, and things." The CIA created a data-mining program called Quantum Leap, which one official told *Fortune* magazine was, "so powerful it's scary."[243]

New York Times columnist William Safire wrote, "This is not some far-out Orwellian scenario. It is what will happen to your personal freedom in the next few weeks if John Poindexter gets the unprecedented power he seeks. This ring-knocking master of deceit is back again with a plan even more scandalous than Iran-Contra."[244]

In 2003, after much public criticism, the office had its funding cut and it was supposedly shut down, although its objectives and operations have continued under other names and in other departments.[245] [246]

As common sense suggests, data mines and surveillance technologies have a high potential for abuse. For example, police officers are known to do background

---

[242] *New York Times* "Pentagon Plans a Computer System That Would Peek at Personal Data of Americans" (November 22, 2002) by John Markoff

[243] *Fortune* "How George tenet Brought the CIA Back from the Dead" (October 13, 2003) by Bill Powell

[244] *New York Times* "You are a suspect" (November 14, 2002) by William Safire

[245] *Electronic Frontier Foundation* "Total/Terrorism Information Awareness (TIA): Is It Truly Dead?"

[246] *National Journal* (Feb. 23, 2006) "TIA Lives On" by Shane Harris

BIG BROTHER

checks on attractive girls they meet in order to learn things about them. In the field, such a practice is called running plates for dates. Police have also routinely sold information illegally for cash to private investigators and have used confidential records to undermine political opponents.

In 2002, a DEA agent named Emilio Calatayud was sentenced to over two years in prison for selling information to private investigators.[247] In the year 2000 a lieutenant in the Charles County, Maryland sheriff's department used private information from the department's databases to influence local elections by releasing information about candidates he didn't like. The lieutenant even deleted a disorderly conduct arrest from the record of the candidate he wanted to become the next sheriff.[248]

In the History Channel's show *Gangland*, which chronicles the histories and activities of different gangs, it was revealed that members of the Detroit gang, the "Best Friends," would pay corrupt cops to find out where rival gang members or drug dealers lived by giving the cops people's license plate numbers or phone numbers. The corrupt cops would then run a background check on them using their internal computers, and give the addresses to the gang. The Best Friends would then assassinate these people.

Stephen Nash started a police accountability group called CopWatch in Denver, Colorado to help prevent police misconduct by monitoring police activity and videotaping police when they were encountering suspects. Because of this, Nash was secretly targeted by police in

---

[247] *Los Angeles Times* "Former DEA Agent Sentenced for Bribery" (December 19, 2002)
[248] *Washington Post* "Board Recommends Firing Officer in Misconduct Case" (October 15, 2000) by Annie Gowen

their database and labeled a "criminal extremist." He only found this out after an unidentified informant in the police department printed out his secret files and sent him a copy, along with a lawyer at the ACLU. Even Nash's wife was labeled a "criminal extremist."

The ACLU contended that the Denver Police Department has inappropriately smeared the reputations of multiple peaceful advocates of nonviolent social change by falsely labeling them or their organizations as "criminal extremist" in their internal databases.[249]

"The few pages of documents we have obtained so far provide an alarming glimpse of the kinds of information the Denver Police Department is recording and the kinds of peaceful protest activity it is monitoring inappropriately," said Mark Silverstein, an ACLU Legal Director.[250]

Echelon

The world's most sophisticated electronic spy system is called Echelon and refers to an advanced system that analyzes nearly every kind of electronic communication in the world, from telephone calls, to even faxes and text messages. A similar system called Carnivore is used for monitoring the Internet, and is likely used in conjunction with Echelon to monitor web traffic, e-mail messages, and websites.

Echelon basically uses systems to intercept most of the world's communication signals by connecting to commercial satellites or trunk communication lines. There had been rumors of the system and its capabilities

---

[249] http://www.aclu.org/free-speech/aclu-seeks-close-secret-files-peaceful-protests-kept-denver-police
[250] Ibid

in the 1980s, and in 1983 James Bamford discussed such technology in his book *The Puzzle Palace* which focused on the National Security Agency. In 1998, the European Parliament published a report titled *An Appraisal of Technologies of Political Control,* that showed the existence of the massive spy system which would later be known as Echelon.[251]

This system is so powerful, for decades, and even today, some people don't believe it is capable of doing what it does. Using Echelon it is extremely simple for the FBI, CIA, NSA, or any number of other agencies to tap into anyone's phone and automatically record conversations between parties. Of course there is supposed to be a warrant for such activities, but routinely this requirement is ignored under the guise of "national security." But Echelon is much more than a simple wire tapping device.

Echelon monitors millions of phone calls in multiple languages at the same time and can actually pick out specific people's voices from among the millions of calls. This is called a voiceprint, and if a specific individual is targeted for whatever reason, if they talk on a telephone, whether it's a payphone on the side of the street, or a complete stranger's cell phone, within seconds their voiceprint will be detected and the system will identify their location and begin recording their conversation.

Equally amazing is Echelon's ability to detect strings of specific keywords from the millions of conversations occurring, and can then record those conversations and identify the parties and their location. For example, if two people are having a conversation and they use several words in succession, such as assassinate, president, rifle,

---

[251] *Los Angeles Times* "U.S.-British Cyber-Spy System Puts European Countries on Edge" (August 16, 1999) by Gary Chapman

and secret service, then in all likelihood that conversation will be detected by the Echelon system and will be flagged for further analysis to determine whether the people were talking about a recent news event, or if they are potentially dangerous individuals who are planning to assassinate the president.

If this seems too complicated, then think again. Google can find a specific set of keywords out of the billions and billions of web pages in a fraction of a second after you search for them. Also, an app for the iPhone called Shazam was released in 2009 that allows people to use their iPhone to pull up the name of practically any song they hear, whether it's on the radio, or playing on a TV commercial. It doesn't matter if there is background noise, or people talking while it is detecting the song, the app still works, and this is all from one tiny iPhone. Just from hearing a few seconds of almost any song, the app identifies it out of the millions of songs available, and then lists the song's title, artist's name, and the album it's found on.

The History Channel aired a show called *Echelon: The Most Secret Spy System* in 2003 that included interviews with intelligence expert James Bamford, and even Mike Hayden, the National Security Agency Director, and in the show it was discussed how Echelon flagged an innocent conversation someone was having because it happened to include several keywords the system was programmed to flag. When a mother was talking about how her son bombed at the school play, meaning he messed up his lines and gave a horrible performance, Echelon detected the keywords "bomb" and "school" and so her conversation was flagged for further analysis to determine if it was a threat.

In the 1998 thriller *Enemy of the State,* Gene Hackman's character makes a comment about this technology saying, "Fort Meade has 18 acres of mainframe computers underground. You're talking to your wife on the phone and you use the word 'bomb,' 'president,' 'Allah,' any of a hundred keywords, the computer recognizes it, automatically records it, red-flags it for analysis. And that was twenty years ago." Most of the viewers thought this was just a Hollywood fantasy, but David Marconi, the screenwriter was obviously aware of Echelon, and a lot of the technology in *Enemy of the State* was based on actual systems.

A respected newspaper in Germany called the *Frankfurter Allgemeine Zeitung* (FAZ) reported that Echelon had collected information at least three months before the terrorist attacks on September 11, 2001 about how Middle Eastern terrorists were planning to hijack aircraft and use them as weapons against symbols of American culture.[252]

Many critics believe Echelon has also been used for political spying, commercial espionage, and blackmail. The *Baltimore Sun* published an article in 1995 talking about how the aerospace company Airbus lost a $6 billion dollar contract with Saudi Arabia in 1994 as a result of the NSA using Echelon to learn that Airbus executives had bribed Saudi officials in attempts to secure the contract.[253] A British journalist named Duncan Campbell along with a New Zealand journalist named Nicky Hager investigated Echelon's use for industrial espionage in the 1990s and uncovered that Americans used the system to illegally spy on a German company called Enercon in order to learn what advanced technology the company

---

[252] *Biz Report* "Echelon Gave Authorities Warning Of Attacks" (September 13, 2001)
[253] *BBC News* "Echelon: Big brother without a cause?" (July 6, 2000) by Martin Asser

was developing for wind turbines.[254] They also say a Belgian company called Lernout & Hauspie had trade secrets stolen from them regarding speech recognition technology because executives were being illegally monitored by Echelon.

In 2001, a European Parliament committee suggested that politicians use cryptography in their communication with each other to protect their privacy from eavesdroppers using Echelon.[255]

Imagine how this system can be, and most likely has been, abused. The president could order the CIA or NSA to look for keywords spoken from specific people to determine if they were aware of a sensitive issue, scandal, or crime. For example, the system could easily implement a search for the keywords "Bilderberg group" or "Bohemian Grove" and cross reference them with the voiceprints of every senator and congressman, so that if any of them were to mention these words during a telephone conversation, then that conversation could be recorded and later listened to so Echelon technicians could know exactly what those people were saying about these very powerful and secretive groups that shape the political and social landscape from behind the scenes.

"Every citizen, or at least every citizen important enough to be worth watching, could be kept for twenty-four hours a day under the eyes of the police."[256]

—*Nineteen Eighty-Four*

Is a certain senator planning on raising the issue of the Bilderberg group on the floor of the Senate, blowing their decades of cover? If so, then a blackmail, intimidation, or coercion scheme would likely be put in

---

[254] Enercon vs. International Trade Commission and Zond Energy Systems
[255] Report A5-0264/2001 of the European Parliament
[256] Orwell, George – *Nineteen Eighty-Four* page 183

place to prevent this security breach and save the Bilderberg group from the unwanted attention that such public comments would bring them. (If you are not familiar with the Bilderberg group then I advise you to research it on your own or read my previous book, *The Resistance Manifesto*.)

Other Snooping Technology

In an episode of *Conspiracy Theory,* a television show hosted by Jesse Ventura, a man Elwood Norris discussed technology he designs for spy agencies and revealed some of his devices' incredible capabilities. Norris first shows Ventura what looks like a small rock and explains, "I can drive by your house...toss that in your front yard...it picks up your security code from your alarm, your cell phone number, and the code to your garage door opener." When Ventura asked who uses such a device, Norris said that the "alphabet agencies" use it, meaning the FBI, CIA, NSA, and other security agencies. The information picked up and stored in the fake rock can then allow investigators (or stalkers or rogue agents) to access a person's home and disable their alarm system, all without being noticed.

National DNA Database

It may become the law one day that every person in America (and perhaps the world) will be required to give a DNA sample that will be stored in a database similar to fingerprint databases. Police officers in numerous states in America have been taking DNA samples of everyone arrested, arguing that it's no different than fingerprints, but others are worried by the practice and see it as a major privacy invasion.

President Obama has publicly stated that he supports forced DNA sampling of those arrested for any reason, saying "It's the right thing to do. This is where the national registry becomes so important, because what you have is individual states—they may have a database, but if they're not sharing it with the state next door, you've got a guy from Illinois driving over into Indiana, and they're not talking to each other."[257]

We know that secretive government agencies often abuse their power, so many wonder what kind of abuses a national DNA database would lead to. With everyone's DNA on file, could certain government agencies then secretly do tests on the DNA or even create human clones from the samples without anyone knowing about it? Could people's DNA be used to see if they have any diseases or are prone to aggressive activities? Could people be unfairly profiled or labeled because of their DNA analysis?

Tax Amnesty Ad

In May 2010, a television ad began airing in Pennsylvania attempting to scare people who haven't paid their taxes into finally paying them. The ad begins with a shot of the earth which then has a crosshair appear over the United States and begins to zoom in as a computerized voice says, "Your name is Tom. You live just off of Fifth Street. Nice car Tom. Nice house." It then goes on to say that if Tom pays his back taxes of over $4000 that he owes to the state of Pennsylvania in the next month, that they will waive the late penalty. The whole time the computerized voice is explaining this in the 30 second ad, the cross hair continues to zoom in from a picture of the

---

[257] *America's Most Wanted* Transcript (March 2010)

whole earth, to the state of Pennsylvania, and then continues onto a single house at which point the words "Subject Located" flash on the screen, and the computerized voice says, "because we do know who you are."[258]

Insider Revelations

Occasionally a high-level insider in government will make a startling and revealing statement about the way government actually functions. One of the most historic revelations was made by President Dwight D. Eisenhower during his departure address in 1961 where he coined the term "military industrial complex."

Eisenhower warned, "In the councils of government, we must guard against the acquisition of unwarranted influence, whether sought or unsought, by the military industrial complex. The potential for the disastrous rise of misplaced power exists and will persist."

The core of Eisenhower's warning was when he said, "We must never let the weight of this combination endanger our liberties or democratic processes. We should take nothing for granted. Only an alert and knowledgeable citizenry can compel the proper meshing of the huge industrial and military machinery of defense with our peaceful methods and goals, so that security and liberty may prosper together."

President John F. Kennedy also made a profound and even more chilling statement about the behind-the-scenes power structure when speaking to the American Newspaper Publishers Association. Audio of this statement is available on the Internet if you search for "JFK on secret societies." While we have all heard

---

[258] *YouTube* "PA Tax Amnesty Ad 'We Know Who You Are'"

several historic JFK sound bites, few in comparison have heard this amazing and candid admission where he said, "The very word 'secrecy' is repugnant in a free and open society; and we are as a people inherently and historically opposed to secret societies, to secret oaths, and to secret proceedings. We decided long ago that the dangers of excessive and unwarranted concealment of pertinent facts far outweighed the dangers which are cited to justify it...For we are opposed around the world by a monolithic and ruthless conspiracy that relies primarily on covered means for expanding its sphere of influence, on infiltration instead of invasion, on subversion instead of elections, on intimidation instead of free choice, on guerillas by night instead of armies by day."

He continued, "It is a system which has conscripted vast human and material resources into the building of a tightly knit, highly efficient machine that combines military, diplomatic, intelligence, economic, scientific and political operations; its preparations concealed, not published, its mistakes are buried not headlined, its dissenters are silenced not praised, no expenditure is questioned, no rumor is printed, no secret is revealed...I am not asking for your newspapers to support an administration. But I am asking your help in the tremendous task of informing and alerting the American people."[259]

President Kennedy's comments echoed what President Woodrow Wilson had said decades early in his 1913 book, *The New Freedom: A Call For the Emancipation of the Generous Energies of a People.* The most widely quoted passage from this book is where

---

[259] President John F. Kennedy Address before the American Newspaper Publishers Association Waldorf-Astoria Hotel New York City (April 27, 1961)

Wilson wrote, "Since I entered politics, I have chiefly had men's views confided to me privately. Some of the biggest men in the United States, in the field of commerce and manufacturing, are afraid of something. They know that there is a power somewhere so organized, so subtle, so watchful, so interlocked, so complete, so pervasive, that they better not speak above their breath when they speak in condemnation of it."

There are a handful of other revealing and unsettling quotes made by high-powered politicians around the world who will occasionally, and perhaps very subtly, betray the establishment's power structure and give people a glimpse of what kind of a system we are really dealing with. Many believe that JFK, Woodrow Wilson and others were referring to the infamous Illuminati secret society, and think that a modern version of the group continues to exist today in the form of secretive good ol' boy networks focused on preserving their wealth and power at any cost. (Read my book, *The Illuminati: Facts & Fiction* for more information on this fascinating subject.)

The Nanny State

The term "nanny state" refers to government regulations and laws that are widely perceived to be overbearing and restrictive in terms of their attempts to regulate economic or social activities that are better off left alone without the government sticking their nose in them. The term comes from the idea that the government is acting as a nanny, trying to protect citizens from themselves, as a nanny does for a small child.

Big Brother technology has allowed the implementation of numerous nanny state policies that impose extra taxes and fines on people for violating laws such as speed limits, driving in bus lanes, or having expired parking meters. There are also Big Brother policies that keep track of the amount of ammunition gun owners purchase, and laws have been proposed to govern the kinds of ingredients in food with the hopes of making people healthier.

Of course, there need to be laws regulating and prohibiting harmful practices from being used by private industries, but as you will see in the following pages, many of these nanny state measures aren't necessarily designed to keep people safe; they are designed to make the government more money.

Red Light Cameras

Everyone is familiar with the dreaded "red light cameras" that automatically issue tickets to people if they drive through an intersection equipped with the system. As of mid 2010, there were more than 441 communities in the United States using the Big Brother ticket machines, including Atlanta, Chicago, Denver, Houston, Los Angeles, New Orleans, New York City, Philadelphia, Phoenix, San Diego, San Francisco, Seattle, and Washington, DC.[260]

Often the tickets for an infraction are $400 or $500 dollars and come to you in the mail, along with several photos of your vehicle from different angles showing you in the intersection while the light is red. There have been many accusations that the intersections equipped with these cameras have the yellow light time reduced in order to catch more people accidentally blowing the red light thus generating more money for the city.

Some states have prohibited the cameras including Nevada, New Hampshire, West Virginia, and Wisconsin.[261] Many other countries around the world also use the red light camera technology, including the United Kingdom, Germany, Taiwan, India, and Israel.

The red light cameras were just the beginning of the Big Brother systems that would later be implemented to automatically issue large fines to motorists.

Bus Lane Enforcement

Some cities are using license plate reading devices to issue tickets to motorists automatically if they stop in a bus lane or other prohibited areas. For example, New York City began testing a system to detect whether taxis stopped in bus lanes to pick up passengers. Taxis frequently use bus lanes, which they're not supposed to do, but now they will automatically be fined $150 for

---

[260] Insurance Institute for Highway Safety "Communities using red light and/or speed cameras as of June 2010"
[261] *WWLTV.com* "Bill Would Ban Red Light Cameras" (April 27, 2009)

each infraction.[262] These systems cross reference every license plate that enters the restricted zone with a list of approved vehicles, and if the vehicle isn't a bus, police car, or emergency vehicle, the driver will be automatically issued a fine.

Hundreds of buses in London, England are equipped with cameras that capture the license plates of vehicles that stop in no-stopping zones, and those drivers are also automatically issued tickets.[263]

Catching Speeders

Motorists are sadly familiar with speed traps, and even the rare incident of airplanes being used to bust speeders on freeways, but until recently most people never envisioned systems that would automatically ticket drivers using license plate reading cameras.

An area in London began testing the "SpeedSpike" system in two different stretches of roads which calculates the average speed between two designated points and can then automatically issue speeding tickets to motorists. The system was created by an American company called PIPS Technology Ltd.[264]

The system uses license plate reader technology to log each vehicle's license plate when it passes the first camera, and then captures it again when it passes the

---

[262] *DOT Press Release* "New York City Department of Transportation: Commissioner Sadik-Khan, MTA Executive Director Sander, Chairman Daus announce camera enforcement of bus lanes to speed transit" (February 23, 2009)
[263]

http://www.jai.com/EN/Traffic/Applications/Pages/Buslaneenforcem ent.aspx
[264] *Telegraph* "New speed cameras trap motorists from space" by Richard Savill (April 20, 2010)

second camera at a different point in the road. It then mathematically figures out each vehicle's average speed depending on the amount of time it took to get between the two cameras, and if the average speed is deemed too fast, then the system knows the vehicle was traveling above the speed limit, and issues a ticket to the owner.

Officials plan on using the system to enforce speed limits on main roads, as well as school zones. When it was first tested, officials said they couldn't publicly comment on it because of "commercial confidentiality." The British Automobile Association said it was, "a natural evolution of the technology that is out there" and didn't think it was Orwellian or sinister.

These systems will probably become as common as red light cameras in the future, striking fear into the hearts (and wallets) of motorists everywhere. Police officers at the Dallas Police Department in Dallas, Texas, were the first to begin using E-ticket machines, rather than the usual ticket pad that required tickets to be filled out by hand that most people are all used to. The E-ticket machines allow officers to write tickets faster and simplify the process of entering them into computer databases, which means—the faster the government can get your money.[265]

There will probably come a time in the not-so-distant future where tickets are automatically debited from your checking account, or if you don't have any money in the bank, then the fine could be levied against one of your credit cards, and if this happens then you'll have to pay interest on the ticket as well.

---

[265] *NBC Dallas Fort Worth* "Traffic Tickets Going High-Tech: E-ticket devices to be tested by 50 motorcycle officers" (December 9th 2010) by Bruce Felps

Automatic Parking Tickets

At some point in the Orwellian New World Order we will see parking meters that automatically ticket vehicles the second the meter expires. This is extremely simple since the meters will be equipped with cameras that capture the license plate number of the vehicle that is parked in the spot at the time the meter expires. As people know, if a parking meter expires and your vehicle is still parked in the spot, you will only get a ticket if a "meter maid" spots the expired meter. Your vehicle could sit in front of the expired meter for thirty minutes or even several hours before the meter maid does their rounds and sees it, but the Orwellian parking meters will fine you the moment your time runs out and will likely issue new fines every few minutes, or every hour, depending on how long the vehicle remains in the parking spot after the meter has expired.

Black Boxes in Automobiles

After the highly publicized problem of accelerators sticking in certain Toyota vehicles in 2010 causing several accidents and deaths since 2007, the Highway Traffic Safety Administration chief David Strickland mentioned that the government was considering making "black boxes" mandatory for all new vehicles which will record data such as a vehicle's speed and breaking effort in order to reconstruct what happened immediately preceding an accident if one were to occur.[266] Toyota recalled more than 8 million vehicles to eliminate the risk of sticking accelerating pedals and the problem was a

---

[266] *Reuters* "Toyota discounts boost sales, US mulls 'black box'" (March 11, 2010) by Kevin Krolicki and John Crawley

major story for months.

Black boxes on vehicles could do more than just record information in the event of an accident. GPS systems installed on vehicles can detect what speed the vehicle is traveling at, and could be used to issue automatic speeding tickets. The GPS systems could easily detect the speed limit for just about any street the vehicle is on, and could automatically issue tickets if the car exceeds the limit. If a car has unpaid parking tickets or an expired registration, then GPS black boxes could also disable the vehicle until these payments were made.

The Virginia Court of Appeals ruled in September 2010 that police did not need a warrant to secretly attach a GPS tracking device on a suspect's vehicle in order to monitor their every move. The Fourth Amendment of the Constitution clearly bans unreasonable searches and seizures, but the Virginia court ruled that because there is no expectation of privacy on a public street, a suspect has no protection against the hi-tech monitoring of their whereabouts. Judge Randolph A. Beales wrote in the opinion that "police used the GPS device to crack this case by tracking the appellant on the public roadways—which they could, of course, do in person any day of the week at any hour without obtaining a warrant."[267]

The Ninth Circuit Court in California has also ruled that secretly placing a GPS device on a vehicle wasn't a Fourth Amendment violation, but the Washington, D.C. Circuit Court held that it was, so this issue could head to the Supreme Court. Since the Virginia and California courts ruled that secretly placing a GPS device on a suspect's vehicle without a warrant is within the law, then one must wonder whether a similar policy will go into

---

[267] *Examiner* "Va. appeals court upholds tracking suspects with GPS" By Emily Babay (September 8, 2010)

effect concerning the use of GPS systems built into people's cell phones. Currently law enforcement officials are legally required to obtain a warrant to track someone's cell phone, but in the New World Order the courts may rule there is no reasonable expectation of privacy considering a person's whereabouts if they are carrying a cell phone since they know it contains a GPS tracking device. Where is the line going to be drawn?

Since there is no reasonable expectation of privacy when someone is standing on a public street, it is legal to videotape and record a person's conversation without their consent, so one must wonder whether it will also become fully legal for law enforcement and other government agencies to secretly eavesdrop on people without a warrant by activating the microphone in their cell phone as a bug, which is a tactic used by the FBI and other agencies after a warrant has been granted.

Is the government going to say that you have no reasonable expectation of privacy if you are carrying a cell phone because there is a microphone built into it? Perhaps the government will change the definition of "reasonable expectation of privacy" and will claim that in today's high-tech society, there is no longer a reasonable expectation of privacy anywhere.

Watching Your Garbage

In the United Kingdom more than 2.5 million trash bins have built-in microchips that weigh the bin's contents as part of a "pay-as-you-throw" program which taxes people based on the amount of garbage they throw away.

In March 2010, an investigation involving Freedom of Information Requests showed that one in five counties in the UK had implemented the Big Brother bins that weigh the garbage and tax the residents accordingly.[268] In 2008, Gordon Brown, the prime minister, had promised to eliminate bin taxes because polls showed it was extremely unpopular among voters, but the practice has quietly increased.

Alex Deane of *Big Brother Watch*, said, "The number of local councils placing microchips in bins is increasing, despite the fact that only one of them has volunteered to trial the Government's pay-as-you-throw scheme. Councils are waiting until the public aren't watching to begin surveillance on our waste habits, intruding into people's private lives and introducing punitive taxes on what we throw away. The British public doesn't want this technology, these fines, or this intrusion. If local authorities have no intention to monitor our waste then they should end the surreptitious installation of these bin microchips."[269]

The "pay-as-you-throw" program also allows city councils to examine people's trash and sell the information to corporations. People are also concerned that data from the chipped bins could show when they were away on vacation, possibly allowing criminals to know when homes were unoccupied, making them easy targets for burglars.

Authorities said the microchips were implemented to help the elderly. A spokesman for the Local Government Association said, "putting microchips in people's bins can allow councils to provide people with a better service that costs less. If an elderly resident needs help getting their bin collected and returned, a microchip quickly flags it up

---

[268] *Daily Mail* "Spy chips hidden in 2.5 MILLION dustbins: 60pc rise in electronic bugs as council snoopers plan pay-as-you-throw tax" by Steve Doughty (March 5, 2010)
[269] Ibid

to the refuse collector, saving time and money."[270]

In 2008, approximately 100 different city councils in the UK investigated the contents of their residents' bins, in order to check to see what kind of garbage was being thrown out by people, and in some cases tried to obtain information on their incomes and lifestyles.

Another possible scenario involving people's garbage may arise after RFID tags are attached to every piece of merchandise replacing the traditional UPCs. Will someone be fined for putting glass bottles in the wrong recycling bin, or if someone accidentally discards cans in the paper bin? RFID tags and sensors installed on recycling bins could not only detect when the wrong materials were placed in the wrong bin, but the tags could also identify who purchased the items, and could issue them a fine for not disposing of them properly.

In Cleveland, Ohio the city began installing RFID tags in recycling bins in order to keep track of how often residents roll their bins out to the curb for collection to make sure they are recycling, and fines them $100 if they are not.[271] A computer on the garbage truck contains an RFID reader that detects the RFID tags attached to the residents' recycle bins, and keeps track of which bins are emptied each week and which ones are not.

If a home's recycle bin has not been placed out by the curb for collection in several weeks, then a trash supervisor will physically go through the person's trash cans to see if that resident is throwing away recyclables in the trash cans, instead of sorting them in the recycle bins. These recyclables include glass, metal cans, plastic bottles, paper and cardboard. If a trash supervisor finds

---

[270] Ibid

[271] *Cleveland.com* "High-tech carts will tell on Cleveland residents who don't recycle...and they face $100 fine" (August 20, 2010) by Mark Gillispie

more than 10 percent recyclable material in the person's trash bin, then that resident is fined $100 for not properly sorting their recyclables.

Cleveland's City Council approved spending $2.5 million dollars on the Big Brother bins in 2010, which were implemented in approximately 25,000 different households at first, and the program is designed to expand to an additional 25,000 households per year until the city's 150,000 residents all use them. A suburb in Washington, DC also announced plans to implement a similar program,[272] and other cities around America are poised to follow.

Ammunition Purchases

Big Brother is scared of people with guns, as all tyrannical and oppressive regimes have been in the past, because an armed population can resist a government aimed at destroying civil liberties or rounding up citizens and sending them to detention centers or death camps. By disarming ordinary law abiding citizens, it also allows a government to grow in size and power because people will need to rely on the police to protect them from dangerous criminals, instead of protecting themselves using their own guns. This allows the police force to grow larger and have more funding. Gun control laws made it illegal for citizens to own guns that aren't registered to them, something that can easily allow officials to do door-to-door weapon confiscations like they did in the aftermath of hurricane Katrina in 2005.[273]

---

[272] *The Washington Examiner* "New recycling bins with tracking chips coming to Alexandria" By Markham Heid (May 6, 2010)
[273] *YouTube* "NRA: The Untold Story of Gun Confiscation After Katrina"

Police can pull up a person's name and instantly see which guns they own, and demand they all get turned in.

While New World Order kingpins continuously attempt to destroy the Second Amendment to the Constitution, there are other Orwellian policies being put into place in attempts to monitor who has what guns, and even how many bullets they own.

As governor of California, Arnold Schwarzenegger signed a bill into law which required stores that sell ammunition to thumbprint customers and log their driver's license for each purchase. Everyone who now buys bullets in California must submit to this procedure, as well as sign for their purchase which is then entered into a federal database that keeps track of how much ammo that person has bought. The database is used to flag people who buy what the government considers large amounts of ammunition, which may then be considered probable cause to investigate the individual further or place them under surveillance.

Schwarzenegger claimed to be against such a policy in the past but later changed his mind saying, "Although I have previously vetoed legislation similar to this measure, local governments have demonstrated that requiring ammunition vendors to keep records on ammunition sales improves public safety."[274]

Sam Paredes, the executive director of Gun Owners of California, said the law treats gun owners like registered sex offenders.

Dr. Big Brother

With the passing of Obamacare into law in March

---

[274] *USA Today* "New California law tracks ammunition sales" (October 12, 2009)

2010, the American government was facing enormous health care costs, and many were pressed to come up with ways to keep these costs down. The Senate Committee on Aging disclosed innovations they were planning as part of the government's new role in the health care industry, and some ideas included video chats with doctors and putting RFIDs on pills so computers could keep track of whether patients are taking their medication or not. The new methods have been called e-Health, e-Care, or telehealth.

"What we're talking about, folks, is using a device like this one," Senator Ron Wyden (D-Oregon) said, as he displayed the small device. "It attaches to the patient's skin and is loaded with drugs that are administered in the exact way that the doctor prescribes—wirelessly."[275]

"That means that a doctor can vary the doses based on the information the doctor is receiving [from the monitor]. The patient doesn't have to go in to the doctor and then the pharmacy to change his or her prescription," he said.[276]

Other devices proposed by the committee were systems that would be attached to patients and monitor things like blood pressure and glucose levels which would then wirelessly report that information over the Internet to their physician. Officials also hope to implement devices that can monitor a person's nutritional intake and ones that could detect whether an elderly person has taken a fall so emergency workers could be alerted.

"Continuous monitoring of vibrations in the floor can detect falls and classify them according to the best choice of first responders—either a 911 call or a visit from a

---

[275] *CNSNews.com* "Senate Panel Previews Electronic Health Technology" (April 26, 2010) by Matt Cover
[276] Ibid

caregiver," proposed Robin Felder of the University of Virginia.[277]

"Emerging technologies allow pills to be electronically outfitted with transmitters to communicate with the user's wristwatch that shows that the pill has been consumed," Felder continued. "Broadband connectivity of these devices would allow the electronic medical record to be updated with regard to medication compliance and efficacy."[278]

Dr. Mohit Kaushal, who is the health care director at the Federal Communications Commission, testified at the Senate Committee on Aging using a video phone in an attempt to promote video chats between patients and doctors as an alternative to office visits.

Eric Dishman, global director of health innovation and policy at Intel, said "Just as e-mail became a new way of interacting with other people that didn't replace all other forms of communication such as phone calls and letters, e-Care uses new technologies to create a new way of providing care that complements—but doesn't replace—all clinic visits."

Dictating Your Diet

Another side effect to the passing of Obamacare are more laws governing the ingredients in food that are considered to be unhealthy. Since the taxpayers were now on the hook for everyone's health insurance, lawmakers were looking for ways to keep people healthier in order to keep down the costs.

A bill introduced in New York tried to ban the use of any salt in restaurant cooking. The bill, A. 10129, states

---

[277] Ibid
[278] Ibid

in part, "No owner or operator of a restaurant in this state shall use salt in any form in the preparation of any food for consumption by customers of such restaurant, including food prepared to be consumed on the premises of such restaurant or off of such premises."

The bill was introduced by Assemblyman Felix Ortiz (D-Brooklyn), and included fines of $1000 for each violation.[279] A coalition of chefs, restaurant owners, and consumers, called the proposed law "absurd" in a press release.

In 2006, the Board of Health in New York City voted to ban restaurants from using trans fats in their food, a law that took effect in July 2008. Trans fats are unhealthy because they raise bad cholesterol and lower good cholesterol, making them worse than saturated fat.

"We don't think that a municipal health agency has any business banning a product the Food and Drug Administration has already approved," said Dan Fleshler, a spokesman for the National Restaurant Association.[280]

Other cities and states are passing laws that require restaurants to list the calorie content on the menus next to each food item.

In New York City, a school actually sent letters to parents of children that were considered fat. "My son, who is very tall for his age and is a little husky, but fit, brought home a piece of paper from his school listing his BMI and stating that he was obese," said Amy Oztan, a mother of two, who received one of the letters.[281] BMI stands for Body Mass Index and comes from a formula

[279] *FoxNews.com* "Chefs Call Proposed New York Salt Ban Absurd" (March 11, 2010)
[280] *MSNBC* "New York City passes trans fat ban" (December 5, 2006)
[281] *ABC News* "Obesity Police Want to Track Your Kid's BMI" (March 4, 2010) by Susan Donaldson James

based on a person's height and weight.

Michelle Obama had started a campaign called Let's Move that involves regular screening of all children's BMI. One major criticism for screening people's BMI is that it doesn't take into account someone's body type such as if they are big-boned or more muscular than an average person.

In *Nineteen Eighty-Four*, every citizen is required to exercise daily in front of the telescreen so they could keep up their strength in order to better serve Big Brother. During one of the sessions, Winston Smith is yelled at by the instructor for not stretching far enough during a toe-touching exercise because the telescreens watched everyone's effort.

While at an elementary school in Washington DC, Michelle Obama told the students that military leaders had informed her that more than one in four children are unqualified for military service because they're too fat and that "childhood obesity isn't just a public health threat, it's not just an economic threat, it's a national security threat as well."[282]

She went on to list all the evils that fat people cause the economy and the health care system and concluded that, "We can't just leave this up to the parents."[283]

It was right around this time that governments approved a ban on soda machines in school cafeterias across the country, and even placed restrictions on school bake sales, in the name of public health.[284] San Francisco even banned toys from most McDonald's Happy Meals

[282] *Politico.com* "Michelle Obama has new warning on obesity" by Mike Allan (December 13th 2010)
[283] Ibid.
[284] *The Minneapolis Star Tribune* – "In St. Paul schools, the not-so-sweet life" by DAAREL BURNETTE II (December 22, 2010)

because officials claimed the toys were enticing children to eat poor quality food.[285]

"Smart" Thermostats

An Orwellian idea that hatched in California and may one day spread around the country, or even the world, involves the government being able to remotely control the thermostat in people's homes in order to turn off the air-conditioning if they feel too much electricity is being used at a particular time and causing strain on the electrical grid.

All new homes built in California have to be equipped with the Big Brother thermostats, and many existing homes as well. The 2008 Building Efficiency Standards (Page 64), known as Title 24, specifically states, "The PCT shall not allow customer changes to thermostat settings during emergency events."

Some government officials also hope to require non-removable FM receivers that connect to other electronic appliances such as water heaters, refrigerators, lights and computers, so these devices could be remotely shut off at will. Michael Shames, executive director of California's Utility Consumers' Action Network said, "The implications of this language are far-reaching and Orwellian. For the government and utility company to say, 'We're going to control the devices in your house, and you have no choice in that matter,' that's where the line is drawn."[286]

Proponents of the "smart" thermostats have failed to

---

[285] *Los Angeles Times* "San Francisco bans Happy Meals" (November 02, 2010) By Sharon Bernstein

[286] *WorldNetDaily.com* "Big Brother to control thermostats in homes?" (January 11, 2008) by Chelsea Schilling

realize that many people can install window air-conditioning units that aren't connected to the home's central thermostat, and will not be able to be controlled by the system. Some homeowners will also find a way to bypass the system without detection.

Fingerprint Scanners

When you think of getting your fingerprints taken, the image of being in handcuffs at the police station is often the first to come to mind, but fingerprint scanners are becoming common ways to check someone's identity, not just to enter a secure area at a government installation, but to pay for lunch at the local school, to enter your local gym, and even to get into Disney World.

For years, Walt Disney's theme parks have used fingerprint scanners to identify ticket holders to make sure that people don't use someone else's ticket.[287] Disney will confiscate any pass that someone attempts to use if it is not theirs.

"The lack of transparency has always been a problem," said Lillie Coney, associate director of the Electronic Privacy Information Center, who believes that the fingerprint scanners are too invasive. "What they're doing is taking a technology that was used to control access to high-level security venues and they're applying it to controlling access to a theme park."[288]

George Crossley, president of the Central Florida ACLU, said, "It's impossible for them to convince me that all they are getting is the fact that that person is the

---

[287] *Eagle Tribune* "Magic Kingdom: Walt Disney World starting to scan fingerprints" (September 3, 2006)
[288] *Newsinitiative.org* "Walt Disney World: The Government's Tomorrowland?" by Karen Harmel (September 1, 2006)

ticket-holder."[289]

It seems comical, but the federal government looked to Disney after the September 11th 2001 terror attacks to learn about security measures including biometrics because their theme parks had been the largest commercial user of biometric scanners. "The government was very aware of what Disney was doing," said Jim Wayman, director of the National Biometric Test Center at San Jose State University.

The company providing the scanners to Disney is believed to be Lumidigm Incorporated which is funded by the CIA, NSA, and the Department of Defense. Lumidigm's CEO Bob Harbour would not admit his company's products were used at Disney, but did say they have a contract with a "major theme park."[290]

Oftentimes companies that use these systems will say that they don't capture the person's actual fingerprint, but instead just look for various points on it and match those up to the points stored in its system, but Raul Diaz, Lumidigm's vice president of sales and marketing, said that such systems can be activated to store the entire image.

In 2004, Sea World in San Antonio, Texas installed fingerprint scanners for people with season passes. It's not just Sea World and the "happiest place on earth" that are using fingerprint scanners to gain entry. 24 Hour Fitness gyms have been using the scanners since at least 2007,[291] and several schools around America have implemented finger scanners as a way for students to pay

---

[289] Ibid

[290] Ibid

[291] *10News.com* "New 24 Hour Fitness System Gives Fingers Workout" by Michelle Krish (January 25, 2007)

for their lunches.[292] It's likely that banks will issue scanners that will either replace or supplement debit card readers at most retailers.

Despite what most people think, fingerprint scanners are not 100% accurate. A Japanese cryptographer and university professor named Tsutomu Matsumoto, tested fingerprint scanners and found that by using gelatin and molding plastic, he could copy someone's fingerprint and beat every major fingerprint reader eight out of ten times.[293] An episode of *Myth Busters* showed the crew was able to fool finger scanners as well.

In 2004, a man named Brandon Mayfield was detained and his home searched immediately after the March 11, 2004 bombing in Madrid, Spain that killed 191 people. The FBI had used their Automated Fingerprint Identification System to link him to the crime, but it turns out that because of a "substandard" fingerprint taken from a bag that contained one of the explosives, their system incorrectly identified him and he was completely innocent.

---

[292] *USA Today* "Finger scans let kids touch and go" by Karen Thomas (February 2, 2006)
[293] *Crypto-Gram Newsletter* "Fun with Fingerprint Readers" (May 15, 2002) by Bruce Schneier

Orwellian Weapons

Over the course of civilization we have seen weapons advance from basic sticks and stones in prehistoric times, to swords and knives after the discovery of iron and steel, and later advancing to guns and missiles, often attached to aircraft or boats that can destroy a target hundreds of miles away. Science fiction literature and films have been filled with stories of lasers and armed humanoid robots that are indestructible killing-machines, but as some people already know, many of these fanciful depictions from the past are now becoming a reality.

While at one time, so-called smart bombs amazed people with their ability to strike strategic targets from long distances; these kinds of weapons are now common knowledge. What is not common knowledge (at least at the time I'm writing this in 2010) are a wide variety of futuristic Orwellian weapons that are already built, or are on the drawing board.

Some of these weapons involve fully autonomous robots that can relentlessly hunt down targets, and even implantable RFID chips that can kill a person when activated, and shock bracelets designed for airline passengers that can electrocute them if they are suspected of posing a threat. These and other weapons, if directed by a tyrannical leader, could squash any kind of resistance and keep every citizen in the world, not only under the watchful eyes of Big Brother, but in his crosshairs as well.

As you will learn in this chapter and the one on artificial intelligence, warnings of a massive robotic massacre, or artificial intelligence systems turning on humans is not only something found in the plots of science fiction movies or the paranoid imaginations of technophobes. It is a very real concern addressed by numerous experts in multiple fields. Big Brother is not just watching us; he is now armed and dangerous.

An Implantable Computer Chip That Can Kill

In 2009, Germany's patent office rejected a patent for an invention dubbed the "Killer Chip," which is basically an implantable RFID similar to the VeriChip said to track visitors from other countries using GPS, and could release a poison into a person's body to "eliminate" them if they become a "security risk." That was at least the Orwellian goal of the Saudi inventor who applied for the patent.

"I apply for these reasons and for reasons of state security and the security of citizens," his application read. German law allows foreigners to apply for patents in the country through a local representative. "Most people apply for a patent in several countries, and this inventor probably did too," Stephanie Krüger of the Patent Office said.[294]

A German Patent and Trademark Office spokeswoman told *Deutsche Presse Agentur* that the inventor's application was submitted in October 2007 and published 18 months later, as required by law, but in Germany, inventions that are unethical or a danger to the public are not approved.

Electric Shock Bracelets for Airline Passengers

A sadistic idea that seems like it would only be implemented for transporting dangerous prisoners was actually proposed for ordinary citizens flying on

[294] *World Net Daily* "'Killer Chip' tracks humans, releases poison" (May 16, 2009) by Jay Baggett

commercial jets that involved making all passengers on airliners wear a tamper-proof shock bracelet that could then be activated to electrocute anyone that the crew thought was potentially dangerous. The Department of Homeland Security has expressed great interest in the so-called EMD (Electo-Muscular Disruption) safety bracelet which was designed by Lampered Less Lethal Incorporated.

A promotional video posted on the company's website shows the device being worn by all passengers on an airline and explained how the company felt it would help keep people safe.[295]

The video starts off by showing footage of the aftermath of the September 11th attacks and goes on to say that facial recognition systems take too much time and would increase the number of flight delays and cancellations. It also says bomb detecting devices aren't effective enough, and that the shock bracelets could stop terrorists once they were on board an aircraft.

It goes on to say that the shock bracelets would make flying more convenient for travelers since they could also be used as their ticket. The video concludes by saying, "We feel if given the choice between taking a flight implementing the added security of the EMD security safety bracelet system, and taking a flight without the additional security, many, if not most passengers, would happily opt for the extra security of the EMD safety bracelet."

I know that this seems like a hoax or a satire to bring attention to Orwellian security measures, but it's not. A search of U.S. patents reveals that a patent was filed for the device in 2002. The application number is 6,933,851, and the description reads, "A method of providing air

---

[295] http://www.lamperdlesslethal.com/video_gallery.asp?video=http

travel security for passengers traveling via an aircraft comprises situating a remotely activatable electric shock device on each of the passengers in position to deliver a disabling electrical shock when activated; and arming the electric shock devices for subsequent selective activation by a selectively operable remote control disposed within the aircraft. The remotely activatable electric shock devices each have activation circuitry responsive to the activating signal transmitted from the selectively operable remote control means. The activated electric shock device is operable to deliver the disabling electrical shock to that passenger."

A letter from a Department of Homeland Security official named Paul S. Ruwaldt was sent to the inventor saying, "To make it clear, we [the federal government] are interested in…the immobilizing security bracelet, and look forward to receiving a written proposal."[296]

The letterhead was from a US Department of Homeland Security office at the William J. Hughes Technical Center at the Atlantic City International Airport (the Federal Aviation Administration headquarters). It was also reported that Ruwaldt had previously met with a rep for the bracelet's manufacturer.[297]

Taser-Firing Flying Robot

In 2007, it was reported that a French entrepreneur was developing a "flying saucer" that could shoot Taser rounds which would electrocute anyone hit by them. He plans for the device to be used to hunt criminal suspects

---

[296] *The Washington Times* "Want some torture with your peanuts?" (July 1, 2008) by P. Jeffrey Black and Jeffrey Denning
[297] Ibid

or zap people in unruly crowds.[298] His invention is basically an Unmanned Ariel Vehicle (UAV) that can hover around like a small radio controlled helicopter that is equipped with Taser rounds.

The controversial Taser gun temporarily paralyzes people by shooting two darts into the body which send electric shocks into the person, and are often abused by police as they electrocute unarmed and often non-threatening people for not complying with an order immediately.

The Taser-firing UAV's creator, Antoine di Zazzo, says that he has been shocked by a Taser more than 50 times during his experiments and claims no side effects. A Taser is different than a stun gun, in that a Taser shoots tiny darts into a person's skin which then carry the electrical current, whereas a stun gun is just a device with two metal prongs on it that are pressed against someone to shock them. Hovering UAVs like Zazzo's design could also easily be armed with pepper spray, knockout gas, or even guns.

Some may think that this technology is still many decades away, but it's not. Police in London deployed a UAV in February 2010 after a suspected car thief was able to evade officers on foot in thick fog. The thermal-imaging cameras built in to the UAV were able to spot the suspect's heat signature, allowing police to track him down and make an arrest.

Several companies are building drones for sale to the general public which may be operated from a laptop computer or even a cell phone. "If the Israelis can use them to find terrorists, certainly a husband is going to be

---

[298] *TGDaily.com* "Death from above - French developing flying TASER-firing saucer" (November 28, 2007) by Humphrey Cheung

able to track a wife who goes out at 11 o'clock at night and follow her," said divorce lawyer Raoul Felder.[299]

An MIT professor named Ms. Cummings, who is developing personal UAVs, commented that she could use a drone to watch her child by planting a transmitter in her lunchbox. "It would bring a whole new meaning to the term hover parent," she said.

She also remarked that, "If everybody had enough money to buy one of these things, we could all be wandering around with little networks of vehicles flying over our heads spying on us…It really opens up a whole new Pandora's Box of: What does it mean to have privacy?"

Frozen Poison Gun

A secret and sinister weapon developed by the CIA, and probably used in multiple assassinations and kidnappings, involves a CO_2 powered gun that shoots a small frozen piece of poison or tranquilizing agent into the target, which leaves no evidence behind of any foul play. This device was actually shown during a congressional hearing when Senator Frank Church questioned then CIA director, William Colby about it.

Transcript:

Senator Frank Church: Does this pistol fire the dart? [Holding up the gun]

CIA Director William Colby: Yes, it does, Mr. Chairman, and a special one was developed which

---

[299] *Daily Mail* "Celebs beware! New Pandora's box of 'personal' drones that could stalk anyone from Brangelina to your own child" (November 8th 2010)

potentially would be able to enter the target without perception.

Senator Frank Church: But also the toxin itself would not appear in the autopsy?

CIA Director William Colby: Yes, so that there was no way of perceiving that the target was hit.

End of Transcript

In a 1998 documentary titled *Secrets of the CIA*, a former CIA agent named Mary Embree explains how it was her job to research poisons that could be used on people which would kill them and make it seem as if they died of a heart attack. She also talks about the frozen poison dart gun, saying, "The poison was frozen into some sort of dart, and then it was shot at very high speed into the person. So when it reached the person, it would melt inside them, and the only thing would be like one little, tiny red dot on their body, which was hard to detect. There wouldn't be a needle left or anything like that in the person."[300]

Hunter-Killer Robots

In the first decade of the twenty-first century, the Pentagon was looking for contractors to build what they called a "Multi-Robot Pursuit System" that will involve packs of robots which "search for and detect a non-cooperative human."[301] In 2005, the Pentagon launched a

---

[300] *Secrets of the CIA* (Turner Home Entertainment 1998)
[301] *New Scientist* "Packs of robots will hunt down uncooperative humans" by Paul Marks (October 22, 2008)

$127 billion dollar project called Future Combat Systems to develop robotic soldiers and was the largest military contract in US history.[302] It seems that real "Terminators" like the ones in the popular Arnold Schwarzenegger films are crossing over from science fiction into science fact.

Several different companies, including iRobot and Foster-Miller, manufacture different radio controlled tank-like robots that are armed with Taser guns, machine guns, and even rocket launchers. The Pentagon and others hope to one day create fully autonomous robots that are so advanced they can basically function on their own without any human intervention, even hunting down and killing people who are programmed as targets to be eliminated. Such systems will be equipped with facial recognition cameras, and likely DNA sniffers that operate like the nose of a tracking dog that can literally smell a suspect and identify him or her out of a large crowd of people and can even track their every footstep in order to hunt them down and either kill them or incapacitate them, depending on the programmed orders.

"If you build a new shopping mall, you could have sniffers all over the place," predicts George Dodd, the father of the "electronic nose" and a researcher with the Highlands Scientific Research Group at the Craig Dunain Hospital in Inverness, UK.[303] Dodd envisions these sniffers as part of security systems in people's homes and offices that will be able to identify intruders.

Police departments in Germany, Holland, and Hungary have been collecting swabs of human scents from crime scenes and putting them into databases, and

---

[302] *New York Times* "Pentagon has sights on robot soldiers" by Tim Weiner (February 16, 2005)
[303] "Millimeter Waves and Mind Control" (March 22, 1997) Alan Yu

George Dodd predicts that in the future every person's individual scent will be stored on a computer similar to fingerprints and DNA. These are some of the capabilities that will be built into robotic terminators.

In 2008, Steve Wright, an expert in police and military technology at Leeds Metropolitan University, predicted that autonomous human hunting robots would soon be fully operational. After news was made of the Pentagon's goals of creating a Multi Robot Pursuit System, Wright said, "What we have here are the beginnings of something designed to enable robots to hunt down humans like a pack of dogs. Once the software is perfected we can reasonably anticipate that they will become autonomous and become armed. We can also expect such systems to be equipped with human detection and tracking devices including sensors which detect human breath and the radio waves associated with a human heart beat. These are technologies already developed."[304]

The US Air Force's *Unmanned Aircraft Systems Flight Plan 2009-2047* report explains how unmanned drones could fly over targets and attack, all without human involvement. The report says that humans will monitor situations rather than being deciders or participants, and that "advances in AI [artificial intelligence] will enable systems to make combat decisions and act within legal and policy constraints without necessarily requiring human input."[305] The Air Force plans to have such devices fully operational by the year 2047. Several pages of the report were classified.

P.W. Singer, a senior fellow at the Brookings

---

[304] *New Scientist* "Packs of robots will hunt down uncooperative humans" (October 22, 2008) by Paul Marks
[305] Ibid

Institution think tank and the author of *Wired for War: The Robotics Revolution and Conflict in the 21st Century* said, "Every mission [that] soldiers go out on in Iraq, there's something (automated) flying over them, maybe an unmanned vehicle scouting ahead of them...When they shoot, the key is what they put their laser on for a drone to fire at....The story of the surge is not the additional troops, it's the air strikes (by machines like Predator drones) going up by a huge amount."[306]

When the Iraq war began in 2003, there were only a handful of ground-based robots in the field, such as radio controlled devices with mechanical arms used to defuse bombs, but a few years into the war there were over 12,000 robots, including Unmanned Arial Vehicles (UAVs) and other ground-based devices being used on a regular basis.[307]

The United States is not the only country with a rapidly increasing number of robotic soldiers. Dozens of other countries have been building a robotic army. In 2009, an Iranian drone was shot down in Iraq, and the Palestinian-based Hezbollah group has used drones to attack Israel on several occasions.

Many fear that lone nuts or small terrorist organizations will obtain robotic soldiers and commit attacks with them on innocent civilians. "I talked to a researcher who told me that for $50,000 worth of robots he could shut down New York for a day. It was pretty convincing. Warfare will go open source," said Singer.[308]

The chair of the Department of Computer Science at the University of Sheffield in England, who is considered a computer and artificial intelligence expert, has also

---

[306] *Forbes* "Robots That Kill For America" by Quentin Hardy (May 14, 2009)
[307] Ibid
[308] Ibid

warned about the dangers of advancing robots. In 2007, Noel Sharkey wrote an article for the *London Guardian* detailing his warnings, where he said, "The deployment of the first armed battlefield robots in Iraq is the latest step on a dangerous path—we are sleepwalking into a brave new world where robots decide who, where and when to kill."[309]

He pointed out the Pentagon's $100 billion dollar Future Combat Systems project working to build killer robots and Unmanned Arial Vehicles (UAVs), saying, "This is dangerous new territory for warfare, yet there are no new ethical codes or guidelines in place. I have worked in artificial intelligence for decades, and the idea of a robot making decisions about human termination is terrifying."[310]

Sharkey warns that, "With prices falling and technology becoming easier, we may soon see a robot arms race that will be difficult to stop,"[311] and urged that legislation be drawn up that would outline a code of ethics for autonomous robots before it's too late. Some experts and military officials worry about robots' ability to determine friendly people from legitimate targets. Robots could be programmed to identify soldiers who are wearing the enemy country's uniforms, or the facial recognition system could be inputted with the faces of the entire enemy's army after a hacker steals that information from them. Every faceprint of American soldiers could be input, and the robots instructed to kill everyone except those people in a specified area, but facial recognition is not 100% accurate. Friendly soldiers may also be equipped with RFID tags that would tell the robots they

---

[309] *The Guardian* "Robot wars are a reality" by Noel Sharkey (August 18, 2007)
[310] Ibid
[311] Ibid

were friendly, and the machines could be programmed to kill any person who is not wearing a tag within the battle zone.

The increasing use of robotic soldiers will change the face of war in many ways. The loss of American soldiers' lives was always a reason for the public to resist entering into a conflict, but perhaps at some point in the future, there will be hardly any risk for human life (for the country with the advanced robotic army, that is), so the public may not protest an ensuing war as much as they have in the past.

Going to war in the past meant that young soldiers would be killed and maimed in battle, but if a country (like America, for example) could send a fleet of robots instead of humans, would-be protesters will likely not resist the decision to go to war. Many people may, in fact, encourage such acts who would have felt indifferent, or even against such action in the past because of the risk to American soldiers' lives.

Robotic Snakes

People have become familiar with the tank-like robots that frequently defuse bombs, and the flying drones that are like large radio controlled airplanes, but an interesting and unexpected design comes in the form of a robotic snake that literally slithers on the ground imitating an actual snake.

The first robot snake was built by Israeli Defense Forces (IDF) and is about 6 feet long and is also equipped with cameras, microphones, and speakers. It is operated by laptop computer.[312] Some envision the snake

---

[312] *The Weekly Standard* "IDF developing battlefield robot snake" by Mary Katharine Ham (June 9, 2009)

slithering through rubble of collapsed buildings in hopes of finding survivors, but the creators also say it could be used to carry bombs, as perhaps a suicide snake bomber, slithering near a target and blowing itself up.

Other robots based on animals are also reportedly in the works, including agile robots modeled after cats and dogs. While the robotic snake built by IDF is designed to operate on land, a Japanese company built a snake robot in 2005 that swims under water like a sea serpent. It's called the ACM-R5 and can be seen operating on videos posted on the Internet.

Big Dog Four-Legged Robot

While most early robots being used by the Department of Defense were not much more than sophisticated miniature radio controlled tanks that rolled around on two treads, designing robots that walk has proved to be a much more difficult task. Creating pilotless drones that fly like radio controlled airplanes or the bomb disposing tread robots like the TALON robots used in the Iraq War are much simpler than designing a system that can balance on two or four legs.

A company called Boston Dynamics was one of the first to create a functioning walking robot they call the Big Dog that walks on four legs using a hydraulic actuation system. The robot is the size of an extremely large dog, standing two and a half feet tall, and is three feet long. Video footage of the Big Dog shows it walking around and being kicked by people as they attempt to throw it off balance and knock it over, but it doesn't appear to lose its footing, and quickly recovers and keeps on walking. The robot is said to be able to carry more than 300 pounds of equipment over 10 miles before refueling, and can walk on rough terrain and up inclines of 35 degrees. Boston Dynamics is funded by the Tactical Technology Office at DARPA.[313]

The designers' goal is to enhance the Big Dog to the point where it can carry supplies for soldiers and follow them practically anywhere on the battlefield, on any terrain. It is highly probably that future versions will also be armed and walk on two legs instead of four.

Killer Wasp Robots

When most people think of a killer robot, they think of a large tank-like machine, or a humanoid-looking robot the size of a person similar to the ones in films like *The Terminator* (1984), *Short Circuit* (1986), or *iRobot* (2004); but in 2008, the Air Force Research Laboratory decided to build tiny radio controlled drones the size of large insects that could actually kill what they called, "high-value targets." The program is called Project Anubis, named after the jackal-headed god of the dead in Egyptian mythology, and is classified, but budget documents reveal that Air Force engineers were successful in developing a "Micro-Air Vehicle (MAV) with innovative seeker/tracking sensor algorithms that can engage maneuvering high-value targets."[314]

These devices are miniature versions of what are called Unmanned Arial Vehicles (UAVs) which refers to aircraft like the popular Predator drones that everyone has heard about in the news. The Predator drones are armed and can launch missiles, and the new Anubis micro drones are also deadly even though they are the size of a large bug. Special Forces have already been using a

---

[313] http://www.bostondynamics.com/robot_bigdog.html

[314] *Wired.com* "Air Force Completes Killer Micro-Drone Project" by David Hambling (January 5, 2010)

larger type of wasp drone made by AeroVironment that weighs less than a pound and can fly three miles away from its operator.

The Air Force's 2008 budget described Project Anubis as "a small UAV [Unmanned Aerial Vehicle] that carries sensors, data links, and a munitions payload to engage time-sensitive fleeting targets in complex environments."[315] The total cost was expected to be $500,000. This was apparently before the devices had been built because a newer budget mentioned Project Anubis as having already been completed, costing $1.75 million dollars.

The tiny drones are believed to be equipped with video cameras and microphones and even small explosives weighing a fraction of a pound, and either drop the explosive device, or the drone itself explodes once it reaches its intended target. Such a tiny drone can easily fly into a building through open doorways or windows and then be detonated once inside.

In the "Big Brother" episode of *Conspiracy Theory* with Jesse Ventura that aired on the TruTV network beginning in December 2009, Ventura interviewed an engineer named Elwood Norris who builds spy systems for the government and explained that they can fly miniature GPS tracking devices, designed to look like a fly with microphones on them, into a person's vehicle (or house) so they can then be monitored without their knowledge.

These tiny bugs give the saying "to be a fly on the wall" a whole new literal meaning, since the "fly" on the wall really may be listening. To give you an idea of how this technology is abused, and how it will be abused even more in the future, all we need to do is turn to the news.

---

[315] Ibid

At a town hall in Charlotte, Vermont, workers renovating the building discovered two electronic bugs that had been planted in the clerk's office, allowing whoever put them there to listen in on meetings and clerk business.[316] The devices were discovered in October 2010, but their batteries had long been dead and were about 10 years old, meaning they were hidden in the town hall building around the year 2000. They were battery powered wireless transmitters that police said could have transmitted to the immediate surrounding area to wherever the person with the receiver was hanging out listening in. The local police said it was a cold case and couldn't even guess who would have planted the bugs or what their motive was.[317]

If someone went through this much trouble to listen in on what was being discussed in some small town hall in Charlotte, Vermont—imagine what kinds of measures are taken to spy on members of Congress, or political activists deemed a threat to the establishment. In the Orwellian nightmare, you can rarely be certain that what comes out of your mouth isn't being overheard and analyzed by Big Brother.

Robots that Feed on Human Flesh

When we think of the power source for a robot, we most often think of them as being battery powered, or even solar powered, but the Pentagon has reportedly been working on one that would run off biomass. The robot is called EATR (pronounced "eater"), which stands for Energetically Autonomous Tactical Robot, and was

---

[316] *Burlington Free Press* "Who would want to bug Charlotte's Town Offices?" by Joel Banner Baird (December 22, 2010)
[317] Ibid.

designed by Robotic Technology Incorporated which says on its website that their robot, "can find, ingest, and extract energy from biomass in the environment (and other organically-based energy sources), as well as use conventional and alternative fuels (such as gasoline, heavy fuel, kerosene, diesel, propane, coal, cooking oil, and solar) when suitable."[318]

Original reports, including one on FoxNews.com, said that the EATR robot would eat animals and even human remains in the battlefield. Dr. Bob Finkelstein, president of Robotic Technology Incorporated (RTI) then released a statement saying that the robot would only be programmed to eat specific kinds of fuel sources. "If it's not on the menu, it's not going to eat it," Finkelstein said. "There are certain signatures from different kinds of materials that would distinguish vegetative biomass from other material."[319]

The company continued to do damage control concerning the initial reports and sent out a press release saying, "Despite the far-reaching reports that this includes human bodies, the public can be assured that the engine Cyclone (Cyclone Power Technologies Inc.) has developed to power the EATR runs on fuel no scarier than twigs, grass clippings and wood chips—small, plant-based items for which RTI's robotic technology is designed to forage."

Cyclone Power Technologies, located in Pompano Beach, Florida created what they call the Waste Heat Engine, which powers the EATR robots, by burning biomass in an external combustion chamber which then generates electricity from heating up water in a closed

---

[318] http://www.RoboticTechnologyInc.com
[319] *FoxNews.com* "Biomass-Eating Military Robot Is a Vegetarian, Company Says" (July 16, 2009)

loop. The designers say that because it would never need to be plugged in somewhere to recharge, the robots could roam on their own for months or years without having to be recharged.

As far as the claims that the EATR robot would not run on dead bodies, the manufacturer didn't deny that this was possible; they just denied this would happen because the robots wouldn't be programmed to do so. Of course in extreme circumstances, such as a major war, this programming could easily be changed.

Electro Magnetic Pulse (EMP)

One possible catastrophic danger of our reliance on modern technology comes from an Electro Magnetic Pulse bomb, or an EMP. This type of weapon sends out a wave of electromagnetic energy that literally destroys every electronic circuit in its path, which can be a few city blocks, a radius of several miles, or even several states.

A nuclear bomb sends out an EMP, and if detonated in the air high above the United States, one could destroy electric devices in a large part of the country, but there are also non-nuclear EMP weapons, and some are small enough to be carried around in a briefcase or back pack. If a non-nuclear EMP was set off in the heart of a major city, for example, everyone's cell phones, laptops, and vehicles will all immediately stop working and be permanently disabled. Street lights, traffic controllers at the airport, police radios, medical equipment at hospitals, and more, would all be completely destroyed without any visible signs of damage. The EMP would basically disable or destroy countless electrical components that we have taken for granted for decades and would practically knock us back to the stone age.

Non-nuclear EMPs are not a theoretical weapon; they

have been built, and although not widely reported in the news, have been used. *CBS News* reported that an EMP bomb was used to disable TV stations in Iraq at the start of the invasion in 2003 and to disable a major power plant in Baghdad.[320] Some reports also say the US used EMPs in the 1991 Gulf War as well.[321] [322]

EMP bombs are not something that only an advanced military can create. An article published in 1996 by a defense analyst named Carlo Kopp, explained that materials to build a non-nuclear electromagnetic weapon are commonly available and concluded, "The threat of electromagnetic bomb proliferation is very real."[323] In 2009, a director at the International Institute for Counter-Terrorism admitted that homemade electromagnetic bombs could become a significant threat.[324]

In the future, small EMP guns will likely be carried by law enforcement and the military which will use them to disable vehicles being used by suspects they are in pursuit of.

LRAD Sound Weapons

A non-lethal weapon that has become popular at protests and demonstrations is the LRAD sound cannon that focuses an ear-piercing high pitched sound at targets in order to cause them such discomfort that they disperse.

---

[320] DefenseTech.org "E-Bomb Explained"

[321] *CBS News* "U.S. Drops 'E-Bomb' On Iraqi TV, First Known Use Of Experimental Weapon" Joel Roberts (March 25, 2003)

[322] *GlobalSecurity.org* "High-power microwave (HPM) / E-Bomb" by John Pike (April 27, 2005)

[323] Department of Computer Science - Monash University "The Electromagnetic Bomb - a Weapon of Electrical Mass Destruction" by Carlo Kopp

[324] *New Scientist* "Aircraft could be brought down by DIY 'E-bombs'" by Paul Marks (April 1, 2009) pp. 16-17

LRAD stands for Long Range Acoustic Device and was developed by a San Diego company called American Technology Corporation.

The small device is often mounted on police or military vehicles and can emit sounds capable of dispersing crowds from up to 300 yards away. The volume control is variable and can range from mildly annoying, to beyond a person's threshold for pain (120-140 dB) which can cause permanent hearing damage at close range.

Smaller, handheld devices will be on the market in the coming years that will be the size of a large flashlight and may be standard equipment carried by police officers or built into Unmanned Ariel Vehicles or other robots.

MEDUSA

Unlike the LRAD acoustical weapon that focuses high volume sound waves at people to cause pain in their ears, a more advanced device called MEDUSA (Mob Excess Deterrent Using Silent Audio) uses microwave pulses that bypass the ears and eardrum and cause noise and pain inside a person's skull.[325] It's interesting that the device's name is *Medusa*, the same as the Greek mythology character that has snakes for hair and turns people to stone if they look at her. The MEDUSA microwave device was created by the Sierra Nevada Corporation for crowd control.

Some people worry that devices like the MEDUSA and others can be used to torture people without leaving external and noticeable evidence of the torture, or that they will be abused by police and military on peaceful protesters.

---

[325] *Gizmag.com* "MEDUSA: Microwave crowd-control raygun" (July 18, 2008) by Loz Blain

Active Denial System

A real life "pain ray" called the Active Denial System literally shoots a microwave beam at people, causing them to feel like their skin is burning.[326] Some believe the device can also disrupt a person's bowels and cause them to literally crap their pants, although this is disputed. The first versions of the Active Denial System were fairly large and had to be mounted on vehicles, but the manufacturer, Raytheon, is working on small portable units that can be easily carried around or mounted on rifles. Raytheon is one of the largest defense contractors that builds weapons for the military, and is the world's biggest producer of guided missile systems.

The Active Denial Systems use a gyrotron to generate powerful magnetic fields called millimeter waves, which are focused at the target and can cause second or third degree burns. Some of the systems were shipped to Afghanistan in 2010, but the military claimed they weren't being used, and were only there "for testing." Of course, shipping a huge unit like that half way around the world only to "test" it doesn't make any sense, since this has been done since at least 2004.[327] Due to the controversy surrounding the weapons it's not surprising the military denies they have been used in battle yet.

"Death Rays"

A retired Colonel from Taiwan's National Defense

---

[326] *Wired.com* "U.S. Testing Pain Ray in Afghanistan" (June 19, 2010) by Noah Shachtman
[327] *Boston Globe* "Ray gun, sci-fi staple, meets reality" (September 24, 2004) by Ross Kerber

Department named Alan Yu learned of deadly Orwellian weapons from working on Taiwan's military budget and having access to classified documents. In a 1997 article he wrote titled, *Millimeter Waves and Mind Control,* he discussed how portable handheld devices were being made that could kill people by using radio waves and leave no evidence.

He wrote, "corrupted undercover career operators can murder anyone as if by natural death (such as induce heart attack, heart failure, or kidney failure, etc.) with the invisible wave weapon. These undercover career operators have been trained professionally in manipulating people's lives and health with their invisible wave weapon. Some recruited young undercover operators will be trained with the murder skill from the senior undercover operators."[328]

His article continues, "For example, in 1995, a former head of Taiwan's National Security Institute died of a 'heart-attack' in a public bath pool in Taipei. This death occurred two days after he announced that he would write a memoir. His widow claimed that her husband has never had any heart problems in his life (supported by his health record history) and requested an autopsy to be performed in order to determine the true cause of his death."[329]

Colonel Yo believes the man was killed to avoid him from discussing state secrets. All that is needed to create a "death ray" is to turn up the power on the Active Denial System, which could easily cause a heart attack, brain aneurism, or organ failure. The HPEM Active Denial System, for example, is used to disable vehicles by

---

[328] *News Post* "Millimeter Waves and Mind Control" by Alan Yu (March 1997)
[329] Ibid

destroying all unshielded electronics, and microwave guns have sent several people to the hospital for injuries during testing.[330]

---

[330] *Wired.com* "Pain Ray Injures Airman" (April 6, 2007) By Noah Shachtman

Artificial Intelligence

Instead of humans being the eyes, ears, and brains behind Big Brother, what if Big Brother became an intelligent being itself? For decades some people have looked forward to (or feared) the day when scientists could create a computer system that would be considered artificially intelligent and would be as intelligent as a human, or even more so. While many scientists have been making tremendous advances towards such a system, others still scoff at the idea saying such a system would be too complex and require too much computing power. Others still cite the free will of human beings, and say that no computer could come close to the intelligence of a human because we have free will, and machines only carry out a specified program.

While this may be true, many of these AI skeptics overlook the idea that animals are intelligent, but are often denied to have a free will in the same manor that humans do. If animals do not have free will, then no matter how intelligent they seem to be, they are simply a biological computer following a program that is hardwired into their brains. Yet, as pet owners can attest, animals of an array of species convey a variety of emotions, from love and fear to anger and loneliness. So is a dog simply following a mental program that it is designed to follow that dictates its behavior, or is it intelligent? Most would agree that dogs are intelligent (to some extent, at least). If animals are intelligent, and they are just following a program hardwired into their brains, then wouldn't it be possible to design a computer system that can simulate (and surpass) this intelligence?

If you were born before 1980, then you remember a

time before telephone systems had voice recognition capabilities and you had to either wait to speak to an operator for them to transfer your call to the appropriate department, or use the automated feature by pressing the assigned number to reach your desired party. Slowly these systems were replaced with more advanced technology that understands your voice commands, and the recording simply asks you what department you need, and the system understands what you say and automatically transfers your call. While this is certainly an incredible task, can this system be considered intelligent?

Is the system that Google and other search engines use to determine what kinds of advertisements to display to you based on your search history an "intelligent" system? Are the characters you fight in a videogame considered intelligent? How exactly does one define an artificially intelligent system, and what are the social, scientific, and legal ramifications if and when a computer system is considered artificially intelligent, or even a conscious being? The most popular method used to test whether or not a computer program is artificially intelligent is called the Turing Test.

The Turing Test

The Turing test was created in 1950 by Alan Turing, a British computer scientist, in order to challenge a human judge to decide whether they were communicating with a computer, or with another human. The test consists of a person (the judge) engaging in a dialog through typing, with a computer program (or at least what may be a computer program). The judge is not told whether they are typing to a computer program or an actual person. If the judge can't determine whether they are having a dialog with a computer program or another person, then the system is said to have a human-level intelligence.

In his 2005 book, *The Singularity is Near*, the respected futurist Ray Kurzweil wrote that he expected computers to have intelligence levels indistinguishable from humans by the end of the 2020s. Kurzweil insists that, "The machines will convince us that they are conscious, that they have their own agenda worthy of our respect. We will come to believe that they are conscious much as we believe that of each other."[331]

Obviously technology has advanced at unthinkable levels since the Turing Test was invented back in 1950, and researchers have been monitoring this rapid advancement each year and anticipating (or fearing) artificial intelligence.

Moore's Law

Moore's Law is a term that describes the growth patterns in computing power as processors get faster and memory capacity increases. The law is credited to Gordon E. Moore, the cofounder of Intel, who in 1965 published a paper observing that the number of transistors able to fit on an integrated circuit was doubling approximately every two years. This trend has continued for over forty-five years, and some experts do not expect it to stop until around 2020 or later.

Moore's Law seems to accurately describe the increasing processing speed of computers each year, as well as their memory capacity, and even the number and size of pixels in digital cameras, which are all increasing near exponential rates. These incredible advances have enabled the communication age and a technological

---

[331] Kurzweil, Ray - *The Age of Spiritual Machines* page 63

revolution after computers transformed from large units that filled entire rooms, into hand-held cell phones that contain more computing power than the first space shuttle that reached the moon in 1969.

The amazing advances seem to be rapidly increasing in accordance with Moore's Law, which leads many computer scientists to forecast that at some point in the coming decades we will see artificially intelligent systems arrive that are much smarter than humans. These anticipated advances have alarmed some experts, causing them to worry that such systems may actually pose a threat to the human race.

Isaac Asimov's Three Laws of Robotics

A popular science fiction writer from the 1940s named Isaac Asimov wrote about advanced intelligent robots in his stories and came up with what he called the three laws of robotics, which he envisioned were necessary to prevent advanced robots from turning against their makers. When Asimov came up with these "laws" they were purely science fiction, but today some scientists are seriously looking at his ideas and are using the three laws as a blueprint hoping to prevent intelligent robots from posing a danger to humans. The three laws follow:

1) A robot may not injure a human being or, through inaction, allow a human being to come to harm.

2) A robot must obey orders given it by human beings except where such orders would conflict with the First Law.

3) A robot must protect its own existence as long as such protection does not conflict with the First or Second Law.

In 2007, computer and robotic experts in South Korea and Japan started drawing up plans for programming moral codes in artificially intelligent robots. An engineer at the South Korean Industry Ministry said, "Robots are becoming more and more intelligent every year to the point where they are virtually thinking for themselves. For this reason we need a code of ethics which all robot manufacturers must build into their machines. The starting point for these ethics should be Isaac Asimov's three laws."[332]

As robots become more intelligent and autonomous, some experts fear that it will become harder to decide who is responsible if and when they injure or kill someone. They ponder whether the designer will be to blame, the user, or even the robot itself. Experts have even discussed whether robots would one day be granted certain civil rights.

A 2007 report from the *BBC* discussed whether robots would one day actually be allowed to own property and foresaw that in the future, legislation would need to be introduced to prevent people from abusing robots. "These questions might sound far-fetched, but debates over animal rights would have seemed equally far-fetched to many people just a few decades ago. Now, however, such questions are part of mainstream public debate," said the article.[333]

Machines Getting Smarter Every Day

Not too long ago in the past, it was considered

---

[332] *Daily Mail* "Robots to be programmed with 'code of morals' so they won't attack humans" (March 7, 2007)
[333] *BBC News* "The ethical dilemmas of robotics" (March 9, 2007)

science fiction to speculate that machines would one day become more intelligent than humans, but as computing power continued to multiply exponentially in the twenty-first century, such claims were starting to come from very well respected scientists and engineers. One of the most popular of these futurists is Ray Kurzweil, who says, "I've made the case that we will have both the hardware and the software to achieve human level artificial intelligence with the broad suppleness of human intelligence including our emotional intelligence by 2029."[334]

Kurzweil is also a transhumanist, and in a 2008 interview with the *BBC*, he said that soon, "We'll have intelligent nanobots go into our brains through the capillaries and interact directly with our biological neurons." These nanobots would, "make us smarter, remember things better and automatically go into full emergent virtual reality environments through the nervous system."[335]

Kurzweil was interviewed at the American Association for the Advancement of Science in Boston, Massachusetts where he and 18 other influential thinkers were chosen to identify the greatest technological challenges facing humanity in the 21st century. Other attendees were Larry Page, founder of Google, and Dr. Craig Venter from the human genome project. Several of the goals the group came up with were to: reverse engineer the brain, secure cyberspace, enhance virtual reality, advance health information, engineer better medicines, and advance personalized learning.

While in the twenty-first century it may be easy to

---

[334] *BBC News* "Machines 'to match man by 2029'" (February 16, 2008) by Helen Briggs
[335] Ibid

see what lies ahead regarding intelligent systems and robotics, it's interesting to note that in a 1968 *Playboy* magazine article, Arthur C. Clark wrote, "In a very few generations—computer generations—which by this time may last only a few months—there will be a mental explosion; the merely intelligent machine will swiftly give away to the ultra-intelligence machine."

Arthur C. Clark is most well known for writing *2001 A Space Odyssey*, where HAL, an artificially intelligent system, begins killing humans on board a space ship in order to prevent them from interfering with its programmed objectives.

It seems that artificial intelligence technology is actually catching up with the science fiction imaginations of the past.

Computer to Play 'Jeopardy!'

IBM designed a computer program to compete against human *Jeopardy!* contestants with hopes of advancing artificial intelligence technology.[336] As many know, IBM had previously developed a program capable of playing chess called Deep Blue which then beat the world champion Garry Kasparov in 1997.

The ability of Deep Blue to play chess is seen as simple compared to designing a program to play a complicated game like *Jeopardy!* because of the wide variety of questions that could be asked. Of course, if the system, called "Watson" after the founder of IBM, Thomas Watson, was connected to the Internet, it would probably easily win since it could scour the Internet for the answers, but for this challenge it will not have access

---

[336] *New York Times* "Computer Program to Take On 'Jeopardy!'" (April 26, 2009) by John Markoff

to the web.

For the project, IBM is looking to develop a new kind of software that can understand human questions and then answer them correctly. "The big goal is to get computers to be able to converse in human terms," said the team leader, David A. Ferrucci, an IBM artificial intelligence researcher.

The Watson program will answer questions with a synthesized voice and will be run on a Blue Gene supercomputer which IBM will move to Los Angeles where the game show is located. The show's producers are considering getting Ken Jennings, a contestant who won a record 74 days in a row and 2.5 million dollars in 2004 to play against Watson.

Artificial Brains

In 2009, scientists in Switzerland claimed that they would be able to create a fully-functioning replica of a human brain by the year 2020. They call it the Blue Brain project, and is headed up by Henry Markram who is the director of the Swiss based Center for Neuroscience & Technology and the Brain Mind Institute. Markram had been working to reverse engineer the human brain for years and claimed that he would be able to accomplish this around the year 2020.[337]

There are other teams working on building electronic brains using large computer mainframes. For example, a team at IBM's Almaden Research Lab at Nevada University used a BlueGene/L Supercomputer to model a mouse brain which consists of about eight million neurons. The first version of the BlueGene computer runs

---

[337] *BBC News* "Artificial brain '10 years away'" (July 22, 2009) by Jonathan Fildes

about one tenth as fast as an actual mouse's brain, a rate that will undoubtedly rapidly increase with advancing technology.

In a talk in 2008 titled "Crossing the Chasm Between Humans and Machines: the Next 40 Years," Justin Rattner, Intel's chief technology officer, spoke seriously on the subject of machines becoming as smart as people. "The industry has taken much greater strides than anyone ever imagined 40 years ago," he said, and admitted that, "machines could even overtake humans in their ability to reason in the not-so-distant future."[338]

Rodney Brooks, a robot designer at the Massachusetts Institute of Technology (MIT) confirmed, "One day we will create a human-level artificial intelligence." Paul Saffo, a technology forecaster at Stanford University said, "Eventually, we're going to reach the point where everybody's going to say, 'Of course machines are smarter than we are.'"

Saffo also made comments showing the dark danger of creating such things. "The truly interesting question is what happens after if we have truly intelligent robots. If we're very lucky, they'll treat us as pets. If not, they'll treat us as food."

While Ray Kurzweil believes, (and hopes) that computers will match and surpass human level intelligence by the year 2029, Intel's Justin Rattner thinks it won't be until at least 2050, and of course others say it will be even longer.

As incredible advances in computers continue, some scientists are understandably getting worried about the implications of computers surpassing human-level intelligence. Some are debating whether there should be

---

[338] *McClatchy Newspapers* "Robots are gaining on us humans" (April 20, 2009) by Robert S. Boyd

restrictions placed on the kinds of research that could lead to a loss of control once intelligent systems are created.

Scientists who met at the Asilomar Conference Grounds on Monterey Bay in California in 2009 largely downplayed the possibility of computers becoming smarter than man or an artificial intelligence system developing from the Internet, but did acknowledge some of the dangers advancing technology had.

The meeting was organized by Dr. Eric Horvitz, the president of the Association for the Advancement of Artificial Intelligence, who also works for Microsoft. The location of the conference was purposefully chosen in an attempt to parallel a meeting in 1975 at the same location where leading biologists met to discuss mixing DNA and other genetic material between different organisms and species. Such technology raised serious ethical questions and the 1975 conference helped to set guidelines for DNA research and experiments.

Dr. Horvitz said, "My sense was that sooner or later we would have to make some sort of statement or assessment, given the rising voice of the technorati and people very concerned about the rise of intelligent machines."

The Association for the Advancement of Artificial Intelligence (A.A.A.I.) decided to draft a report that would assess the possibility of "the loss of human control of computer-based intelligences," as well as the ethical, legal, and socioeconomic issues that are connected to such intelligences arising. Dr. Horvitz said sensitive or potentially dangerous technology and research should be contained in highly secure laboratories as a precaution.

Some scientists, however, were only made more uncomfortable by the meeting after learning about the emerging artificial intelligent systems and their likely implications on the world. Tom Mitchell, a professor of artificial intelligence at Carnegie Mellon University, said, "I went in very optimistic about the future of A.I. and thinking that Bill Joy and Ray Kurzweil were far off in their predictions," but that, "The meeting made me want to be more outspoken about these issues and in particular be outspoken about the vast amounts of data collected about our personal lives."

Technological Singularity

The "technological singularity," sometimes simply called "the singularity" refers to a theoretical time in the future when an artificial intelligence is created that is able to learn and advance technology at a faster pace than humans are able to comprehend. According to this idea, once machines exceed human intelligence, they will improve their own designs and functions in complex ways that are too difficult for humans to understand.

The term, "the singularity" is credited to Vernor Vinge who is a retired mathematics professor at San Diego State University and a science fiction writer, who in 1993 wrote about such an event possibly happening in the future, and coined the term. In his paper titled, *The Coming Technological Singularity,* he wrote, "Within thirty years, we will have the technological means to create superhuman intelligence. Shortly after, the human era will be ended."

The idea of an "intelligence explosion" by intelligent machines that would design even more intelligent machines was also proposed by a mathematician in 1965 named I. J. Good. In more recent times, many other prominent professionals and experts have spoken about such events.

Bill Joy, the founder of Sun Microsystems, a popular computer chip manufacturer, warned of such an event in an article published in a 2000 edition of *Wired Magazine* titled "Why the Future Doesn't Need Us."

He wrote, "From the moment I became involved in the creation of new technologies, their ethical dimensions have concerned me, but it was only in the autumn of 1998 that I became anxiously aware of how great are the dangers facing us in the 21st century."[339]

He continues, "I was also reminded of the Borg of *Star Trek,* a hive of partly biological, partly robotic creatures with a strong destructive streak. Borg-like disasters are a staple of science fiction, so why hadn't I been more concerned about such robotic dystopias earlier? Why weren't other people more concerned about these nightmarish scenarios?"

"By 2030, we are likely to be able to build machines, in quantity, a million times as powerful as the personal computers of today—sufficient to implement the dreams of Kurzweil and Moravec."

"Given the incredible power of these new technologies, shouldn't we be asking how we can best coexist with them? And if our own extinction is a likely, or even possible, outcome of our technological development, shouldn't we proceed with great caution?"

"How soon could such an intelligent robot be built? The coming advances in computing power seem to make it possible by 2030. And once an intelligent robot exists, it is only a small step to a robot species—to an intelligent robot that can make evolved copies of itself."

He goes on to say that we are rapidly approaching the point of no return with no plan, no control, and no breaks; and ponders, "Have we already gone too far down the path to alter course?"

---

[339] *Wired Magazine* "Why The Future Doesn't Need Us" (August 4, 2000) by Bill Joy

He also discusses his fears that self-replicating robots and nanotechnology could soon surprise us the way news of the first cloned animal did. He concludes by saying, "This crystallized for me my problem with Kurzweil's dream. A technological approach to Eternity—near immortality through robotics—may not be the most desirable utopia, and its pursuit brings clear dangers. Maybe we should rethink our utopian choices."

In 2008, an organization called Singularity University in Silicon Valley began offering courses to prepare a "cadre" to shape advancing technology and help society cope with the ramifications of what they see as the coming singularity.

Techno-Utopianism

Technological utopianism refers to the belief that scientific and technological advances will one day bring about a utopia where humans can live in luxury and enjoy an abundance of goods and services that are all built and maintained by robots and/or artificially intelligent systems.

Such an idea has been portrayed in science fiction books and films, as well as cartoons like the *Jetsons*. Proponents envision that in the future, things like cooking, cleaning, and manual labor will be done by robots, allowing people to have an abundance of free time to enjoy themselves with 3D entertainment, interactive video games, or other leisure activities or hobbies. It's difficult to reconcile these ideas because often people's jobs have been replaced by new technology, leaving them unemployed and with job skills that aren't needed anymore. Such displacements don't allow the individual to then live a comfortable life of luxury, but instead place tremendous stress on them as they scramble to find a new place in the job market to provide for their family and pay their bills. Techno-utopian dreamers somehow often overlook practical scenarios involving advancing technology.

If we look back at history to the industrial revolution, we can see that many people thought this would bring about a techno-utopia since manual labor could be reduced by advanced machinery, but instead, people were needed to design, build, operate, and maintain the new machines, and such developments didn't ease American's work load at all. Quite contrary, Americans are working longer hours now than in years past, and in the last few generations we have seen the need for both husband and wife to work in order to make ends meet.

In the 1990s when the Internet became widely popular and the dot-com craze started, techno-utopian dreams were revived once again. Many of the key players in the computer revolution were counter-culture figures such as Steve Jobs, founder of Apple Inc., who was a hippie who smoked pot and used LSD, but later grew into a suite-wearing businessman.

While computers and the Internet have changed the world and our culture in vast ways, are people working less and retiring earlier? No. Sure, there are exceptions such as people who created a business model and developed it into a successful money making operation and became wealthy in a short period of time, but these are the rare exceptions. It seems that jobs and careers are similar to energy, in that they simply change form and cause people to scramble to learn new skills as their positions are eliminated.

As you know, the dot-com bubble burst after the rampant speculation of permanent prosperity and instant millionaires came crashing down to reality. The belief in techno-utopianism may at times gain a tremendous following of people who can cite all kinds of reasons and evidence for why it will soon occur, but they will inevitably be disappointed when reality sets in.

Techno-utopian dreamers believe that technological growth will lead to the end of economic scarcity, and that this will then eliminate every major social evil such as crime. What they overlook is the fact that some people steal for the thrill of it, and some people kill out of rage, and some people like to gain and abuse power just for the sake of power.

Zeitgeist the Movie

A popular set of films on the Internet is *Zeitgeist the Movie*, and its sequel *Zeitgeist: Addendum* which were produced by a man using a possible pseudonym of "Peter Joseph." The films attempt to expose the New World Order, the 9/11 attacks, and the Federal Reserve banking system, while simultaneously attacking Christianity and claiming that Jesus never existed. For the sake of this analysis, we will focus primarily on the techno-utopia described in the sequel, *Zeitgeist: Addendum.* A thorough analysis of the other aspects of the films can be found in my book, *The Illuminati: Facts & Fiction.*

In October of 2008, *Zeitgeist* part 2, or the *Addendum,* was released as an Internet film and began with a discussion about the private Federal Reserve banking system and its implications on the economy and society, but then took a turn into the bizarre. A large part of *Zeitgeist Addendum* promotes the idea that civilization will not need money anymore after we design and build sophisticated robots and mechanical systems to perform most of the tasks that humans now have to accomplish. The producer, "Peter Joseph," and the proponents of what is called the Venus Project, envision a techno-utopian society where machines will do all the work for us, and people will then be able to spend their time enjoying themselves and living in luxury. The film pushes the idea that these advanced machines will be able to create an abundance of everything we need, and can cook and clean and do all kinds of manual labor, so that people can then live like they're on a permanent vacation and explore their creative side.

Of course it seems as if the producer was high on marijuana when he wrote the script, and to any educated person the film seems like a pipe dream, but a lot of younger viewers fully support the techno-utopian ideas and believe the picture of the future painted in the film will soon be a reality.

Who wouldn't like a world where you wouldn't have to work? Seems like a great idea on the surface, until you actually look at the logistics of such an idea. Unfortunately the supporters of this film cannot grasp the reality of a medium of exchange, nor the value of rare artifacts or the need for human labor, and that even if sophisticated machines or robots are able to replace a fair amount of human labor, there will always be countless jobs that they will not be able to do: from teaching children, to various service oriented jobs or research and development. Such a techno-utopia has been the dream of many who envisioned microwave ovens, cell phones, and laptop computers as the tools which would free mankind from the burdens of work, but such inventions have only complicated the issue.

Since the *Zeitgeist* series is blatantly anti-religion, particularly anti-Christianity, many of the Zeitgeist supporters attack anyone who addresses the fallacies in the film often saying critics must be brainwashed from religion and too old fashioned to change with the times.

Aside from his attacks on Christianity in his first

film, "Peter Joseph" is also anti-Second Amendment and said that in his vision of the future, people wouldn't need to own guns anymore since there would be no crime. In an interview, when he was asked about people who didn't want to go along and participate in his supposed utopian New World Order, he basically said the people would need to be re-educated.[340]

Peter Joseph seems to have attempted to establish himself as some sort of cult leader by promoting what he calls the Zeitgeist Movement, which is seen as a group of activists who desire to change society into the kind envisioned in his films. In June 2010, the movement claimed to have over 400,000 members,[341] which consist of people who have signed up for an e-mail list.

Supporters of the so-called Zeitgeist Movement dream of a society with no money, no private property, mass automation of manual labor and tedious tasks, and artificial intelligent systems to make ethical judgments, perhaps replacing human judges and juries, which they claim are biased and not objective. While these ideas seem to be taken right out of a science fiction novel, or someone who lacks critical thinking skills, Peter Joseph seems to actually believe in them and has a fair number of supporters who agree with him. It is unclear exactly how these people will usher in their techno-utopia, but somehow they feel they deserve it.

On October 8, 2008, some supporters of the Zeitgeist Movement smashed several windows in a building at Oklahoma State University and spray painted "Zeitgeist Movement" on the pavement in some sort of attempt to "fight the system." It's extremely unlikely that the

---

[340] *The Alex Jones Show* (October 15, 2008) Interview with Peter Joseph
[341]
http://www.thezeitgeistmovement.com/joomla/index.php?Itemid=50

"Zeitgeist Movement" will formulate into an actual social movement or affect any kind of social changes whatsoever, but the *Zeitgeist* films show how appealing fanciful dreams of a techno-utopia are for people.

An Analysis of Ray Kurzweil's Predictions

I thought it would be beneficial to analyze the predictions of the respected futurist Ray Kurzweil, especially since one of his books, *The Age of Spiritual Machines*, was published in 1999, and contains his technological forecasts for the decades to come. At the time I'm writing this analysis, it is the year 2010, so we can look back at Kurzweil's predictions for the year 2009 that he made ten years earlier in order to see how they pan out. We will also look at his predictions for the future and discuss the likelihood of them being accurate. His book contains chapters on his vision of the future and what technology we will have in the years 2009, 2019, 2029, and 2099.

Kurzweil's Predictions For 2009

In 1999, Kurzweil looked ahead ten years and predicted that by 2009, "Personal computers are available in a wide range of sizes and shapes, and are commonly embedded in clothing and jewelry such as wristwatches, rings, earrings, and other body ornaments. Computers with high-resolution visual interfaces range from rings and pins and credit cards up to the size of a thin book."[342] Well, with the release of smart phones such as the Black Berry and the iPhone, one could argue that computers do come in all shapes and sizes, but as far as his prediction of

---

[342] Kurzweil, Ray - *The Age of Spiritual Machines* page 189

them being "commonly" embedded in clothing and jewelry, this didn't happen.

He was more accurate, though, when he stated, "Computer displays have all the display quality of paper—high resolution, high contrast, large viewing angle, and no flicker. Books, magazines, and newspapers are now routinely read on displays that are the size of, well, small books."[343]

Amazon.com released their e-book reader, *Kindle*, in 2007, which was later followed by Barnes and Noble's *Nook*, and e-books could be read on iPhones and other smart phones as well. In April 2010, Apple Inc. released the iPad, which they advertised as an e-book reader among other things.

The iPad also sounds a lot like what he described here, where he said, "Students of all ages typically have a computer of their own, which is a thin table-like device weighing under a pound with a very high resolution display suitable for reading."[344] Most students in 2009 had laptop computers, and while they weighed more than a pound, they were certainly amazing creations that had wireless Internet access and could be used to watch videos or read e-books.

Back in 1999, Kurzweil also stated that in 2009, "Telephone communication is primarily wireless, and routinely includes high-resolution moving images,"[345] which, thanks to smart phones with video cameras and color screens, this is what we have. Many people now don't even have a "home phone" and only have their cell phones. He also predicted, "Computers routinely include moving picture image cameras and are able to reliably

---

[343] Kurzweil, Ray - *The Age of Spiritual Machines* page 190

[344] Kurzweil, Ray - *The Age of Spiritual Machines* page 191

[345] Kurzweil, Ray - *The Age of Spiritual Machines* page 193

identify their owners from their faces."[346] Well, he was right again, because all laptops come standard with a tiny camera and microphone built into them, and any laptop can be installed with facial recognition software used as a security measure to only allow the owner to use it. Tiny video cameras were also common in cell phones in 2009.

While we now take iTunes and downloadable mp3s for granted, in 1999 the music industry was running scared of people downloading their music on peer-to-peer networks like Napster. Kurzweil predicted by 2009 that, "Most purchases of books, musical 'albums,' video games, and other forms of software do not involve any physical object, so new business models for distributing these forms of information have emerged."[347]

While he may have been wrong by using the word "most," he was certainly correct that an extremely large number of people purchase software, videogames, and music from websites and instantly download them, instead of having to physically go to a store and buy them on a disk. Kurzweil also saw the future of On-Demand movies and services like Netflix, YouTube, and podcasts of popular radio shows, saying, "Users can instantly download books, magazines, newspapers, television, radio, movies, and other forms of software to their highly portable personal communication devices." [348]

Not surprisingly, Kurzweil also mentioned that privacy would become a major concern for people, and as you know, identity theft became a popular fear as we relied more and more on technology. "Privacy has emerged as a primary political issue. The virtually constant use of electronic communication technologies is

---

[346] Kurzweil, Ray - *The Age of Spiritual Machines* page 190
[347] Kurzweil, Ray - *The Age of Spiritual Machines* page 195
[348] Kurzweil, Ray - *The Age of Spiritual Machines* page 193

leaving a highly detailed trail of every person's every move," he said.[349]

It's also interesting to read that Kurzweil foresaw a large portion of the population would become politically neutralized, saying, "Although not politically popular, the underclass is politically neutralized through public assistance and the generally high level of affluence."[350]

Not all of his predictions for 2009 came true, however. One such prediction was concerning the economy, which he was embarrassingly wrong about when he said, "Despite occasional corrections, the ten years leading up to 2009 have seen continuous economic expansion and prosperity due to the dominance of the knowledge content of products and services. The greatest gains continue to be in the value of the stock market."[351] Now it is understandable that he is a technology expert, not an economist, so his failed economic forecasting shouldn't detract from his insight into technological advances.

Also, while he did foresee the use of unmanned flying drones to be used in wars, he believed that humans would be mostly far removed from the scene of battle, sadly, a prediction that was far from accurate with the fatalities and injuries to soldiers and innocent civilians in the wars in Iraq and Afghanistan. He did, however, envision small UAVs (Unmanned Arial Vehicles) the size of birds or smaller,[352] which did come true in 2009 and 2010, although such devices were still in their infancy.

---

[349] Kurzweil, Ray - *The Age of Spiritual Machines* page 195
[350] Kurzweil, Ray - *The Age of Spiritual Machines* page 196
[351] Kurzweil, Ray - *The Age of Spiritual Machines* page 194
[352] Kurzweil, Ray - *The Age of Spiritual Machines* page 197

Kurzweil's Predictions for 2019

Looking further ahead, he says by the year 2019 computers will be so small that they'll practically be invisible and that we will have displays built into our eye glasses and contact lenses which will replace old fashioned LCD monitors.

He insists that reverse engineering of the human brain will have inspired the architecture of machine-based neural networks and says a $4000 computer will have the same computing power as a human brain (20 million-billion calculations per second).

"Keyboards are rare, although they still exist. Most interactions with computing is through gestures using hands, fingers, and facial expressions and through two-way natural-language spoken communication. People communicate with computers the same way they would communicate with a human assistant, both verbally and through visual expression," he says.[353]

"Paper books and documents are rarely used or accessed....Most learning is accomplished using intelligent software-based simulated teachers. To the extent that teaching is done by human teachers, the human teachers are often not in the local vicinity of the student."[354]

He also says that people will be hooked up to virtual reality systems that can simulate pressure, temperature, textures, and moistness, and says that "sexual interactions with other human partners or simulated partners" will be the "preferred mode of interaction, even when a human partner is nearby."[355]

---

[353] Kurzweil, Ray - *The Age of Spiritual Machines* page 203
[354] Kurzweil, Ray - *The Age of Spiritual Machines* page 204
[355] Kurzweil, Ray - *The Age of Spiritual Machines* page 206

He goes on to say that people will begin having relationships with automated personalities, including automated lovers, and writes that "automated personalities are superior to humans in some ways, such as having very reliable memories, and if desired, predictable (and programmable) personalities."[356]

He forecasts that the military will widely use very small flying weapons, some the size of insects, a concept that the military has already budgeted for, and is working towards. **(See *Orwellian Weapons*)**

By 2019, Kurzweil believes that some reports will claim that computers have passed the Turing Test, but he insists that these systems will not meet all the criteria of an artificially intelligent system for a few more years.

"Public and private spaces are routinely monitored by machine intelligence to prevent interpersonal violence," he says, and "privacy continues to be a major political and social issue with each individual's practically every move stored in a database somewhere."[357]   It's interesting to read his forecast of "machine intelligence" that he says will prevent violence, because as you may recall from the chapter on surveillance cameras, in 2010 these systems were already in their early stages with pre-crime cameras that detect "hostile" speech based on the volume, speed, and pitch of conversations the microphones pick up.

He also writes that in this period of time the "human underclass" will continue to be an issue and that the difference between those "productively engaged" in the economy and those who aren't, will be complicated.

---

[356] Kurzweil, Ray - *The Age of Spiritual Machines* page 206
[357] Kurzweil, Ray - *The Age of Spiritual Machines* page 206-207

Kurzweil's Predictions for 2029

This is where his predictions start to get scary. Much of them sound like science fiction or fantasies coming from an over-active imagination, but Kurzweil is supposedly an expert, and was able to fairly accurately predict the kinds of technology that would be used in the year 2009 when he wrote his book ten years earlier. While some of these predictions for 2029 may seem fanciful, some of them are certainly extremely likely to occur.

Instead of people wearing a blue tooth piece on their ear to talk on their phone, Kurzweil believes that, "Cochlear implants, originally used just for the hearing impaired, are now ubiquitous. These implants provide auditory communication in both directions between the human user and the world wide computing network."[358] This is certainly believable, but what is even more disturbing is that he says similar devices will be implanted in our eyes.

"Displays are now implanted in the eyes, with a choice of permanent implants or removable implants (similar to contact lenses). Images are projected directly onto the retina providing the usual high-resolution three-dimensional overlay on the physical world."[359]

He also envisions neural interfaces will be as common as cell phones were in the beginning of the twenty-first century, saying, "neural implants based on machine intelligence are providing enhanced perceptual and cognitive functioning to humans. Defining what constitutes a human being is emerging as a significant legal and political issue. The rapidly growing capability

---

[358] Kurzweil, Ray - *The Age of Spiritual Machines* page 221
[359] Kurzweil, Ray - *The Age of Spiritual Machines* page 220

of machines is controversial, but there is no effective resistance to it."[360]

If this isn't unsettling enough, he also alludes to the fact that the majority of humans on earth will not even be needed anymore, and will be completely replaced by machines. "There is almost no human employment in production, agriculture, and transportation," he says.[361]

If there is no human employment in production, agriculture, or transportation, as Kurzweil predicts, then what kinds of jobs are those people going to have? What he doesn't mention is that elite politicians, environmentalists, and businessmen have a strong desire to massively reduce the world's population in order to (as they believe) preserve the earth's natural resources. Wealthy elitists like Ted Turner and Prince Philip have publicly stated their desire to reduce the population by several billion people. The elite's ideologies behind population reduction are discussed at length in my book, *The New World Order: Facts & Fiction.*

Kurzweil's Predictions for 2099

If you thought his predictions for the year 2029 were far-fetched, or just plain disturbing, what Kurzweil believes life will be like in 2099 is truly bizarre. "A software-based intelligence is able to manifest bodies at will: one or more virtual bodies at different levels of virtual reality and nanoengineered physical bodies using instantly reconfigurable nanobot swarms."[362] What he is saying, basically, is that billions of tiny nanorobots that all communicate with each other, will be able to work

---

[360] Kurzweil, Ray - *The Age of Spiritual Machines* page 222-223
[361] Kurzweil, Ray - *The Age of Spiritual Machines* page 222
[362] Kurzweil, Ray - *The Age of Spiritual Machines* page 234

together to assemble themselves in the shape of whatever they want, similar to the T-1000 Terminator robot from the Arnold Schwarzenegger movie *Terminator 2*.

He also says that computer systems will be completely artificially intelligent, and will even be smarter than the entire human race's intelligence combined.[363]

Humans, he says, will almost all have computers implanted in their brains and will all be cyborgs. "Even among those human intelligences still using carbon-based neurons, there is ubiquitous use of neural implant technology, which provides enormous augmentation of human perceptual and cognitive abilities. Humans who do not utilize such implants are unable to meaningfully participate in dialogues with those who do."[364]

Only time will tell just how accurate these predictions are. While his visions of the year 2009 were very accurate, this could be in part because much of the technology that became popular around that time was already in the works when he wrote his book in 1999. It's not that difficult to see how emerging technology will become commonplace in the near future, but extrapolating accurate predictions thirty years and one hundred years into the future are likely much more difficult. Depending on what year you are reading this book, you will be able to make a more accurate assessment of the timeline Kurzweil outlines in his writings.

Even if Kurzweil is dramatically wrong in his visions of future technology, the kinds of invasive and dehumanizing systems that will undoubtedly be created in the coming decades should be a cause for alarm, and precautions should be made today to ensure that we do

---

[363] Kurzweil, Ray - *The Age of Spiritual Machines* page 105
[364] Kurzweil, Ray - *The Age of Spiritual Machines* page 234

not become a mindless species of cyborgs, or the slaves of artificially intelligent robots.

Cybernetic Organisms

A cybernetic organism is a living creature that consists of both biological systems, as well as artificial systems, and is often seen as being a person or other organism that has enhanced abilities due to advanced technology. The term *cyborg* is often used as a shortened version of *cybernetic organism* and is a popular term used in science fiction to describe a creature that is part man, part machine. The term cyborg was coined in 1960 by Manfred Clynes and Nathan Kline in a paper where they outlined how cybernetic systems could be used to allow humans to "meet the requirements of extraterrestrial environments," as they traveled in space to other planets.[365]

Characters such as the Borg from *Star Trek*, and the *Six million Dollar Man* from the 1970s TV series are examples of popular cyborgs from science fiction, which is where most people believe is the only place that cyborgs are found. Quite surprising is the fact that cybernetic organisms are actually real, although they are not nearly advanced as the ones in the movies…yet.

As far back as 2004, a cybernetic brain was able to fly a flight simulator for an F-22 fighter jet.[366] This cyborg brain was built from 25,000 neurons extracted from a rat's brain which sits in a petri dish. The brain is still alive. Dr. Thomas DeMarse, professor of biomedical engineering at the University of Florida said, "It's essentially a dish with 60 electrodes arranged in a dish at

---

[365] "Cyborgs and Space" in *Astronautics* (September 1960) by Manfred E. Clynes and Nathan S. Kline
[366] *CNN.com* "Brain in dish flies flight simulator" (November 4, 2004)

the bottom, over that we put the living cortical neurons from rats, which rapidly begin to reconnect themselves, forming a living neural network—a brain."

An article on CNN.com in 2004 discussing the system mentioned that "living networks" could be used to fly actual unmanned aircraft in the future, and not just a flight simulator. This cyborg rat brain was reported to have "learned" to control the flight simulator. With the partial rat brain consisting of only 25,000 neurons, one can only imagine what could happen if and when complete brains, or the brains of larger animals are used. A dog's brain has 160 million neurons, for example, and a chimpanzee's has more than six billion.

A similar cyborg brain was created at the Georgia Institute of Technology which operates a small mechanical body instead of a flight simulator. The designers call it the Hybrot, meaning hybrid-robot, which also uses a portion of a rat's brain. The researchers are hoping that their creation will start to actually learn.

"Learning is often defined as a lasting change in behaviors, resulting from experience," said Steve Potter, the bio-medical engineer on the project. "In order for a cultured network to learn, it must be able to behave. By using multi-electrode arrays as a two-way interface to cultured mammalian cortical networks, we have given these networks an artificial body with which to behave," he said.[367]

In 2007 Charles Higgins, an associate professor at the University of Arizona, built a small robot that is controlled partially by the brain of a moth. Higgens attached electrodes to a part of the moth's brain that deals with sight, which then causes the robot to respond

---

[367] *Science Daily* "Georgia Tech Researchers Use Lab Cultures To Control Robotic Device" (Apr. 28, 2003)

depending on what the moth is seeing.

Higgens said in the future, "Most computers will have some kind of living component to them. In time, our knowledge of biology will get to a point where if your heart is failing, we won't wait for a donor. We'll just grow you one. We'll be able to do that with brains, too. If I could grow brains, I could really make computing efficient."[368]

Higgens insists that he would draw the line at using monkey or human brains for cybernetic creations, but mentioned that someday these new hybrid computers could become artificially intelligent. "Computers now are good at chess and Word and Excel, but they're not good at being flexible or interacting with other users. There may be some way to use biological computing to actually make our computers seem more intelligent," he said.

Monkey Equipped with Mechanical Arm

In 2003 scientists at Duke University's Medical Center in Durham, North Carolina attached a neural interface to a monkey's brain that allowed it to move a mechanical arm by using its thoughts. The monkey would just think about using its own arm, and its brain signals were intercepted by the neural interface and caused the mechanical arm to move the same way its own arm would have. The monkey was able to grab things and feed itself with the cybernetic arm.[369]

"It's quite plausible that the perception is you're extended into the robot arm, or the arm is an extension of

---

[368] *Computer World* "Scientist: 'Hybrid' computers will meld living brains with technology" (December 3, 2007) by Sharon Gaudin
[369] *Washington Post* "Monkeys Control Robotic Arm With Brain Implants" (October 13, 2003) by Rick Weiss

you," said the University of Washington's Eberhard E. Fetz, a pioneer in the field of brain-machine interfaces.

"It moves much like your own arm would move," said Dr Andrew Schwartz of Pittsburgh University. The scientists said they would soon upgrade the system so that the users could transmit their mental commands to machines wirelessly instead of having them physically wired into the brain.[370]

The monkeys used in the experiment had bundles of wires protruding from their head after they had holes drilled through their skulls to implant the interfaces into their brains. Miguel Nicolelis, the scientist in charge of the experiments, insisted the monkeys liked the experiment. "If anything, they're enjoying themselves playing these games. It enriches their lives," he said. "You don't have to do anything to get these guys into their chair. They go right there. That's play time."[371]

Man Tests Mechanical Hand

In Italy a man who lost his forearm in a car accident was equipped with a cybernetic arm in 2003, similar to the one that was tested on monkeys several years earlier. In this instance, the mechanical hand was just part of a test and was not a permanent thing.

Scientists implanted electrodes into the nerves at the end of the man's severed hand and connected them to the mechanical hand and he was able to wiggle the fingers and grab things. The project was called LifeHand. You may recall in one of the *Star Wars* films, the lead character, Luke Skywalker, had his hand cut off which

---

[370] *BBC News* "Brain-controlled 'robo-arm' hope" (February 18, 2005) by Michelle Roberts
[371] *Washington Post* "Monkeys Control Robotic Arm With Brain Implants" (October 13, 2003) by R. Weiss

was then replaced by a mechanical hand that he used throughout the rest of the trilogy.

After the surgery which implanted the electrodes in the patient's arm, he only took a few days to master the robotic hand. Scientists said the device was able to receive and obey 95% of the commands from the man's nervous system. "It felt almost the same as a real hand," said the patient.[372]

Paolo Maria Rossini, a neurologist who lead the procedure, said the patient "didn't have to learn to use muscles that do a different job to move a prosthesis, he just had to concentrate and send to the robotic hand the same messages he used to send to his own hand."[373]

Transhumanism

Transhumanism is a fringe belief system, some call it a movement, of people who are hoping or attempting to use technology to improve human beings mental and physical characteristics and abilities. Such technologies will lead to what supporters call "human enhancement." Some of the ideas brought forth by transhumanists are noble, such as helping the handicapped or curing disease, but many also dream of one day eliminating aging and even death and transforming ordinary humans into cyborgs that live forever. Most transhumanists are atheists.

The term *transhumanism* is symbolized by H+ and comes from the idea that humans can transform themselves into beings with dramatically improved abilities compared to what a natural born human has in

---

[372] *Associated Press* "Experts: Man controlled robotic hand with thoughts" (December, 2 2003) by Ariel David
[373] Ibid

regards to strength, mental capabilities, and communication. Much of the "enhancements" come from cybernetic devices like neural interfaces that will turn an ordinary person into a cyborg. The emergence of nanotechnology is looked at as a major primer that will jumpstart the transhumanist revolution. Nanotechnology refers to the manipulation or assembly of matter on an atomic scale, or structures between 1 and 100 nanometers in size. One nanometer is one billionth of a meter. Nanotechnology has a wide range of applications, mainly in electronics and medicine.

In 1986 a man named Eric Drexler published a book titled *Engines of Creation: The Coming Era of Nanotechnology,* which was one of the first to discuss the future possibilities of nanotechnology to dramatically extend the human lifespan and use nanorobots for various science fiction-like tasks.[374]

Ray Kurzweil believes that, "Nanobots launched into our bloodstreams could supplement our natural immune system and seek out and destroy pathogens, cancer cells, arterial plaque, and other agents....We will be able to reconstruct any or all of our bodily organs and systems, and do so at the cellular level."[375]

In her 1992 book *Science as Salvation,* Mary Midgley discussed transhumanist goals of achieving immortality and called their ideas quasi-scientific dreams and self-indulgent, uncontrolled power-fantasies driven by pseudoscientific speculation and the fear of death.[376]

---

[374] Drexler, Eric - *Engines of Creation: The Coming Era of Nanotechnology* (Bantam Doubleday Dell; 1st edition June 1986)
[375] Kurzweil, Ray - *The Age of Spiritual Machines* page 140
[376] Midgley, Mary – *Science as Salvation: A Modern Myth and its Meaning* (Gifford Lectures) (Routledge 1992)

A Closer Look at
Nineteen Eighty-Four

Let's now take a closer look at the story elements of *Nineteen Eighty-Four* and see how the novel reflects our current society in many ways, not just in terms of privacy-invading technology and the watchful eyes of Big Brother. The story of Winston Smith, the lead character, and the world in *Nineteen Eighty-Four* also involves very insightful elements describing the socioeconomic structure and the drastic differences in lifestyles between different segments of society. Orwell also highlighted a perpetual state of war and the propaganda that kept society supporting it. As you read through the novel, it is impossible not to notice numerous other parallels between the storyline and our actual reality. The book is one of the scariest instances of life imitating art, and critics of Big Brother will sometimes say that *Nineteen Eighty-Four* was not meant to be used as an instruction manual.

Social Structure

In the novel, the government consists of "the Party" which itself is made up of Inner members and Outer members, each with dramatically different privileges. The Inner members have access to luxuries such as real food and refreshments, and live in spacious and well-furnished homes, while the Outer members are given small food rations and live in dilapidated housing projects. A step below the Outer members on the socioeconomic scale are the Proles (or proletariats) who live in deplorable conditions like a third world country and are seen as immoral and out of control animals who are not given any of the "luxuries" of Party members.

Orwell explains, "Heavy physical work, the care of home and children, petty quarrels with neighbors, films, football, beer, and above all, gambling filled up the horizon of their minds. To keep them in control was not difficult...All that was required of them was a primitive patriotism which could be appealed to whenever it was necessary to make them accept longer working hours or shorter rations. And when they become discontented, as they sometimes did, their discontentment led nowhere, because being without general ideas, they could only focus it on petty specific grievances."[377]

A steady supply of "Victory Gin" provided by the government kept people mildly intoxicated, and contributed to their apathetic attitude. In the story, the political ideology is described as *Ingsoc*, which stands for English Socialism, and is the justification for the severe government control and regulation of goods and services. Even having children is regulated by the government and a couple must be approved before they start a family.

Life wasn't always so controlled and joyless. After what is called the Revolution, the Party gained power and created a society where each individual is reduced to nothing more than a worker, working for the sake of the Party, and under the constant supervision of Big Brother.

The population of the Proles was massive compared to Party members, and Orwell notes that if they would only realize the strength that they had in numbers, they could rise up and overthrow the Party and Big Brother in an instant.

"Why was it that they could never shout like that about anything that mattered?" Winston lamented after

---

[377] Orwell, George – *Nineteen Eighty-Four* page 63

hearing a group of people yelling in the streets over a petty quarrel. The reason for their poor living condition was their lack of education and their own ignorance. The Party did everything they could to prevent them from becoming enlightened.

"For if leisure and security were enjoyed by all alike, the great mass of human beings who are normally stupefied by poverty would become literate and would learn to think for themselves; and when once they had done this, they would sooner or later realize that the privileged minority had no function, and they would sweep it away. In the long run, a hierarchical society was only possible on a basis of poverty and ignorance."[378]

The Control of Information

George Orwell knew the power of propaganda, thus the Party controlled all information such as the newsreels shown on the telescreens, and the publishing of all newspapers and books. They even wrote the songs people would sing, created the games children played, and produced the entertainment people enjoyed.

"They [the citizens] could be made to accept the most flagrant violations of reality, because they never fully grasped the enormity of what was demanded of them, and were not sufficiently interested in public events to notice what was happening."[379]

In our society we have Operation Mockingbird which has manipulated the mainstream media since the 1950s and functions as a propaganda arm of the establishment, and a gate-keeper to contain important information, preventing it from reaching the public. Most people are

---

[378] Orwell, George – *Nineteen Eighty-Four* page 168-169
[379] Orwell, George – *Nineteen Eighty-Four* page 138

also distracted by entertainment news such as celebrity gossip and sports, which divert people's attention away from important issues and allows government corruption to run rampant.

A *memory hole* is another term coined by Orwell, and means the alteration or disappearance of inconvenient or embarrassing documents, photographs, transcripts, or other records, in a way that attempts to make it seem as though something never happened and the information never even existed. For example, if an embarrassing story is posted online after slipping past the editors but is later brought to their attention, sometimes they may change a headline, remove parts of the story, or just delete the entire story altogether in an attempt to contain certain information and prevent it from being known or spreading around. When this happens, the information is said to have disappeared down the memory hole.

In *Nineteen Eighty-Four* there is a scene where Winston Smith had to edit newspapers from the past (which was part of his job) and change the amount of chocolate rations that were allowed to each person per week. In reality, the amount decreased from 30 grams to 20 grams, but Smith had to make it seem like the ration had actually increased from 15 to 20. A visibly happy friend of Winston later passes him in a hallway and cheerfully says, "Did you hear they're going to increase the chocolate rations from 15 grams to 20 grams per week," and is so brainwashed by Big Brother that he doesn't realize the number had actually been reduced and not increased. All past documentation showing anything different had been removed from existence.

All information about a person who betrays Big Brother or the Party is also completely removed from all records, and that person becomes an "unperson" and is executed. It is made as if they never even existed. Near the end of the novel, the main antagonist, O'Brien, tells Winston, "Who controls the past controls the future. Who controls the present controls the past." Any information the Party didn't want people to have access to anymore simply disappeared into a memory hole (meaning it was destroyed) and was quickly forgotten about by everyone. With no physical evidence or record of a piece of information, there was no longer any way to verify whether a fact was true or not. The truth was what the Party said it was.

In a very ironic situation in 2009, Amazon.com deleted a large number of copies of *Nineteen Eighty-Four* from their Kindle electronic book readers. Customers had purchased e-book copies of *Nineteen Eighty-Four* which were then sent wirelessly to their Kindle reader, but after it was discovered that the publisher who listed that particular Kindle version for sale did not actually have the rights to the novel, the copies were deleted by Amazon from customer's own Kindle e-book readers, and disappeared into a memory hole.[380] Customers were not told what had happened, and the copy of the book simply vanished from their e-book reader because they are all wirelessly connected to Amazon.com and the company controls which files are stored on the Kindle unit.

Another one of countless incidences where important information disappears down a *memory hole* as a result of government intervention was with the case of the pulling of an episode of Jesse Ventura's television show, *Conspiracy Theory*. After the "Police State" episode first aired on Friday November 26th 2010, it was scheduled to be replayed the following week as a lead-in for the new episode, but it mysteriously never aired again.

---

[380] *New York Times* "Some E-Books Are More Equal Than Others" (July 17, 2009) by David Pogue

The episode's description was also pulled from TruTV's website, the cable channel airing program. It covered secretive FEMA prison camps and terrorist fusion centers which collect and data mine information to look for terrorists or anyone who may be a threat to the government's tyranny. The episode was pretty disturbing.

After websites and blogs started to buzz with speculation, it was then revealed by the show's producers that the U.S. government put pressure on the network to kill the episode from airing again, so they did.[381] The information in episodes of *Conspiracy Theory* is so powerful that the government doesn't want people watching it so they put pressure on the network to make one of the most damaging episodes disappear. People who recorded that episode on their DVRs at home then started reporting that the episode was missing from their DVR unit. Apparently the cable company had even removed the recorded episodes in an attempt to dump them down a memory hole.

Perpetual State of War

Society is stuck in a lengthy war with another superpower and the ongoing battle is used as an explanation for various food and supply shortages that people must endure. The telescreens announce victories on the battlefield that always bring the war "within measurable distance of its end," but it continues on, and on and society continues to support it.

While this war continues, the enemy superpower they are supposedly fighting keeps changing, and nobody seems to notice. First they are fighting Eastasia (and

---

[381] *Infowars.com* "Police State episode of hit Ventura show covering FEMA camps pulled from air" (December 3, 2010)

allies with Eurasia), but later they are said to be battling Eurasia, and allies with Eastasia, but nobody notices. It's kind of like the switch from fighting the "War on Terror" in Afghanistan starting in 2001, shortly after the 9/11 attacks, and later shifting to the War in Iraq in 2003 which then continued for many years.

Winston finds a girlfriend named Julia who feels the same way he does about the Party, society, and Big Brother, and the two discuss finding the Brotherhood, an underground and secret Resistance movement that is plotting to overthrow the Party and restore freedom. As they discuss finding the Brotherhood (called *The Resistance* in the film version) they begin unraveling the extent of the lies coming from the Party. When discussing the perpetual war, Julia remarks, "The rocket bombs which fell daily on London were probably fired by the government itself, just to keep people frightened."[382] It's stunning that Orwell included this reference to false flag terrorism in the storyline, a very real and ruthless strategy used by governments around the world throughout history. A false flag attack means a country (or group) attacks themselves and blames it on some other country or group in order to justify a massive military response that is seen as a retaliation for the (fraudulent) attack against them.

In the novel, Orwell also explains that the war Oceania is fighting isn't a real war, but that it is a fabrication that the ruling Party needs to continuously go on in order to destroy the fruits of society's labor, thus ensuring a continuous shortage of goods which maintains the social structure that the ruling elite has constructed.

The Party would print up "atrocity pamphlets" outlining the crimes allegedly committed by the enemy,

---

[382] Orwell, George – *Nineteen Eighty-Four* page 156

and distribute them to the citizens of Oceania so they could see how evil the enemy was that they were fighting and the horrors of war were constantly in their mind and reinforced the reason they had to work so hard for so little.

Winston comes to discover, "The essential act of war is destruction, not necessarily of human lives, but of the products of human labor. War is a way of shattering to pieces, or pouring into the stratosphere or sinking in the depths of the sea, materials which might otherwise be used to make the masses too comfortable, and hence, in the long run, too intelligent."[383]

"In the past, the ruling groups of all countries, although they might recognize their common interest and therefore limit the destructiveness of war, did fight against one another, and the victor always plundered the vanquished. In our own day they are not fighting against one another at all. The war is waged by each ruling group against its own subjects, and the object of the war is not to make or prevent conquests of territory, but to keep the structure of society intact."[384]

According to the novel, if society was not at war, and the goods they manufactured were put to use to improve the living conditions of everyone, then the ruling elite would lose their power because the wealth would be more evenly distributed. It is for this reason that the Inner Party continues their manufactured and fraudulent war, which then keeps them in control of the infrastructure and assets, and prevents everyone else from rising out of poverty.

---

[383] Orwell, George – *Nineteen Eighty-Four* page 169
[384] Orwell, George – *Nineteen Eighty-Four* page 177

The Personification of the Party

A man named Big Brother is supposedly the head of the Party, and his picture is plastered on walls in every building and on every street to constantly remind everyone that "Big Brother is watching you." There is actually no one named Big Brother, or at least not anymore, but the people didn't know this, or even consider it. He is a face attached to personify the Party and give it the appearance and feeling of being human. Orwell explains, "Big Brother is the guise in which the Party chooses to exhibit itself to the world. His function is to act as a focusing point for love, fear, and reverence, emotions which are more easily felt toward an individual than toward an organization."[385]

In reality, a similar method is used with the President of the United States (and the leaders of other countries as well). The president is believed by many to be the man in charge, and the most powerful man in the world, but he is simply a spokesman and puppet for the ones who are really running the show. When people are mad at the policies they must obey or conditions they find themselves and their country in, they point to the president and blame him, believing it's all his fault. This makes them feel better by having an individual to blame and focus their anger on. The president is a personification of the party, and even the entire country.

A similar personification has been used with Osama bin Laden in the War on Terror. For years the American government blamed this one man for all of the problems in the world, even though bin Laden had been dead since at least 2005. The myth of a living bin Laden has been perpetuated by the American establishment and an

---

[385] Orwell, George – *Nineteen Eighty-Four* page 213

occasional video tape or audio message is released to the public, supposedly of the man, but such video taped messages are always from old videos and contain typical "death to America" and "death to Israel" messages, and nothing new is ever discovered.

Experts highly doubt that "new" audio messages claimed to be from bin Laden are actually even him. In 2006, Bruce Lawrence, a professor at Duke University and an expert on Osama bin Laden, said he believed bin Laden was dead and that audio messages purported to be from him were in fact not, but for political reasons were claimed otherwise.[386]

The myth that Osama bin Laden remains alive and is directing his global terrorist organization, Al Qaeda, is a monumental lie that is continuously spread to the public to keep them in a state of fear, and is used as the reason for the War on Terror to continue.

Most of the ignorant public has been led to believe that this one man is responsible for every terrorist attack in the world, as if he is some untouchable mafia kingpin out of a comic book who personally orders every incident. He is the boogie man and the face of terrorism, and his myth has been kept alive to justify the ongoing "War on Terror." He should be called Osama Bin Elvis, because he never dies, and there are always reports of bin Laden sightings, similar to Elvis Presley sightings by people who believe Elvis faked his death and is still alive.

If you find my claims about Osama bin Laden and the War on Terror absurd, then you have a long way to go in your awakening process to undo the years of brainwashing and social conditioning you have been a victim of. As Orwell said, "It might very well be that

---

[386] *WTVD-TV ABC 11* "Duke Professor Skeptical of bin Laden Tape" (January 19, 2006) by Amber Rupinta

literally ever word in the history books, even the things that one accepted without question, was pure fantasy."[387]

Osama bin Laden is used to fulfill the same role that Emmanuel Goldstein plays in *Nineteen Eighty-Four*. Goldstein is the bad guy, and the ultimate evil. "All subsequent crimes against the Party, all treacheries, acts of sabotage, heresies, deviations, sprang directly out of his teaching. Somewhere or other he was still alive and hatching his conspiracies," Orwell wrote. [388]

Winston starts to see through the myth of Goldstein and at one point when a "new message" from Goldstein was aired on the telescreens attacking Big Brother and the Party, Smith called it, "an attack so exaggerated and perverse that a child should have been able to see through it."[389]

Julia also saw through the propaganda, saying, "The tales about Goldstein and his underground army, were simply a lot of rubbish which the Party had invented for its own purposes."[390]

Telescreens

A major component of Big Brother in *Nineteen Eighty-Four* are telescreens, which are television screens that can also see and hear what is in their immediate surroundings and are monitored by the Thought Police who make sure no one is saying anything bad about Big Brother or the Party. Telescreens are mounted in every home and also continuously communicate Party propaganda to society and cannot be turned off (accept by

---

[387] Orwell, George – *Nineteen Eighty-Four* page 66

[388] Orwell, George – *Nineteen Eighty-Four* page 10

[389] Orwell, George – *Nineteen Eighty-Four* page 11

[390] Orwell, George – *Nineteen Eighty-Four* page 135

Inner Party members, for a brief period of time). These telescreens watched and listened to every member of the Party, and nobody dares question their authority. Such an act would amount to Thought Crime and would cause one to be imprisoned and killed. The telescreens and microphones are continuously monitored and even facial expressions and body language can be understood by the Big Brother system. No one dares even whisper a word of disagreement or doubt about the Party or Big Brother.

"It was terribly dangerous to let your thoughts wonder when you were in any public place or within range of a telescreen. The smallest thing could give you away. A nervous tic, an unconscious look of anxiety, a habit of muttering to yourself—anything that carried with it the suggestion of abnormality, of having something to hide."[391]

As you've learned in *Big Brother: The Orwellian Nightmare Come True,* real life telescreens now exist, along with pre-crime cameras, facial recognition systems, store cameras that alert customer service if you loiter in an isle too long; cameras that allow bosses to watch, listen, and talk to their employees, and more. It's getting to the point that no matter where you are (even in a school bathroom) you may be within reach of the watchful eyes and ears of Big Brother.

Orwell wrote, "the telescreen received and transmitted simultaneously. Any sound that Winston made, above the level of a very low whisper, would be picked up by it, moreover, so long as he remained within the field of vision which the metal plaque commanded, he could be seen as well as heard...You had to live—did live, from habit that became instinct—in the assumption that every sound you made was overheard, and, except in

---

[391] Orwell, George – *Nineteen Eighty-Four* page 55

darkness, every movement scrutinized."[392]

When George Orwell wrote his book, computer technology was nonexistent. Color TV had not been invented yet, there were no microwave ovens, answering machines, VCRs, cassette players, or even eight-track players. In 1949, the most advanced technology was black and white television. Systems like Echelon, Carnivore, facial recognition cameras and other Big Brother technology are becoming common knowledge in the twenty-first century, but at the time *Nineteen Eighty-Four* was first published, this technology was limited to the creative imaginations of science fiction writers, or dismissed as insanity.

Modern surveillance systems are even much more powerful than what Orwell imagined. As the cliché goes, the truth *is* stranger than fiction. In a move that would have caused a national outcry just a decade earlier when people weren't so desensitized to Orwellian measures, in December 2010, the retail giant Wal-Mart began using video screens at the checkout stands at around 600 hundred different locations in the United States to repeatedly play a brief message from the head of the Department of Homeland Security, Janet Napolitano, informing shoppers that the Department of Homeland Security has "teamed up" with Wal-Mart in order to help keep your community safe from terrorists.

It is very odd and disturbing to have one of the world's largest corporations teaming up with a federal police force to encourage shoppers to be informants and to spy on their family, friends, and neighbors; because they want you to believe that people everywhere may be plotting a terrorist attack against the government. Everyone already knows they can dial 911 to reach the

---

[392] Orwell, George – *Nineteen Eighty-Four* page 2

police for any reason, and people frequently abuse it and call to report that a cashier at McDonald's wouldn't refund their money, or for a variety of other stupid reasons.[393]

With 911 operators already overloaded with unimportant calls, and police resources being wasted when they could actually be legitimately used to stop or solve crime, just imagine the mess after the population tips off authorities over every little suspicion as a result of their minds being filled with paranoia from the mainstream media for years, telling everyone that there's a boogey man around every corner who may be secretly plotting some kind of terrorist attack in your neighborhood.

A Snitch Culture

The few people living in the dystopian world described in *Nineteen Eighty-Four* who were still able to think critically and independently were afraid to speak their mind out of fear that others would report them as traitors to the Party and enemies of Big Brother. The Thought Police are a secret police force that use telescreens, snitches, and entrapment in order to intimidate the population in attempts to prevent Thought Crime, and to also discover Thought Criminals, and arrest and punish them. A Thought Criminal is anyone who dares think anything bad about Big Brother or the Party.

People, and particularly children, have all been turned into spies and are encouraged to report Thought Crime to the authorities. "Nearly all children nowadays

---

[393] *TheSmokingGun.com* "A McNuggets 'Emergency' Floridian called 911 three times over McDonald's chicken shortage" (March 3, 2009)

were horrible," Orwell wrote. "They adored the Party and everything connected with it. The songs, the processions, the banners, the hiking, the drilling with dummy rifles, the yelling of slogans, the worship of Big Brother—it was all a sort of glorious game to them."[394] That was in *Nineteen Eighty-Four*, but unfortunately we also find parallels within our own society.

The Department of Homeland launched a program where they decided to "partner" with the Boy Scouts to "prepare youths for more traditional jobs as police officers and firefighters."[395] *The New York Times* ran an article in 2009 discussing a drill the children were involved in where they used fake rifles and had to confront a "disgruntled Iraq War veteran" who became a domestic terrorist. The article showed a photo of some kids holding fake rifles and dressed up in SWAT gear.[396]

A British website called ClimateCops.com designed for children ages 7 to 11 features cartoons and downloadable materials urging children to become "climate cops" who keep a watchful eye on their parents to see if they are wasting electricity. Children download a "Climate Crime Case File" to write up "tickets" for their parents to make sure they "don't commit those crimes again (or else)!" The site also tells children that they "need to keep a watchful eye" on their parents to prevent future energy violations.

In the nightmarish world of *Nineteen Eighty-Four*, children were, "systematically turned against their parents and taught to spy on them and report their deviations. The family had become in effect an extension of the Though Police. It was a device by means of which

---

[394] Orwell, George – *Nineteen Eighty-Four* page 21
[395] *The New York Times* "Scouts Train to Fight Terrorists, and More" by Jennifer Steinhauer (May 13, 2009)
[396] Ibid

everyone could be surrounded night and day by informers who knew him intimately."[397]

In an interview with *ABC News*, President Obama's top legal advisor, Attorney General Eric Holder, announced that the most dangerous terrorist threat to America wasn't radical Islamic terrorists from the Middle East who travel to the United States with the sole intention of blowing something up. No. He said the new #1 threat to America is American citizens who have been born and raised in the United States, but for whatever reason, have come to identify with Osama Bin Elvis (Laden), the immortal boogey man. This announcement came close to ten years after the September 11th 2001 terrorist attacks when the world was getting tired of the prolonged wars in the Middle East so the establishment needed to ensure Americans' minds were still continuously filled with fear.

"What I am trying to do in this interview is to make people aware of the fact that the threat is real, the threat is different, the threat is constant," Holder said. "It is one of the things that keeps me up at night. You didn't worry about this even two years ago—about individuals, about Americans, to the extent that we now do. And—that is of—of great concern."[398]

He continued, "The threat has changed from simply worrying about foreigners coming here, to worrying about people in the United States, American citizens—raised here, born here, and who for whatever reason, have decided that they are going to become radicalized and take up arms against the nation in which they were born."

---

[397] Orwell, George – *Nineteen Eighty-Four* page 118

[398] *ABCNews.com* "Attorney General's Blunt Warning on Terror Attacks" by Jack Cloherty and Pierre Thomas (December 21, 2010)

Holder wasn't even talking about radical Islamic terrorists like the kind that had been presented as the boogey men we should all fear for the last few decades. Holder's statement was an attempt to paint practically anyone of any race, religion, age, political affiliation, etc., as a potential "domestic extremist" who authorities want you to believe may attack the government or innocent civilians for any number of reasons at any time.

Several years earlier the federal government had secretly distributed literature to law enforcement agencies that listed what police should look for concerning possible "domestic terrorist activity." The eight-page MIAC Report, leaked in March 2009 listed bumper stickers showing support for Congressman Ron Paul, owning gold coins, and having possession of certain documentary films as things authorities should look for.[399]

A similar Department of Homeland Security report titled *Right-wing Extremism: Current Economic and Political Climate Fueling Resurgence in Radicalization and Recruitment,* warned officials that returning Iraq War veterans may turn on the American government and that "rightwing extremists" are recruiting supporters who are concerned about illegal immigration, restrictions on firearms, and the loss of US sovereignty.[400]

As the Orwellian nightmare was rapidly coming true, Big Brother saw the resistance building and worried about a revolution.

Many people believe that Nazi Germany's secret police (the Gestapo) terrorized ordinary German citizens under orders from Nazi leaders, but history shows that the

---

[399] *The MIAC Report: The Modern Militia Movement*
[400] World Net Daily *Homeland Security on guard for 'right-wing extremists'* April 12, 2009

majority of investigations into citizens were launched because someone tipped off authorities.

One of the world's most respected historians specializing in World War II Europe, Professor Robert Gellately of Florida State University, explains, "There were relatively few secret police, and most were just processing the information coming in. I had found a shocking fact. It wasn't the secret police who were doing this wide-scale surveillance and hiding on every street corner. It was the ordinary German people who were informing on their neighbors."[401]

In his writings Gellately explains that most Germans who turned in others didn't do so because they were doing anything suspicious or talking negatively about the Nazi party. Most people were turned in because of greed, jealousy, and petty differences, rather than because of a legitimate threat or suspicion that a person may be an actual enemy of the state.

There were many instances of people turning in their business partners so they could gain full control of the businesses they shared together. Jealous lovers turned in rival suitors in order to keep them away from their boyfriend or girlfriend, and people turned others in because they lived in an apartment that was in high demand. Others who became informants did so because it was the first time an authority figure valued them and they felt important through this process.

Gellately also emphasizes that German citizens who tipped off Nazi authorities about someone knew what horrific fate they would find, but didn't care because of the financial or social rewards that person would receive in return. While such despicable behavior was once restricted to tyrannical regimes like Nazi Germany,

---

[401] http://www.fsu.edu/profiles/gellately/

Stalinist Russia, or Mao Tse-tung's China, it is heart-breaking that the once great United States of America has succumbed to this same kind of erosion from within, as a result of corruption at the top.

An iPhone app with the Orwellian name of the *PatriotApp* functions as a way for people to send seemingly anonymous tips in the form of text messages to various government agencies including the FBI, EPA (Environmental Protection Agency), CDC (Center for Disease Control), and more, to report anything suspicious or illegal. On the surface this may seem like a reasonable function, but just like the post-911 legislation bill, *The Patriot Act*, the Patriot App is anything but patriotic.

The App was created by a company called Citizen Concepts which was formed by people with strong ties with DHS and DoD, according the company's website, PatriotApps.com[402] The description in the Apple App Store says that the PatriotApp is, "the world's first iPhone application that empowers citizens to assist government agencies in creating safer, cleaner, and more efficient communities via social networking and mobile technology."[403]

The description also says the App, "Deputizes your iPhone," giving people the impression that they are a member of the secret police now that they have been "deputized" like something out of an old western film. Such an impersonal form of communication also reduces the discernment that people will use when thinking about reporting someone or something. A phone call to 911 or the police would be fairly personal and the tipster would be invested in the process, but by simply clicking a few

---

[402] http://www.patriotapps.com/Team html Gives the background info on several team members who designed the Patriot App.

[403] Apple Inc.'s app store description for the Patriot App

boxes and typing a short text message, this reduces the humanity in the overall process of informing authorities that something may be wrong. Such an impersonal act practically eliminates an informant's analysis of the situation, preventing them from giving it a second thought, thus dramatically reducing the quality of the tip.

During the 2008 presidential campaign in America, then candidate Barrack Obama made a startling statement revealing his desire to implement a program involving ordinary citizens like you and me as spies who feel like they're empowered and part of the Department of Homeland Security, the FBI, or other law enforcement agency. Obama openly stated, "We cannot continue to rely only on our military in order to achieve the national security objectives that we've set. We've got to have a civilian national security force that's just as powerful, just as strong, just as well-funded."[404]

Then, immediately after becoming president, the Obama administration began implementing one Orwellian policy after the next. We saw the telescreens go up in Wal-Mart, the 'if you see something...say something' snitch campaign. The MIAC report and more. The "civilian national security force" he was talking about was every American being turned into a paranoid rat. This will undoubtedly lead to a rash of invalid "tips" and complains, and a larger bureaucracy (and police force) will be needed to address these floods of tips.

Relationships

Friendships, romantic relationships, and families are all shunned by the Party in *Nineteen Eighty-Four* to

---

[404] *YouTube* - Barack Obama speech during his 2008 Presidential Campaign Calls for Civilian National Security Force.

"prevent men and women from forming loyalties which it might not be able to control...the only recognized purpose of marriage was to beget children for the service of the Party."[405] Families are almost nonexistent, since each individual must give his or her full allegiance and love to Big Brother and the Party.

Those children that were born were all brought up in government institutions and indoctrinated from the time of birth. The government realized that if people had personal friendships and strong family ties, they would join together and overthrow Big Brother. Again, we find a reflection of our own society in Orwell's words. While in America sexuality is not repressed like in the novel, the effects of hyper-sexuality and broken families serves the same purpose and severely limits the ability of people to join together and stand up for their rights against a New World Order.

With rampant family dysfunction, divorces, out of wedlock births, and children who don't even know who their father is, society is in such chaos in regards to interpersonal problems, that many people aren't concerned with larger social issues because their own life is such a mess and they are constantly engaged in domestic disputes, money problems, and other obligations. Most people just don't care about what is going on with the government because they have their own personal problems to deal with.

A Heartless Society

Society was so inhumane in *Nineteen Eighty-Four* that they regularly enjoyed watching video clips of war footage that were shown on the telescreens to see the

---

[405] Orwell, George – *Nineteen Eighty-Four* page 58

destruction of their enemy's soldiers. Winston remarked once that the audience was amused and laughed hysterically when a helicopter began shooting a fat man and riddled his body with bullets as he tried to swim away from his capsized ship. It was the highlight of the broadcast.

He describes how the audience was easily stirred into an angry mob and that, "a desire to kill, to torture, to smash faces in with a sledge hammer, seemed to flow through the whole group of people like an electric current."[406] Since Big Brother was basically God, there was no room for religion either. One character who worked in the Ministry of Truth was arrested and killed for allowing the word "God" to remain in a poem he was supposed to censor.

The Big Brother system has stamped out most feelings of empathy. O'Brien says, "never again will you be capable of ordinary human feeling. Everything will be dead inside you. Never again will you be capable of love, or friendship, or joy of living, or laughter, or curiosity, or courage, or integrity. You will be hollow. We shall squeeze you empty, and then we shall fill you with ourselves."[407]

A massive thirty year analysis published in May of 2010 showed that college students are dramatically less empathetic today than students in the past. "College kids today are about 40 percent lower in empathy than their counterparts of 20 or 30 years ago, as measured by standard tests of this personality trait," said Sara Konrath, a researcher at the University of Michigan Institute for Social Research.[408]

---

[406] Orwell, George – *Nineteen Eighty-Four* page 12

[407] Orwell, George – *Nineteen Eighty-Four* page 228-229

[408] *HealthDay News* "Today's College Students More Likely to Lack Empathy" (May 28, 2010)

"The increase in exposure to media during this time period could be one factor," she said. "Compared to 30 years ago, the average American now is exposed to three times as much nonwork-related information. In terms of media content, this generation of college students grew up with video games. And a growing body of research, including work done by my colleagues at Michigan, is establishing that exposure to violent media numbs people to the pain of others," said Konrath.

The study also showed that the students were less likely to feel concerned about the less fortunate, and even their own friends. Today's students were said to be the most self-centered and narcissistic individuals in recent history.

Another reason believed to cause the increase in narcissism and lack of empathy, aside from massive exposure to violent media, was the emergence of social networking sites which give people the ability to "tune out" and not respond to interactions online, and this could be translating into a learned behavior that manifests itself during face-to-face interactions.

Foreign Countries Painted as Enemies

When one country is having tensions with another, or if two countries are approaching an armed conflict, the entire "enemy" country and all of its occupants are usually portrayed as "hating freedom" or being ruthless savages who want to kill the citizens of the other county. This is rarely ever true, of course, and most often it is one corrupt leader butting heads with another corrupt leader, or one country fabricating complete lies in order to spark a war for economic reasons. The vast majority of citizens of both countries want the same things out of life. They don't want any problems. They just want to be safe and have a stable economy, and be able to enjoy a few of life's pleasures and spend time with family and friends. Most informed citizens in the "enemy" country are just as upset about their corrupt leader as citizens of the opposing country.

Other people, perhaps the majority, unfortunately, believe the propaganda produced from their own country and literally hate everyone from the "enemy" country. You could see this during the War in Iraq, with many moronic Americans wanting to kill all Arabs, or Muslims, or nuke the entire Middle East and "turn it into a glass parking lot." Such ignorance is the fuel that the establishment needs to continue its operations. Orwell interestingly noted, "If he [people in general] were allowed contact with foreigners he would discover that they are creatures similar to himself and that most of what he has been told about them is lies."[409]

"The citizen of Oceania is not allowed to know anything of the tenets of the other two [enemies] philosophies, but he is taught to execrate [denounce] them as barbarous outrages upon morality and common sense."[410]

In an insightful documentary that aired on PBS in the spring and summer of 2010 called *Rick Steves' Iran*, the host traveled to Iran and spoke with people about their country and the growing tensions with the US. Multiple Iranians said that they have no problem with America or the American people. One woman clearly stated that the governments have problems with each other, but the people should be friends. The woman went on to say that it was unfortunate that Iran had a theocracy where the religious leaders ran the government and she called it

---

[409] Orwell, George – *Nineteen Eighty-Four* page 174
[410] Orwell, George – *Nineteen Eighty-Four* page 175

Iran's main problem.[411]

This is quite the opposite of what the American establishment would like people to believe. The Iranians, we are told, all hate Americans, and want us dead. This false belief aids the establishment's military industrial complex and supports the everlasting "War on Terror."

Power Hungry Officials

Just as the "enemies" of a country are always cast in the darkest light, the leader of the homeland is almost always painted as a heroic and virtuous man who must protect the poor citizens of his land from the evildoers. "Everywhere is the same pyramidal structure, the same worship of a semi-divine leader," notes Orwell.[412]

We see billboards and t-shirts in America with the image of the president featured on them like they are rock stars; and no matter who the president is, their supporters will always lash out and attack anyone who questions their authority. If someone disagreed with President George W. Bush, then they were called un-American and said to support the terrorists. People who resisted President Obama were simply called racists. The strategy is the same no matter which party is in power. Most people are ideologically blind, and don't even notice the major shortcomings of their own party or leader.

At one point in Orwell's story, Winston muses that he now understands the how, but he had yet to understand the why. He knew how the Party and Big Brother were able to operate in total power, but he had yet to understand why they did this. He later realized it was for the power itself.

---

[411] *Rick Steve's Iran* Avalon Travel Publishing; DVD edition (2010)
[412] Orwell, George – *Nineteen Eighty-Four* page 175

O'Brien tells him, "The Party seeks power entirely for its own sake. We are not interested in the good of others; we are interested solely in power. Not wealth or luxury or long life or happiness; only power, pure power."[413] O'Brien concludes, "Power is power over human beings. Over the body—but above all, over the mind."[414]

The infamous political player, Henry Kissinger, famously stated that "power is the ultimate aphrodisiac" and many have heard of Lord Acton's dictum, which states that power tends to corrupt, and absolute power corrupts absolutely. Power is what dirt-poor street gang members are after because its feeling is better than any drug. Power is what organized mob bosses are after more than the money they pull in, and power is what politicians desire, more than "serving" their country. And just like drug addicts will do all kinds of illegal and immoral things just to get a fix, the same is true of those addicted to power.

An Erosion of the Language

In *Nineteen Eighty-Four*, the language that people spoke was being reduced down to basic nouns and verbs in a purposeful attempt to dumb people down. The language was called Newspeak and each year a new dictionary would come out with the approved words for society, and each year it got smaller and smaller. The goal was to eliminate most of the words, and thus eliminate people's thoughts and ways to express themselves to keep them mentally enslaved.

In one scene a coworker of Winston's was bragging

---

[413] Orwell, George – *Nineteen Eighty-Four* page 234
[414] Orwell, George – *Nineteen Eighty-Four* page 236

that in a few more generations people "wouldn't be able to have a conversation like this" because the language will be so eroded.

Just as the residents of Oceania were losing the ability to express themselves verbally due to the eroding language, we can see a similar phenomenon in our culture with the decline of reading and education. People's foul mouths and the reliance on text messaging also shows their inability to articulate ideas. People's vocabulary seems to be shrinking, along with their IQs.

Double Think

The concept of *Double Think* means to "know and not to know, to be conscious of complete truthfulness while telling carefully constructed lies, to hold simultaneously two opinions which cancelled out, knowing them to be contradictory and believing in both of them."[415] Orwell used the slogan "War is Peace, Freedom is Slavery, Ignorance is Strength" to illustrate Double Think. It was the slogan of the Party and captured the depths of the backwards and illogical beliefs of society. Unfortunately we find equally backward beliefs in our own society and Double Think is not just a concept found in *Nineteen Eighty-Four*.

Everyone is familiar with the Patriot Act legislation that was passed after the 9/11 attacks in 2001, eliminating various Constitutional liberties, and is anything but patriotic. The name "Patriot" Act was carefully chosen to imply the new laws were patriotic and is a perfect example of Double Think since it is completely the opposite of anything patriotic or American.

In a segment of Alex Jones' documentary

---

[415] Orwell, George – *Nineteen Eighty-Four* page 31

Terrorstorm: A History of Government Sponsored Terrorism, the camera crew interviews random people on the streets of London to discuss the increasing surveillance, and one woman proclaims, "I think we should give up liberty for freedom," clearly not realizing the illogical and blatant contradiction of her own words.

The concept of Double Think often applies to war. "Peace keeping" troops are often there to kill the enemy, and it is often said that we must "fight for peace." Comedian George Carlin saw the irony in the terms and once said, "fighting for peace is like screwing for virginity." In America, the Department of Defense use to be called the Department of War until 1947 when the name was changed to improve its image. It should really be called the Department of *Offense,* not Defense, but in true Orwellian style, its name reflects the opposite of what it is.

When the commercial for the Little Buddy GPS tracking device said parents can "build trust" by forcing their children to wear a GPS tracker—this is another example of Double Think—since using the product is an obvious sign of not trusting your child.

Double Think is essentially a blatant lie that can easily be identified by an enlightened person, but is fully believed by the ignorant masses. It's like when a store advertises that people should "spend more to save more" and customers actually believe they're saving money by spending it.

Double Think uses misnomers and false terms to purposefully label things incorrectly, and such names are often the exact opposite of what the thing really is or does. People with minimum critical thinking skills often accept the word or phrase on face value, and don't realize it masks something else.

The Ministry of Love

The Ministry of Love is basically the police force and prison system in *Nineteen Eighty-Four* and is anything but loving. They look out for, and arrest people who betray Big Brother and the Party. Violators are taking to the much-feared Room 101 where they are tortured and brainwashed to love Big Brother.

The Ministry of Plenty

The Ministry of Plenty is in control of the food rations and the manufacture and supply of goods and services. Periodically the Ministry of Plenty publishes reports that claim the standard of living has increased, along with the amount of food rations people are entitled to, but in reality, the standard of living has continuously declined. As with the other departments of government in the novel, its name reflects exactly the opposite of what it says, and the Ministry of Plenty is really the reason for scarcity.

The Ministry of Peace

The Ministry of Peace is responsible for the perpetual war that plagues society and uses up or destroys the fruits of people's labor to prevent an increase in the standard of living for the lower levels of society.

In America, we have the Department of Defense, which is really the Department of War, and actually used to be called that, until the name was changed in 1947 to give it a better image. In true Orwellian fashion, the department's name is meant to hide the fact that it is really a Ministry of War.

The Ministry of Truth

The Ministry of Truth, found in the novel, is a misnomer and in reality serves as exactly the opposite of what its name implies and is responsible for the falsification of historical events, and determines what the "truth" is and then disseminates it in the media and historical records. The massive building is described as being in the shape of a pyramid.

The Ministry of Truth also provides the citizens of Oceana with all of their newspapers, films, textbooks, plays, and novels. They have a special department for proletarian literature that "produced rubbishy newspapers, containing almost nothing except sport, crime, and astrology, sensational five-cent novelettes, films oozing with sex, and sentimental songs."[416]

It is basically the heart of the massive propaganda machine that is entirely under the direction of the Party.

---

[416] Orwell, George – *Nineteen Eighty-Four* page 38

Conclusion

As a reader approaches the end of Orwell's novel, one begins to hope that *The Resistance* will jump into action and members of the Inner Party would turn on the Big Brother system, or that the Proles or Outer Party members would rise up and start a revolution to restore freedom, but unfortunately this doesn't happen.

Winston and his girlfriend Julia are both captured by the Thought Police and taken to Room 101 to be "re-educated." Winston then realizes that O'Brien, who he thought was his friend and working with *The Resistance*, actually only pretended to, in order to entrap Winston. O'Brien, then, as it turns out, is also in charge of punishing Winston for Thought Crimes and his disloyalty to Big Brother. As he is torturing Winston, he tells him what the future will be like once Big Brother has wiped out all resistance. He explains, "There will be no curiosity, no enjoyment of the process of life. All competing pleasures will be destroyed. But always—do not forget this, Winston—always there will be the intoxication of power, constantly increasing and constantly growing subtler. Always, at every moment, there will be the thrill of victory, the sensation of trampling on an enemy who is helpless. If you want a picture of the future, imagine a boot stamping on a human face—forever."[417]

After unbearable torture and lecturing from O'Brien, Winston eventually abandons all thoughts of resistance and actually comes to love Big Brother. "You must love Big Brother. It is not enough to obey him; you must love

---

[417] Orwell, George – *Nineteen Eighty-Four* page 238-239

him," O'Brien says.

One must seriously consider whether people who resist the real Big Brother system and the New World Order will find the same fate that Winston Smith did. Is it too late to stop the Orwellian system described in *Nineteen Eighty-Four* from actually being built? One must hold onto the hope that no matter how far along the Big Brother system is, that there are a large number of educated people who are ready to resist it and stand up against it.

Orwell explained, "If there was hope, it must lie in the proles, because only there, in those swarming disregarded masses, eighty-five percent of the population of Oceania, could the force to destroy the Party ever be generated...But the proles, if only they could somehow become conscious of their own strength, would have no need to conspire...If they chose they could blow the Party to pieces tomorrow morning."[418]

We are the proles. The hope lies with us. We must create safeguards and checks and balances to minimize abuse by government and private industry. We must actively counter propaganda and lies, and hold corrupt government officials accountable for their crimes. Only an educated and alert public can counter the invisible empire and their Orwellian dreams. We must use the tools of advanced technology to enhance and simplify the human experience, not to stifle it or destroy it. We must stay strong in the face of immense opposition and remember what Martin Luther King Jr. said when he proclaimed, "He who passively accepts evil is as much involved in it as he who helps to perpetrate it. He who accepts evil without protesting against it is really cooperating with it."

---

[418] Orwell, George – *Nineteen Eighty-Four* page 61

We outnumber the elite Illuminati thousands to one, and if we can awaken our fellow man to see the system that we are all victims of, and if we can lift the veil of ignorance and apathy then we can unite and restore our communities, our country, and the world with the inalienable rights that we have been endowed by our Creator. We know that Big Brother is watching us, so let's show him what we're capable of.

Down with Big Brother!